PHILOSOPHY OF RELIGION A–Z

Forthcoming Volumes in the Philosophy A–Z Series

Philosophy of Religion A–Z

Patrick Quinn

First published in the UK 2005 by Edinburgh University Press Ltd.
First Published in the United States in 2005 by
PALGRAVE MACMILLAN™
175 Fifth Avenue, New York, N.Y. 10010 and
Houndmills, Basingstoke, Hampshire, England RG21 6XS.
Companies and representatives throughout the world.

PALGRAVE MACMILLAN is the global academic imprint of the
Palgrave Macmillan division of St. Martin's Press, LLC and of Palgrave
Macmillan Ltd. Macmillan® is a registered trademark in the United
States, United Kingdom and other countries. Palgrave is a registered
trademark in the European Union and other countries.

ISBN 1-4039-7266-4 hardcover
ISBN 1-4039-7267-2 paperback

Library of Congress Cataloging-in-Publication Data
is available from the Library of Congress.

10 9 8 7 6 5 4 3 2 1

Printed in Finland

Contents

Series Editor's Preface

Theology and philosophy often ask the same questions, or at least questions that look similar. Both seek to understand highly theoretical issues and employ reason in coming to their solutions. Yet religion and philosophy are often pitted against each other, as though the traditional rivalry between Athens, representing philosophy, and Jerusalem, standing for religion, is a constant feature in our intellectual culture. Perhaps it is, and certainly it would be difficult to understand philosophy unless one took on board a whole range of religious issues as both important and intriguing. For much of their joint histories philosophy and religion have worked side by side, each illuminating and arguing with the other. Although a good deal of emphasis in religion is placed on what is higher than reason, or on the limits of reason, faith is itself, of course, a notion highly susceptible to philosophical analysis, and all the propositions of religion are capable of being put forward as rational beliefs to be argued for and possibly accepted. Religion is an area in which our personal and emotional lives are very much tied in with our beliefs. The role of philosophy has often been to try to establish some distance and clarity in what is otherwise a highly subjective issue. Patrick Quinn's book brings out the interwoven nature of the two disciplines and indeed the two forms of life, and will serve as a useful guide to how some of the key expressions in both religion and philosophy are to be understood.

Oliver Leaman

Introduction

The relationship between philosophy and religion is a long one and has been marked historically by varying degrees of closeness, compatibility, suspicion and even hostility. Philosophers try to analyse religion by asking questions about the kind of evidence that supports religious belief, notably in the existence of God or divinity, however understood. They also examine what constitutes authentic religious experience and how, if at all, this may be explained from a rational point of view. There is also the more general issue concerning the intrinsic capability of philosophy to deal objectively and adequately with the phenomenon of religion given the subjective perceptions that colour all our views, especially about religious faith and its effects, not least in the world of today. Our interpretation of the significance of religion is naturally shaped by the way in which we see our world and this determines the extent to which our attitudes towards religion may be positive, negative or, as far as possible, neutral.

Many people, including many philosophers, would argue that there should be some rational basis for religious faith, though others would have sympathy with the 'leap of faith' beyond reason approach so enthusiastically advocated by the philosopher, Kierkegaard. The relationship between faith and reason is considered and lived out in a variety of ways by human beings both on a personal and political level as history shows. For the believer, however, religious faith is not merely an interesting theoretical option nor primarily a subject for

philosophical investigation but rather signifies the disposition
to believe in God or divinity, however understood, as well as,
or alternatively, in a transcendent dimension to human life in
the cosmos in which one lives. This is demonstrated in the efforts of believing communities to commit themselves to a life
of faith and its requirements in the respective cultures of belief
which ground their understanding of what is true. Those who,
like philosophers of religion (some of whom themselves will
be religious believers), try to rationally analyse the nature and
expression of religious truth will inevitably be confronted by
the transcendent character of religion as a phenomenon that
claims to concern itself with what is believed to go beyond the
limits of human thought and language. This is the challenge
of religion for philosophy and philosophers and is what constitutes the philosophy of a religion as a most intriguing area
for investigation and analysis by those curious and interested
enough to explore its possibilities.

Preparatory Note Although many faiths are discussed in the
pages that follow, the Christian calendar is used throughout
the text for chronological purposes. This is for convenience
only and should not be taken to signify that the Christian
faith has priority over others in the context of this book.

Acknowledgements

I wish to thank a number of people who helped me in various ways during my work on this project. First and foremost, I wish to thank Professor Oliver Leaman, the editor of the Philosophy A–Z series, who invited me to write this book on the philosophy of religion and who has been extremely helpful, as usual, all along the way with suggestions and advice, not to mention great patience. My thanks to the staff of the Edinburgh Press with whom I was in contact and especially to Jackie Jones, Head of Publishing and Deputy Chief Executive, who was most helpful and very patient, especially during the later stages of the work with deadlines to be met. My thanks to Felicity Marsh for her very careful editing and thorough scrutiny of the presentation of the text which made it all the more readable as a result. A special mention too to those many philosophy students over the years in the various colleges where I have taught and tutored on courses on the philosophy of religion, especially at University College Dublin and Oscail National Distance Learning Centre at Dublin City University and also at All Hallows College, Dublin. Their contributions to the subject during our discussions on religion have always been personally stimulating and helpful to me in straightening out my own ideas about how philosophy and religion interact. During my final revisions of the text in late February 2005, I received the sad news of the death of a very valued friend, Dr Paul Campbell-Tiech. It is only fitting that I pay tribute to him here by way of acknowledging his contributions over the years to my own understanding of religion and of life generally. Whenever we met, our exchange of views on these and many other subjects was always stimulating, helped no doubt by the inevitable and welcome glass of good red wine. I shall greatly miss our conversations together and Paul's kind and generous presence.

My thanks to my son, Stephen, and to Maeve Doherty, and to my daughter Barbara for helping me with the technical difficulties that arose with the computerised version of the text, especially as regards the problems with e-mail attachments. Finally, and not least, my thanks to Marion, my wife, who, as always, was patiently supportive and encouraging of my efforts when more urgent household duties demanded attention, especially during the Christmas period.

I must also acknowledge the following texts which proved extremely useful and which are included in the bibliographical section: *A Dictionary of Philosophy* by Peter A. Angeles, the *Pocket Dictionary of Apologetics and Philosophy of Religion* by Stephen C. Evans and *Faith and Reason* edited by Paul Helm.

Finally, I should say that due to the demands of text size, not to mention time constraints, I had to be necessarily selective about the choice of entries. Some readers may object to omissions of topics and thinkers which they would have liked to have seen included but that can't be helped and all I can offer is the hope that the entries here are sufficiently representative of philosophers and topics generally associated with the philosophy of religion.

The book is aimed at a wide audience: at readers with a general interest in the area, at philosophy students at graduate and postgraduate levels, at students of theology and those who study anthropology and culture, as well as anyone interested in the psychology and sociology of religion. I would also hope that teachers of religion of senior students in their final years at secondary and high school level will find this book a useful reference guide to the subject.

Philosophy of Religion A–Z

A

Abraham: described in the Book of Genesis (12 et seq.) in the Hebrew Bible or Old Testament as the first of the patriarchs, the father of Isaac and the founder of the Jewish people, to whom and to whose people God promised special divine protection.

See **Judaism**

Further reading: The Jerusalem Bible

Absolute, The: denotes what is the most ultimate in reality and is often applied to God or the divine, however conceived of. The Absolute is totally unconditioned, unrestricted, complete, perfect and pure, and in Hegel's philosophy represents that towards which all things dialectically evolve.

See **God, Hegel**

Further reading: Helm (1999)

Absurd, The: refers in twentieth-century existentialism to reality as perceived to be irrational and ultimately meaningless. In Sartre's *Being and Nothingness*, for example, it is stated that 'it is absurd that we are born, it is absurd that we die'. Camus, in *The Myth of Sisyphus*, claims that the absurd nature of reality confronts us with the possibility of suicide since life's apparent pointlessness compels us to overcome an endless number of obstacles that never diminish. Central to Camus' concept of the absurd, as with Sartre's, is the disjunction between our expectation of an ultimately meaningful rational life, however understood, and the inevitable impossibility of this ever being realised in practice. Camus' solution is for us to remain stoical and to endure whatever adversities we encounter. This constitutes the heroic stance of the existentialist hero who finds meaning in the struggle to survive.

See **Camus, Existentialism, Sartre**

Further reading: Blackham (1962); Camus (1973, 1983); Sartre (1946)

Aesthetics: concerns the philosophical analysis of beauty which, for some philosophers, demonstrates the transcendent nature of reality, sometimes in a religious and theological way. A number of Christian philosopher–theologians, especially in the Middle Ages, regarded Plato's treatment of beauty (for example in *Symposium*) and Plotinus's account of it in *Ennead* IV.8.1 as well as Pseudo-Dionysius's definition of beauty as a divine attribute (in his text, *De Divinis Nominibus*) as of primary theological significance. God thus came to be understood as beauty itself, and when combined with the Platonic/Neoplatonic treatments of the ineffable Good (for example in Plato's *Republic* and Plotinus's *Enneads*), the result was a conception of God as the essence and source of beauty. In the twentieth century, Stephen MacKenna and Iris Murdoch emphasised the centrality of beauty to life and to art in the context of religious and philosophical thought and in the cosmos generally. Both argued that it represented the transcendent in a world in which the question of God's existence was being seen as ever more problematic.

See **Beauty, Christianity, God, Stephen MacKenna, Iris Murdoch, Plato, Plotinus, Pseudo-Dionysius, Religion**

Further reading: Dillon (1991); Dodds (1936); Hamilton and Cairns (1963); Murdoch (1992)

Afterlife, The: describes the post-mortem state of existence as in, for example, Plato's dialogue, *Phaedo* and Aquinas's treatment of the subject in Book IV, *Summa Contra Gentiles* and in other works like *The Egyptian* and *Tibetan Book*(s) *of the Dead.*

See **Death,** *The Egyptian Book of the Dead, The Tibetan Book of the Dead,* **Heaven, Hell, Immortality,** *Phaedo,* **Plato,** *Psyche,* **Soul, Spirit**

Further reading: Hamilton and Cairns (1963); Quinn (1996)

Agathon: meaning the Good in Plato's *Republic*, that which is beyond being and in the light of which one can see reality.

See **The Good, Iris Murdoch, Plato, Plotinus,** *Republic*

Further reading: Hamilton and Cairns (1963)

Agnosticism: the state of not knowing whether God exists or not. Agnosticism is sometimes seen as close to atheism and even indistinguishable both from it and also from negative theology in that the latter argues that God is known best by being unknown. Knowing by not knowing is traditionally associated with Socrates and with the mystical religious approach, sometimes described as 'the dark night of the soul' in Christian writings. Knowing God negatively is also important in the writings of Maimonides who strongly argued in his *Guide of the Perplexed* that this form of knowledge represents the closest way one can come to know God best. St Thomas Aquinas also subscribed to this 'agnostic' view, and, following Maimonides, philosophically and theologically explored the negative way in his own writings, for example in Book I of *Summa Contra Gentiles* and in Question 1, Article 2 of his Exposition of Boethius's *On the Trinity*. However, Aquinas did insist that having positive knowledge of God was also valid and complemented the 'negative way' with both combining in the analogical knowledge of God. The latter involves a comparison between the likeness that exists between God and creatures while simultaneously acknowledging the infinite distance between them. There is an interesting philosophical precedent to this in Plato's dialogue, *Parmenides*, where knowing and not knowing the One are dialectically explored. In the twentieth century, in his classic text, *Language, Truth and Logic*, A. J. Ayer claimed that using a term such as 'God' was literally meaningless since there was no empirical basis for God's existence. This meant, according to Ayer, that the kind of language used was metaphorical and emotive, designed to evoke feelings of psychological conviction that God does in fact exists.

See **A. J. Ayer, God, Hume, Maimonides, Socrates, Negative Theology,** *Via Negativa*

Further reading: Ayer (1971); Helm (1999); Maimonides (1963); McInerney (1998); Hamilton and Cairns (1963); Quinn (1996)

Al-Farabi (870–950): was an Islamic philosopher and logician of Turkish origin who represented a very significant link between Greek philosophy and Islamic thought. His logical commentaries covered the whole range of Aristotelian logic and he developed a cosmological and metaphysical system based on Plotinus's emanationist views. Al-Farabi's concept of God is similar to Aristotle's Unmoved Mover, that is to say thought thinking itself. Moreover, God is the First Being from whom derives, through a process of progressive emanation and over-flowing, the successive orders of intellect, soul and prime matter. Once it has fulfilled its destiny in the higher intelligible world, the soul is able, by joining with the Active Intellect, to re-enter its original place in that higher world. The theory that the world is an eternal everlasting emanation from God led to questions being asked by Islamic theologians about how such claims could be reconciled with the Islamic doctrine that the world is created in time *ex nihilo* by the divine action of God. Questions also arose concerning whether the human soul as conceived by al-Farabi is merely part of the world soul, which moves the heavenly spheres and the terrestrial world below, or is, as Muslims believe, created by God as immortal and capable of surviving death to be miraculously re-united with its body in the afterlife. Al-Farabi also thought of humankind as a link between the intelligible realm and the material world of generation and corruptibility and he concluded that human beings, with their nutritive, perceptual, imaginative and rational faculties, can only achieve their ultimate goal of happiness and well-being in the context of the wider human society. The Islamic state, ruled by the wise religious–theological leader, provides this social context. This is clearly a theological development of the political vision of the ideal state outlined in Plato's *Republic*. Al-Farabi, who seems to have been convinced that Plato and Aristotle shared a common approach on essential matters, thus absorbed Platonist/Neoplatonist thought into the Islamic intellectual tradition, thereby contributing substantially to the development of Islamic Neoplatonism, with all its philosophical and religious implications. In his own life, he lived simply and sparsely, interested solely in learning and teaching, and, as his biographer Ibn Abi Usyabi'ah (d.1270) described him, a person 'pure in heart, superior in intelligence, averse to the world and contented with the necessities in life, following in the footsteps of ancient philosophers' (Fakhry 2002 p. 157).

See **Ibn Rushd, Ibn Sina, Islam**

Further reading: Fakhry (2002); Leaman (1999)

Al-Ghazzali, Abu Hamid Muhammad (1058–1111): born in the eastern Iranian city of Tus, where he also died, by his early thirties he was a pre-eminent legal scholar and teacher in Baghdad. However, to combat the scepticism he had induced in himself by his philosophical–religious thinking, he decided to adopt the practices of Sufi mysticism in an attempt to recover his religious certainty. He claimed to have succeeded in this task, and after ten years of travel and ascetic contemplation and at the invitation of the sultan, he resumed his teaching in his final years. His famous work, *The Incoherence of the Philosophers*, argues that although some Islamic philosophers such as al-Farabi and ibn Sina claimed to have provided absolutely unassailable arguments on important issues in theology and in metaphysics, in fact they could not satisfactorily demonstrate these claims. In addition, and more seriously, al-Ghazzali insisted that some of their assertions were simply heresies in disguise. The *Incoherence* is thus a crucial work in the area of the philosophy of religion since it challenged the viability of undertaking philosophical–religious enquiries in the context of Islam, given philosophy's potential, at least according to al-Ghazzali, for subverting Islamic faith. Ibn Rushd (Averroes) took this attack so seriously that he set out to refute al-Ghazzali's position in his own book, *The Incoherence of the Incoherence*, and he also argued in other texts that religion and philosophy are in harmony, not in conflict with each other, as al-Ghazzali claimed. Ibn-Rushd's solution to the problem of the apparent conflicts of interest between the religious and philosophical forms of knowledge is set out in his classic theory of interpretation, which anticipates later developments in Western philosophy and the case made for a theological hermeneutics by some six hundred years.

See **Al-Farabi, Ibn Rushd, Creation, Emanation, Faith, Islam, Mysticism, Philosophy, Religion, Ibn Rushd, Ibn Sina, Sufism, Theology**

Further reading: Al-Ghazzali (1997); Leaman (1999)

Alienation: for Karl Marx means the disconnection between oneself and one's labour sold for the benefit of others. He argued that within this context, religion, notably Christianity, intensified the experience of alienation, especially among the working classes, because it promised false hope beyond this world and one's present environment in a fantasy heavenly world of perfect happiness and bliss. Religion thus constituted the 'opium of the people', a drug that induced the delusion in the masses that it was possible to escape the unique reality of this world for a fantasy one elsewhere.

In existentialism, alienation represents the experience of not belonging to the world that we inhabit in that we feel like strangers in it and disconnected from it, almost as if we were exiles, but from where or what we do not know. The themes of disconnection and exile are frequently explored in the latter Camus' writings while other existentialists, such as Heidegger and Sartre, ascribe importance to an original state of feeling that one has been thrown into the world. This sense of alienation and disconnection, which is related to the apparent lack of meaning in life and the seeming absence of rationality about reality as a whole, is also linked to whether or not one accepts the existence of God. The existentialist philosopher, Gabriel Marcel, who accepts God's existence, interprets reality as a mystery of which we too are part, to be wondered at for what it is. Philosophy in his view takes the form of ongoing reflection about the essential mysteriousness of reality, which can lead to the conviction that there is a divine dimension to it all through the immanent, yet transcendent, presence of divinity. Others like Sartre and Camus, who reject or take issue with the possibility of God's existence, interpret reality as being ultimately pointless. In that context, human life is seen to provide the only possible affirmation of meaning, albeit subjectively worked out.

See **Camus, Existentialism, Marcel, Marx, Sartre**

Further reading: Camus (1983); Marcel (1948); Marx (1977)

Analogy: from the Greek *analogia*, *analogos* meaning 'reasoned proportion' or 'ratio' it refers to the similarities and resemblances between things. According to Aquinas, our knowledge of God is analogical in that, at one level, we come to realise that we do not know what God is (*via negativa*) whereas at another level, we can come to know God positively in certain ways (*via positiva/affirmativa*), for instance as being good, just, loving and merciful. The way of analogy respects both of these approaches by acknowledging that God, while transcendently unlike and beyond everything else, nevertheless has something in common with what he has created such as, for example, existence, life and thought. Such analogical knowledge is typically expressed through analogical language.

See **St Thomas Aquinas, God, Metaphor, Negative Theology, *Via Negativa, Via Positiva***

Further reading: Quinn (1996)

Angels: believed to be spiritual beings or intelligences often described as mediators between God and humankind.

References to angelic beings are found in many religious traditions including Judaism, Christianity and Islam and in the writings of philosophers such as Plato (who used the term *daemon* for example in *Symposium* 202e–203a) and Plotinus (in his treatise on guardian angels in *Ennead* III.4). Aquinas also wrote extensively about angels, for instance in *Summa Theologica* Part 1 Qq's.50–63, and often compares the intuitive and swift angelic intellect with the slower rational human mind.

See **St Thomas Aquinas, Boundary Being, Christianity, Daemon, Plato, Plotinus**

Further reading: Quinn (1996)

Anselm, St (1033–1109): monk and Bishop of Canterbury who reiterated St Augustine's view of faith and knowledge as belief seeking understanding. According to St Anselm, faith is prior to and provides the context for understanding, so it is not the case that we understand first in order to believe but rather that we believe in order to understand. This is stated at the outset of his famous ontological argument for the existence of God in *Proslogion*. If God is defined as a being than which nothing greater can be conceived or thought, then God must exist, since it is greater to exist in reality than just in the mind as notional or conceptual. Aquinas regarded this as an invalid proof, claiming that it defined God into existence. However, the fascination of Anselm's argument has led to continuous debate about its structure and validity right down to the present day and it has been examined by many philosophers including Descartes and Kant in the seventeenth and eighteenth centuries and contemporarily philosophers such as Hartshorne and Alvin Plantinga in the twentieth century. The fascination of the ontological argument undoubtedly lies in the way in which a particular concept is transformed into ontological (as distinct from notional) reality, although Anselm did insist that this concept was unique.

See **St Thomas Aquinas, Arguments for the Existence of God, Kant**

Further reading: Plantinga (1968)

Anthropomorphism: attributing human attitudes and qualities to a non-human subject or being. Christian belief in the divinity of Jesus is sometimes seen by other faiths as an example of this. In the nineteenth and twentieth centuries, Ludwig Feuerbach, Karl Marx and Sigmund Freud argued that belief in God and in the divine attributes represented the need (perhaps escapist in nature) to personify human qualities and ideals in something external that was conceived as supremely perfect.

See **Christianity, Freud, Feuerbach, Karl Marx**

Aquinas, St Thomas (1225–74): the most important Christian theologian–philosopher of the Middle Ages whose best known work is *Summa Theologica* (1267–72) which he was never to complete. He was also author of an earlier philosophical-theological compendium, *Summa Contra Gentiles* (1258–59) as well as of numerous other works (Anthony Kenny estimates that Aquinas wrote 8,500,000 words). His main concerns were the existence and nature of God, the divine attributes, the relationship between God and creation (specifically human creation), the ways in which one can come to know God, the relationship between faith and reason, the nature of the human soul and its embodiment and, in the latter context, the relationship between the mind and the senses. He claimed that it was naturally possible, though very difficult, to come to know God through positive, negative and analogical knowledge. However, faith, which, in his case meant Christian faith in the revealed word of God initially to the Jewish people and subsequently through Jesus Christ to his apostles and disciples, provided much greater knowledge of what God is and about the nature of the divine–human relationship, than is possible to acquire by natural human reason. Faith, Aquinas insists, is not in conflict with reason but rather complements the efforts of natural reason to know God. The final stage of knowledge, also supernatural as is the case with Christian faith, consists in the beatific vision of God face to face, in the company of the blessed in heaven, which is the ultimate purpose of human life and fulfils all human desires for happiness. It is in this context that Aquinas's predominant preference for the Aristotelian philosophical approach is to be understood, though it should also be said that St Thomas, when it was necessary, employed insights from the tradition of Platonism. His enormous corpus of writings is not only impressive but represents medieval Christian philosophy and theology at its best. The relevance of many of his texts to the philosophy of religion is evident and his thinking gave rise to the tradition of Thomism and Neothomism among Catholic thinkers. Some would argue, though, that the preference of the Catholic Church for Aquinas's philosophical and theological approach prevented philosophers from other traditions from accepting his philosophical views as being independently critical in their own right since there was a perception (and still is) that they were substantially influenced by and biased towards the conclusions of the Roman Catholic faith. The latter view is set out in Bertrand Russell's *History of Western Philosophy*. In recent years, however, especially since the Second Vatican Council in Rome (1962–5) which introduced more recent and contemporary philosophical approaches by some Catholic theologians present at it, there has been less emphasis and interest, generally speaking, in Aquinas's theology and philosophy among Catholics, among priests and the clergy generally. This, paradoxically, has enabled Aquinas's philosophy to be taken more seriously by scholars, including those from other traditions. As regards his religious philosophising, though Christian in perspective, it does offer many valuable insights into how religious faith can be analysed and explained, a development which can only be positive for the contemporary appreciation of St Thomas's philosophical views.

See **Afterlife, Aristotle, Beatific Vision, Christianity, Death, Faith, God, Immortality, Anthony Kenny, Neoplatonism, Philosophy of Religion, Plato, Proclus, Reason, Soul, Theology, Thomism** (including **Neothomism**)

Further reading: Burrell (1986); Copleston (1955); Kenny (1980, 1993); McInerney (1998); Quinn (1996)

Arguments for the Existence of God: The question as to whether or not it is possible to prove God's existence by human reason is a central topic in the philosophy of religion. It implies questions about what is meant by 'God' and 'human reason' and what kind of criteria are used to prove or disprove the existence of God. Issues also arise about the impact on theistic belief of being able to prove or disprove the existence of God. In *The Unknown God* (2004) Anthony Kenny restates his agnostic position which began, he says, during the period spent as a Roman Catholic priest in the early 1960s when he came to seriously doubt whether God's existence could be established by human reason. After deciding not to continue as a priest, he set out to investigate philosophically the validity of proofs for God's existence, beginning with Aquinas's five ways, which Kenny concluded in his book, *The Five Ways*, were seriously flawed in that they were based on an outdated Aristotelian cosmology and contained fallacious arguments. Kenny subsequently claimed that the God of scholastic and rationalist philosophy does not exist though he accepts that God can be conceived in other ways and thus leaves open the possibility of God's existence. Over the course of his work, Kenny has become much more interested in viewing religious discourse, including discourse about God, as reflecting a poetic rather than a scientific mode of thought and language. Questions therefore arise for philosophers of religion about their own degree of bias for or against the possibility of proving God's existence, and raising the question of whether indeed there can be any wholly objective proof for or against God's existence. Some have suggested that it is beyond the capacity of human reason to establish this one way or the other. Believers might also add that what is essential is faith in God and in God's revelation to human beings. These kinds of concerns have historically drawn philosophers into an analysis of the precise nature of the relationship between faith and reason. The issue was famously discussed in Christian, Jewish and Islamic philosophical and religious thought. From the beginnings of Christianity as a missionary religion to the Greek world, Christian thinkers who were educated in Greek philosophy discussed this relationship. Later St Augustine's analysis was followed by that of many others, including St Anselm of Canterbury and particularly St Thomas Aquinas, both of whom set out to demonstrate how God's existence might be established by reason. The latter's five ways exemplify such attempts and are based on one's sensory experience of the world. Their common conclusion that there is a being whom people call God specifically derives from (1) the existence of motion which argues for an Unmoved Mover, (2) the experience of causality that argues for an Uncaused Cause, (3) the experience of possibility and necessity which implies the existence of an ultimately necessary first being,

(4) the knowledge that existing entities are more or less good, noble, etc. which argues that there is a perfect being and, (5) the purposefulness and goal-driven nature and activities of things in the world, notably the non-intelligent entities, which argues for cosmic design and order instituted by an intelligent being. Although there is considerable debate about the validity of the five ways (as in the critique of Anthony Kenny), Aquinas himself was convinced about them. Aquinas's thesis was that faith and reason are not essentially in conflict with each other but rather complement one another in a harmonious relationship of partnership in the search for the most important kind of knowledge, that is knowledge about God. However, for Aquinas it remained true that faith immeasurably adds to and more perfectly enhances what can be discovered by our natural reason. An example of this is that though natural reason can establish that God exists, Christian faith teaches that God is a Trinity of Divine Persons and Creator of the universe, and the Redeemer God–Man, Jesus Christ, who suffered and died for the sins of humankind and rose from the dead in glory to lead humankind to the eternally happy face-to-face vision of God after death. Other Christian thinkers like Duns Scotus and William of Ockham also presented arguments for God's existence and this tradition continued after medieval times, though in different forms, into the era of modern philosophy and beyond. In the seventeenth century, for example, Western Christian thinkers such as Descartes and Leibniz provided arguments for the existence of God. Descartes stated that our clear perception of a standard of perfection must imply the existence of a perfect being, namely God, while Leibniz claimed that the answer to the metaphysical question as to why there is something rather than nothing lies in the existence and nature of the first necessary and uncaused Cause, God.

Blaise Pascal, the French mathematician, declared that God's existence can be accepted as the best option to gamble on since if God does not exist, we have nothing to lose and if God does exist, then so much the better for us. However, from the eighteenth century onwards, Western philosophers became more sceptical about the validity of arguments for God's existence and this is particularly evident in the writings of Hume and Kant. Hume, an agnostic, and Kant, a Christian, dismissed for different reasons the possibility of inferring from one's experience of the world that God exists and some Enlightenment thinkers wrote scathingly of religion, especially of Judaism (Kant) and Christianity (Tom Paine). Kant declared that religion is the subject matter of faith rather than philosophy and later Kierkegaard suggested that taking a 'leap of faith' that goes far beyond reason is necessary if we are to meaningfully relate to God. Other philosophers, particularly David Hume, argued that accepting God's existence is based more on psychological and emotional needs rather than reason and this interpretation was also a feature of the writings of, among others, Friedrich Schleiermacher, Ludwig Feuerbach, Karl Marx and the physician–psychoanalyst, Sigmund Freud, all of whom perceived belief in God's existence as originating in the emotional and imaginative psychological life of human beings. In the twentieth century, thinkers such as Sartre, A. J. Ayer and Richard Dawkins rejected the existence of God as being incompatible with, respectively, human freedom and the absurdity of reality (Sartre), the requirements of language and the nature of science (Ayer and Dawkins). On the other hand, Gabriel Marcel was convinced that a self-reflective metaphysical approach facilitated the recognition of the mystery of the divine in reality. Bertrand Russell, who rejected God's existence, nevertheless continued to be fascinated by religious belief as did Ludwig

Wittgenstein from a different point of view, and both continued to grapple with the religious question at various stages throughout their lives. Islamic thinkers have also been very interested in the existence and nature of God and the relationship between faith and reason. Al-Kindi (died c. 866/873), often described as the first philosopher of the Arabs, identified God as the One and he defined the True One as essentially constituting an absolute unity, eternal and infinite, transcending all genera and species, susceptible neither to generation nor corruption, and immovable. The One is the cause of all other entities that possess unity and is the creator and preserver of everything created. Al-Kindi was also convinced that creation took place in time *ex nihilo* (from nothing). Al-Farabi also discussed God as First Being and the Cause of all existing things. According to al-Farabi, God is primordially and supremely perfect, eternal, wholly complete, necessary and actual and not composed of matter nor form. God is unique and does not derive his being from anything else, has no end other than himself, is wholly separate from matter, is intellect in action, is living as thought thinking itself and love loving itself. Through his superabundant goodness, the First Being overflows and gives rise to the whole hierarchy of existing entities which al-Farabi proceeded to examine in some detail. Ibn Sina (Avicenna) came to conceive of God as necessary being from the distinction between what is contingent and what is necessary. That which is conceived in itself must necessarily exist and can be equated with 'that being, which, if it is supposed not to exist, an absurdity will ensue', according to ibn Sina. By contrast, what is contingent may or may not exist without any absurdity being attributed. On the basis of this distinction, ibn Sina developed his famous proof for the existence of God as necessary being which was known up to the time of Leibniz, whose

proof is similar. Ibn Sina argued that whatever has being must either have a reason for its being or not. If it
does, then it is contingent. If it does not, then it is necessary in its being and if this is so, then the case is established. If, however, being is contingent, then there must
be a reason for this and if this reason is itself contingent, and if there is a chain of such contingent reasons,
then there is no being at all, which is absurd since we
know that there are beings. Therefore contingent beings
are ultimately explained by the existence of a necessary
being. Ibn Sina goes on to argue that this necessary being is essentially one and without any cause whatsoever.
The other great Islamic thinker, ibn Rushd, in response to
al-Ghazzali's attack on philosophy as a subversive influence on Qur'anic faith, set out his own arguments for
God's existence in the context of what he claimed to be
a harmonious relationship between religion and philosophy. The proofs for God's existence, according to ibn
Rushd, are based on the principle that all existing things
are suited to human existence and needs, which also
obliges us to develop a greater understanding of what
surrounds us as a means of coming to know God. The
existence of inanimate objects and the activities of the
natural world and the motions of the heavens imply, he
claims, 'a Producer of life and a Gracious Giver of it, who
is God Almighty'. Secondly, the invention of things in the
universe indicates the existence of an inventor, God. In
making this claim, ibn Rushd rejects the view that because God is transcendent it is impossible to argue from
created effects to the existence of their Creator. Similar
and indebted to Islamic religious thought and discourse
or *kalam*, is a corresponding body of thought in the Jewish tradition, especially in the writings of medieval Jewish
philosophers like Dawud b. Marwan al-Muqammis (early
ninth century), who subsequently became a Christian,

and Saadia ben Joseph al-Fayyumi (842–942). Just as Islamic civilisation, and much earlier still, Christian culture, absorbed aspects of the classical world, especially in terms of philosophical and scientific thought, so too did Judaism with regards to how belief in God, divine creation, divine justice and the afterlife and other related issues, came to be analysed and understood. This process was probably initiated by the Jewish thinker Philo who lived in Alexandria in the first century AD who used Platonic philosophical analysis in his exegesis of the Hebrew Bible (Christian Old Testament). In the twelfth century AD, Abraham Ibn Daud, who lived in Spain between 1110 and 1180, argued, following Aristotle, that the explanation of motion or change lies in the existence of an immobile Prime Mover and the greatest of all the medieval Jewish philosophers, Moses ben Maimon or Moses Maimonides wrote extensively about what can be known of God's existence and attributes in his classic work, *Guide of the Perplexed*. Another Spanish-born Jewish thinker, Shem Tov ben Falaquera (c. 1225–95) distinguished between the prophetic and the scientific paths to truth where in the former case, the truth is obtained without study or searching while the latter involves examining, scrutinising and understanding everything that exists since the only proof for God's existence lies in the reality that is before our eyes. Hasdai Crescas (d. 1412 at Saragossa) argued that the essence of the infinite God cannot be attained by the human mind, a conclusion that is evident from a philosophical point of view and most importantly from revelation. There are thus no proofs for God's existence, according to Crescas, though we know that God exists since he is the Cause, as Creator, of the world that we apprehend. Without God, there would be no world, and we can positively conceive of God, if only in a limited way, just as we can have some idea of what is infinite from our knowledge of what is finite. Moreover, existence cannot be predicated of God and creatures in the same way since there is an essential difference between them. Thus, in the Jewish tradition, as with Christianity and Islam, and in other religious traditions, there is a certain consensus of agreement that human reason, although limited in scope, is capable of presenting arguments that can establish divine existence. At the time of writing, the status of arguments for God's existence still remains very much an open question and still provokes considerable debate on all sides.

See **Al-Farabi, Al-Ghazzali, Al-Kindi, St Anselm, St Thomas Aquinas, Aristotle, St Augustine, A. J. Ayer, Belief, Christianity, Dawkins, Faith, Feuerbach, Freud, God, Hume, Ibn Rushd, Ibn Sina, Islam, Judaism, Kant, Anthony Kenny, Kierkegaard, Leibniz, Gabriel Marcel, Maimonides, Karl Marx, Reason, Religion, Bertrand Russell, Sartre, Friedrich Schleiermacher, Wittgenstein**

Further reading: Averroes (2001); Fahry (1997); Helm (1999); Jamil-Ur-Rehman (1921); Kenny (1986, 1992, 2004); Leaman (1999); McInerney (1998); Marx (1977); Paine (1984); Rowe (1998); Seckel (1986); Sirat (1990); Wittgenstein (1980)

Arguments from Design: the range of arguments for God's existence based on the perceived purposeful design of the universe.

See **Arguments for the Existence of God, Leibniz**
Further reading: Leibniz (1973)

Aristotle (384–22 BC): student and subsequently close colleague of Plato's at the Academy. Following the latter's death, Aristotle, after some years travelling, set up his own school, the Lyceum. As with Plato's writings, Aristotle's address a comprehensive range of subjects,

many of which are identifiably scientific in nature including physics and biology. He also wrote on psychology and
politics, ethics and metaphysics, drama and economics
and on many other subjects. Unlike the Platonic writings,
most of which are found in the form of dialogues, the
Aristotelian texts available are written in an identifiable
'text book' style and Aristotle's scientific interests pre-
dominate throughout. His conclusion about the Unmoved Mover as the ultimate source of change was later
used by Aquinas, among others, to establish the existence
of God. St Thomas based much of his own philosophical approach on that of Aristotle, as did others in the
Christian tradition, and this is also true of thinkers in the
Islamic and Jewish traditions, particularly ibn Sina, ibn
Rushd and Moses Maimonides. Although Aristotle does
not convey the impression of being hugely interested in
religion and theology, he does write about God in some of
his texts, such as in Books VIII and IX of *Nichomachean
Ethics*. His views on the rational *psyche* as the substantial
principle of human life and the relationship between the
senses and the intellect influenced later theories about the
human soul and about how we naturally acquire knowledge, especially those of St Thomas Aquinas.

See **St Thomas Aquinas, Creation, Death, God, Ibn
Rushd, Ibn Sina, Maimonides, Plato, Reason, Soul**

Further reading: Ackrill (1981); Barnes (1982, 1984);
Leaman (1999a); Quinn (1996)

Asceticism: involves self-denial in the form of austere practices and abstention from worldly pleasures, particularly
for religious reasons. Such practices may include fasting,
limited sleep, isolation from others and restricted communication with them, physical hardships and other kinds
of deprivations. Those who aspire to a life of holiness
and closer contact with the divine, often welcome an ascetic life style as individuals or as members of a religious

community. The underlying principle of asceticism is that by withdrawing from this world through practices of self-denial, people are more likely to more freely pursue a life of holiness and closer union with God or divinity, however conceived. There is a considerable body of literature on the subject including Plato's dialogue, *Phaedo* (especially 65a–67b), which provides some philosophical background for asceticism. Here Socrates argues strongly for distancing the *psyche* from its state of physical embodiment in this world as a necessary condition for attaining psychic perfection, enlightenment and happiness through purification. Plotinus also advocated an asceticism of the spirit in order to focus more clearly on the journey towards the One. Likewise in many religious traditions including Christianity, Judaism, Islam, Hinduism and Buddhism, asceticism exemplifies the path towards God and the divine through self-denial. Some religious objections to asceticism warn of the dangers involved in certain extreme forms of self-denial that may be physically and psychologically harmful. It has been suggested, for example, that Simone Weil's ascetic practices, which hastened her death, were the result of psychological rather than religious motivation. Though she claimed that she was fasting in solidarity with her French compatriots who had to suffer the Nazi occupation of France, others have perceived her behaviour as extreme and unbalanced and most likely the result of her psychological problems dating from her early childhood. A more general theological caution warns against the attraction of withdrawing 'from the world'. This, it is argued, if carried to extremes, might be interpreted as a lack of respect or even disdain for God's creation and divine immanence.

See **Buddhism, Christianity, God, Hinduism, Mysticism, Plato, Plotinus, Religion, Ninian Smart, Soul, Sufism, Simone Weil**

Further reading: Netton (2000); Smart (1971, 1989)

Atheism: denies both that God or a particular kind of God or divinity exists and the possibility of any supernatural presence or intervention in the natural world. Since the nineteenth century, particularly, atheism has become a dominant feature of Western thought for a whole variety of reasons and has shaped the writings of such thinkers as Karl Marx, Nietzsche, Sartre, Camus, A. J. Ayer, Bertrand Russell and Richard Dawkins among many others. One form of atheism exhorts people to confront the reality of a non-theistic world and adjust their lives accordingly rather than believing in God out of emotional, psychological, cultural or social needs. It is thus presented as a mature contemporary response to what the world is by contrast with what are regarded as less well-informed views of religious believers which belong to an earlier age of ignorance, fear, superstition and immaturity characterised by magical thinking and a lack of adequate scientific knowledge which too often allowed religious–political power to dominate people's lives. Atheism is thus seen to represent a new maturity in human thought, which, by rejecting the existence of God, facilitates a more rational approach to how one should live in the empirically verifiable world. Some atheistic approaches are indifferent to or even tolerant of religious beliefs although others are explicitly hostile. The latter would include the views of Marx, Sartre and Richard Dawkins. Bertrand Russell, curiously enough, while deploring the anti-scientific and punitive dogmatism, as he saw it, of the Catholic Church, saw a demonstrable social value in religion in that believers are exhorted to be morally well disposed towards their fellow human beings in society.

See **A. J. Ayer, Camus, Dawkins, Faith, God, Hume, Karl Marx, Nietszche, Philosophy of Religion, Religion, Russell, Sartre**

Further reading: Ayer (1936); Camus (1973); Hume (1975); Marx (1977); Russell (1961); Sartre (1946)

Augustine of Hippo, St (AD 354–430): born in Thagaste
in Roman North Africa (present day Morocco) at a
time when the empire was being undermined by various
barbarian invasions, Augustine was to have an extremely powerful and long-lasting effect on subsequent
Christian thought, especially through the Middle Ages
and also during the Reformation. His mother, Monica,
who greatly influenced him throughout her life, was a
Christian whereas his father was not, although he was
baptised before he died, and Augustine himself did not
become a Christian until he was 33. He was educated
in Carthage where he later taught rhetoric, and subsequently in Milan, where he came to Christianity via
Manicheism and Platonism. The Manichees expressed
revulsion at physical reality and argued for the necessity of extreme forms of asceticism. They believed in a
permanent conflict between the Power of Light and the
Power of Darkness (from which evil resulted), and Mani,
their founder, borrowed from Christian thought, including from the New Testament. Augustine was with the
Manis for ten years before becoming suspicious of their
views, then became interested in scepticism and finally
took up Platonism where he was particularly attracted
by the philosophy of Plotinus and Porphyry, as well as
by Plato's writings. This led him towards Christianity
and under the influence of St Ambrose, the Archbishop
of Milan, he decided to become a baptised Christian.
He was subsequently ordained priest and Bishop of
Hippo. Augustine favoured Platonism as the philosophical approach most suitable for Christians and his writings explore the relationship between human reason
and Church teachings. *The Confessions* describe his personal journey towards God culminating in his Christian
faith and, in addition, Augustine wrote extensively
on a vast range other theological and philosophical
topics.

See St Thomas Aquinas, Belief, Christianity, Faith, Neoplatonism, Philosophy, Plato, Plotinus, Porphyry, Reason

Further reading: O'Meara (1997)

Averroes See **Ibn Rushd**

Avicenna See **Ibn Sina**

Awe: the believer's attitude of wonder, reverence and respect for God or the divine and/or at the wondrous nature of reality. This is said to constitute the basic religious stance expressed as worship and contemplation. Philosophers, particularly Aristotle, recognise the importance of awe at what exists as the basis of all reflection, including the scientific, and ibn Rushd, among others, perceived such reflection as leading towards a theological understanding of God.

See **Beatific Vision, God, the Holy, Stephen MacKenna, Iris Murdoch, Rudolf Otto, Plato, Plotinus, the Sacred**

Further reading: Eliade (1959); Murdoch (1992); Otto (1923)

Ayer, A. J. (1910–89): educated at Christ Church, Oxford and later philosophy lecturer and professor at Oxford and the University of London, Ayer exerted considerable influence on twentieth-century British philosophical thought. His writings reflect what came to be known as analytic philosophy. His classic work, *Language, Truth and Logic* (1971), which outlined his linguistic analytic approach, resulted from his contacts with the Vienna Circle of philosophers. The principal theme of this and his other works is that only analytic statements (where subject and predicate are in some way identical) and statements whose references can be empirically verified are meaningful. On these grounds, Ayer rejected meta-physics as a meaningful philosophical discipline and also denied the existence of God on the grounds that such a claim was expressed in language that contained no empirical reference, according to his criterion of empirical verifiability. The latter, which he later modified somewhat without substantially changing it, stated that

> a sentence is factually significant to any given person, if, and only if, he knows how to verify the proposition which it purports to express – that is, if he knows what observations would lead him, under certain conditions, to accept the proposition as being true, or reject it as being false.

Since metaphysical, religious and, in some respects, ethical statements, cannot be empirically tested in this way, these forms of discourse are meaningless or nonsensical (having no sense). Ayer regards them as probably psychological in inspiration and claims they are emotive, even poetic in purpose. It is arguable, however, that Ayer's own criterion of empirical verifiability is itself incapable of being empirically verified and more than likely represents his belief rather expressing a testable hypothesis. His contact with the Vienna Circle which highly respected Wittgenstein's *Tractatus Logico-Philosophicus* led Ayer to admire the author although Ayer was unhappy with Wittgenstein's later approach to the relationship between language, thought and reality which was set out in *Philosophical Investigations*. There was also a clear difference between the two men on the nature of religious discourse which was always highly valued by Wittgenstein once it was properly located in the religious system of reference which he claims to admire. By contrast, A. J. Ayer follows Hume's approach and claims that such discourse is inferior to scientific and empirically-based discourse and reflects the purely psychological, emotional and poetic dimensions of human existence. It should be noted in passing, however, that in some respects Ayer's linguistic theory does carry resonances of the *via negativa*, especially as set out in Maimonides' *Guide of the Perplexed*.

See **Agnosticism, God, Hume, Maimonides, *Via Negativa***

Further reading: Ayer (1936)

Beatific Vision: The direct face to face post-mortem vision of God in the ultimate and supremely blissful state of perfect happiness. Many religious philosophers claim that this non-bodily vision represents the ultimate end and goal of all human endeavour since it is this vision that constitutes everything that human beings search for, whether they are aware of it or not. The paradox, according to the twentieth-century philosopher–theologian Bernard Lonergan, is that, although *visio Dei*, or the 'vision of God', represents the ultimate goal of all intelligent beings, seeing God in this way can only be achieved supernaturally, that is, in a way that transcends the natural capacity of created intelligent beings. Aquinas wrote extensively about the beatified happiness that results from the vision of God, for example in *Summa Contra Gentiles* Book IV, although these sentiments are prefigured by earlier thinkers. Plato's *Symposium*, for example, describes the essence of beauty as not having 'the form of a face, or of hands, or of anything that is of the flesh' but is above and beyond everything else ineffably subsisting of itself in an eternal oneness (211ab). For Christian thinkers like Aquinas, though the beatified experience is said to occur after death in a non-bodily state, questions arise as to what bodily resurrection adds to the separated soul's vision of God. There are also questions about whether or not the beatific vision can occur in some temporary way and Aquinas argues that 2 Corinthians 12:1–6 means that St Paul must have had a transitory vision of God which is explained by a temporary suspension of the sensory powers. St Thomas's intriguing account is to be found in *Summa Theologica* II–II Q.175 and in *De Veritate* Q.13 and represents a brave attempt to analyse how this extraordinary experience might have happened.

See **The Afterlife, St Thomas Aquinas, Plato, Plotinus, Soul**

Further reading: Quinn (1996)

Beauty: in the philosophy of religion, beauty is perceived to have special religious significance as exemplifying the essence of God and demonstrating the divine presence and creative power in reality. Influenced by Plato's *Symposium* (for example 211ab) and Plotinus' treatise on beauty (*Ennead* IV.6.1), many Christian medieval philosophers identified the divine essence with the essence of beauty and Aquinas describes it as a transcendental property of being which expresses being as that which has integrity or perfection, right proportion, splendour of form and is pleasing to the senses. Some twentieth-century writers such as Stephen MacKenna and Iris Murdoch regarded beauty as signifying the religious and the transcendent. They argue that if one attends to the world in which one lives, the cosmos can be seen as beautiful and this should influence those who consider it in this way to live a life of goodness and aesthetic appreciation.

See **Aesthetics, St Thomas Aquinas, God, Stephen MacKenna, Iris Murdoch, Plato, Plotinus**

Further reading: Dillon (1991); Dodds (1936); Murdoch (1992)

Belief: a state of mind in which trust, faith and confidence are placed in a person, idea or thing. There is the conviction to the point of certainty that some propositions are true irrespective of being (at least during the period of belief) unprovable. Giving assent to propositions of this kind can be based on a range of inter-related factors: intellectual, psychological, emotional, social, historical and so forth and results in what can be described as a world view. The latter, as one's 'culture of conviction' (G. A. Cohen's phrase), is derived from one's personal–social environment of origin, though it can be and sometimes is subsequently modified or discarded to be replaced, for a variety of reasons, by a different way of seeing the world. The relationship between one's believed way of seeing things and one's rational efforts to understand reality is of great philosophical interest and is examined in Western thought in the writings of Plato and Aristotle, and from the Middle Ages onwards down to the present day where it is interestingly explored by philosophers such as Michael Polanyi and G. A. Cohen. Plato's *Theaetetus* (206e et seq.) teases out the relationship between knowledge and correct belief while Aristotle argues that we cannot go back *ad infinitum* in terms of proof but must begin with certain assumptions. The relationship between belief as religious faith and other kinds of knowledge was extensively explored by such Christian thinkers as Augustine, St Anselm and St Thomas Aquinas, by Jewish thinkers such as Moses Maimonides and in Islam by ibn Rushd (Averroes) and others. St Anselm claimed that it is not the case that we understand in order to believe but rather that it is in the context of belief (which, for him, was Christian belief) that we come to understand reality. Aquinas argued that belief as Christian faith is compatible with reason since faith does not destroy reason but completes and perfects it. In particular, it extends our knowledge of God and the divine presence in reality. In the Islamic tradition, there was also considerable discussion about the impact of philosophical/scientific knowledge on Islamic belief, and this was also examined in the Jewish tradition. Our beliefs about reality, which may or may not include religious beliefs, are thus a function of our cultures of conviction to which we subscribe on the basis of trust and which thereby determine how we see reality. As part of our respective cultures of conviction, belief as religious belief, is therefore situated between knowledge and opinion, in that the believer is certain of the truth of the theological propositions to which assent is given but which, by definition, cannot be fully proven. David Hume's analysis of belief as psychological in nature, aimed at strengthening our convictions about how we wish to perceive reality, is also a valuable contribution to the philosophical study of this subject.

See **Al-Ghazzali, Arguments for the Existence of God, Faith, St Anselm, St Thomas Aquinas, Hume, Miracles, Polanyi**

Further reading: Cohen (2000); Costello (2003)

Bergson, Henri (1859–1941): French-born Jewish philosopher, many of whose writings contain philosophical observations concerning religion which includes his references to the importance of intuition (for instance in his *Introduction to Metaphysics*) and his concept of *elan vital* or life-force which, in his book, *Creative Evolution*, appears to be identified with God. He also wrote about the nature of the relationship between duration and the self (*Time and Free Will*) and analysed the connection between morality and religion (*The Two Sources of Morality and Religion*). His writings were looked upon with suspicion by some philosophers (especially by some Catholic academics and by the Catholic Church) as anti-intellectual and there may be some suggestions of pantheism in his concept of *élan vital*. He did think of becoming a Catholic as he grew older but decided to remain in the Jewish faith out of solidarity, given the political climate that existed in Europe in the 1930s and early 1940s.

See **God, Immanence, Gabriel Marcel, Mysticism, Religion**

Further reading: Bergson (1977, 1983)

Berkeley, George (1685–1753): Irish Anglican cleric who studied for the ministry and eventually became Bishop of Cloyne in County Cork. A radical thinker who, on reading John Locke's *Essay Concerning Human Understanding*, developed his own theory of knowledge, which was informed by his theological perspective. For Berkeley, only minds (finite human minds and the infinite mind of God) and ideas exist and matter is a concept of the mind. His arguments are presented in *A Treatise Concerning the Principles of Human Knowledge* (1710) and *Three Dialogues between Hylas and Philonous* (1713). However, Berkeley's principal concerns were theological and pastoral and, in middle age, one of his radical projects, which failed due to lack of finance, was to set up a missionary university in Bermuda which would cater not only for colonial American settlers but also for members of the indigenous Native American population.

See **God**

Further reading: Berkeley (1962)

Bhagavad Gita: meaning 'The Song of the Lord' is possibly the most popular Hindu scripture available in the West. It constitutes part of the great Indian epic, the *Mahabharata* and represents for many Hindus the essence of their religion, outlining as it does the different paths to salvation.

It contains a long dialogue between the hero, Arjuna, and his chariot driver who unknown to Arjuna is really the Lord Krishna, the most important incarnation of the god Vishnu. Arjuna is concerned about the prospect of killing fellow humans including his own relations and friends but he is advised by Krishna to do his duty in a disinterested way fitting to his membership of the warrior caste. Part of the argument for doing so involves belief in the soul's immortality and its ability to inhabit different bodies, a claim which lessens the finality of death. There is also a discussion on the nature of the highest deity and the introduction of the view that God is the self and the originator of all that exists in the universe. It states that one should do one's duty selflessly and also for the sake of God. There are different interpretations of this text with some arguing that violence is being condoned and others, like Gandhi, claiming that one is not to reject the struggle against evil within oneself but rather to avoid engaging in physical violence against those whom we consider to be enemies.

See **God, Hinduism**

Further reading: Mascaro (1962)

Bible, The: from Greek *biblion* for book, it refers to the Old Testament or Hebrew Bible and to the sacred writings of Christianity which comprise the Old and New Testaments, and, in the Roman Catholic Church, the Apocrypha. The Old Testament describes God's special relationship with the Jewish people chosen by him, while the Christian Bible (Old and New Testaments) depicts the culmination of God's covenant with Abraham and Moses in the new Covenant with God through Jesus Christ as God-made-man in a new and radical relationship with Jews and Gentiles (non-Jews) who are called to be followers of Jesus through faith in His divinity as divine

Messiah and second Person of the Trinity of God as Father, Son and Holy Spirit.

See **Christianity, Erasmus, Judaism, Luther, The Reformation**

Further reading: The Jerusalem Bible

Bioethics: The study of the ethical problems that arise from medical/biological research with its progressive technological developments and the applications of these in the area of life, from the perspective of human rights, responsibilities and duties, including those involved in research in the area of medical science. Examples of issues include abortion, embryonic development outside the womb, eugenics, euthanasia, foetal research and genetic manipulation, terminal intervention in comatose states, screening and therapy and brain manipulation. While this area, strictly speaking, is the concern of ethics, it does raise questions for philosophers of religion as regards, for example, the religious status of bioethical activities and the compatibility of the latter with certain principles and practice in many religious traditions, including Christianity, Judaism, Islam and the Jehovah Witnesses, to name but a few.

See **scientism**

Further reading: O'Neill (2002)

Body, The: discussions about the nature and role of the human body before and after death and its relationship with the human soul take on considerable importance in the philosophy of religion. For those who believe in the resurrected body, for example, philosophical questions arise concerning the kind of embodiment that would then exist. Part of the difficulty lies in conceiving and stating just what the human body is as the dimension of physicality or corporeality that constitutes the human being. Questions arise, for example, as to whether it is a physical substance (Plato and Descartes) which may impede intelligent and religious activities or is exclusively constituent of and reducible to individual human life without remainder. In the religious context, it has been suggested that it is important for 'the body' to be subservient to one's spiritual life through, for example, certain forms of self-denial and ascetic practices. Linked with this is a more extreme concept of the human body as the source of evil, and in its early days, Christianity was influenced to some extent in this direction by Gnosticism, Manicheism and even Platonism so that some Christian thinkers, St Augustine, for example, tended to conceive of human bodiliness in a negative way. However Aquinas affirmed the importance of human bodiliness by positively defining the individual human being as 'this flesh, these bones'. He did, though, struggle with some conceptual difficulties when he speculated philosophically and theologically about the beatific vision of the resurrection which, for him, required some explanation of the status of human bodiliness in the blissful experience of the beatific vision, as regards what did the body 'add to' the spiritual enjoyment of God in this state. Nevertheless he contrived to depict human bodiliness as positively contributing to the beatific experience in that it defined the latter as subjectively a human experience for those who were beatified. He does, however, describe the beatified resurrected human body, in *Summa Contra Gentiles* Book IV for example as a spiritualised body (*corpus spirituale*) in that it appears brilliant and glorious, is not hampered by physical spatial conditions, and indeed does not seem to function physically as human bodies naturally do before death as regards growth, ageing, needing nourishment or enjoying sexual experiences. Questions thus arise as to what kind of bodiliness could possibly be involved in the beatified state. By contrast,

Aquinas claims that the resurrected bodies of the damned will be dark (compared with the brilliance of beatified bodies) and will constitute a heavy burden for their souls. They will also be subject to physical punishments of the most persistent and excessive kind which will continue unbearably without end. For Platonism, where the human body can be regarded as a vessel bearing the soul and sometimes conceived of as imprisoning the latter and a physical impediment to its path to transcendence (as in Plato's *Phaedo* and in some of Plotinus's writings), it is thus perceived as a contaminating physical influence on its psychic partner.

See **St Augustine, St Thomas Aquinas, Beatific Vision, Empiricism, Hume, Manicheism, Neoplatonism, Plato, Plotinus,** *Psyche,* **Soul**

Boethius (AD 480–525/6): author of the classic text, *The Consolation of Philosophy*, Roman statesman and consul, philosopher and a man of considerable learning who read Greek and Latin and had extensive knowledge of the writings of Plato, Aristotle, Cicero and other classical writers. It was his ambition to translate all the works of Plato and Aristotle and to demonstrate the essential agreement between them, a project never to be completed due to his imprisonment and execution. He did, however, translate Aristotle's logical treatises and other key texts and wrote extensively on philosophy, theology, music, geometry and mathematics, and, most importantly, was crucial in the transmission of classical thinking to the medieval world. He wrote *The Consolation of Philosophy*, his most famous work, when he was imprisoned by the emperor Theodoric and faced execution. The book remains a classic text in the philosophy of religion and is written in prose and poetry and dialogue form where Boethius converses with Lady Philosophy about his fate and state of dejection and near despair while being imprisoned awaiting execution. The text can be seen as a philosophical and theological attempt in literary form by Boethius to extract some meaning from his terrible predicament. The issues discussed include the meaning of life and how to see it from the correct perspective, the gratitude one should have for the good things acquired, the limitations of human life before death, where perfect happiness can truly be found, God's providence and human freedom, the question of evil and, most of all, the need to take a positive view of reality in the face of adversity, however extreme. What is perhaps most interesting about Boethius's approach is that, although he was a Christian, the consolation offered seems to take the form of a religious Platonism with no mention whatsoever of Christ or the Christian view of salvation, although there are many significant references to God. Whether that suggests that Boethius reverted to pure philosophy as a consolation and means of coping with his imminent execution, rather than taking a more explicit Christian stance in the face of death, remains an intriguing question. In many ways, this text echoes Plato's account of Socrates' defence in the *Apology* and also the Book of Job. It deservedly remains a perennial classic in the philosophy of religion and retained a strong influence well into and beyond the Middle Ages and indeed into contemporary times.

See **Afterlife, Aristotle, Christianity, Death, God, Neoplatonism, Philosophy, Plato, Socrates**

Further reading: Boethius (2002)

Boundary Being: A phrase used to describe how the human being or human soul is situated at the interface of the bodily temporal world, on the one hand, and of the intelligible, spiritual, eternal realm, on the other. Uniquely comprising a form of being that is structured in terms of existence, life and thought, this 'boundary' theory originates in the writings of Plato and represents a Neoplatonic interpretation of human reality which is set out, for example, in the writings of Philo, Plotinus, Proclus and others. It influenced Christian and Islamic thought and is to be found in the writings of St Augustine, Gregory of Nyassa, Nemesius, Maximus of Chrsysopolis, St John Damascene and St Thomas Aquinas, among others, and in the thought of some Islamic philosophers, including ibn Sina. Aquinas's boundary image of the human soul (as substantial principle of human life and as intelligent substance) sits uneasily at times with his Aristotelian philosophical viewpoint, for example in *Summa Theologica Part.* I Q.89.Art. 1 where he examines whether or not the human soul can function intelligently after death and in *On Being and Essence* where the human soul is depicted both as the form of human life and as the lowest of the intelligent substances. The tension of this 'in-between' or interfacing form of existence is said to be resolved when the spiritual and intelligible dimension takes total control over human existence in the ultimate transcendent state, by metaphysical or supernatural means, which then ensures the radical spiritualisation of one's mode of existence in the vision of divine being.

See **Hierarchy of Being, St Thomas Aquinas, Neoplatonism, Plato, Proclus, Soul**

Further reading: Quinn (1996)

Buber, Martin (1878–1965): Jewish philosopher with central interests in theology (including Hassidism) and education, born in Vienna, renowned for his classic work *I and Thou* published in 1923. He is also the author of *Between Man and Man* (1946) which contains some of his views on education. His book, *Eclipse of God* (1952) contains many essays on the relationship between philosophy and religion. Buber's interest in the nature of relationships and specifically in how one should relate through dialogue with the Other as uniquely Other (I–Thou), rather than as subject to object (I–It) is explored in his book *I and Thou*. The implication is that the I–Thou discourse reveals the Eternal Other, God, as the ultimate, absolute mysterious Other. In a later essay 'Religion and Philosophy' contained in *Eclipse of God*, he distinguishes religion from philosophy and claims that whereas the I–It relationship finds its highest illumination and concentration in philosophy, the I–Thou relationship achieves its highest intensity and transfiguration in religious reality. The philosophy of religion must continually take this distinction into account since this gives rise to the question as to how the philosophy of religion can do ever do adequate justice to the nature of the religious experience.

See **God, Judaism, Maimonides, Mysticism, Philosophy of Religion**

Further reading: Buber (1958, 1988)

Buddhism: one of the great religions of Asia which, mainly since the latter part of the twentieth century has also enjoyed some popularity in the West. The early period of Buddhism, which began about the sixth century BC and lasted until the first century AD, consists of the time when the Buddha lived and when the teachings and practice of Buddhism were consolidated. Born c. 586 BC in India, Siddhartha Gautama grew up in some luxury but eventually, after he married and became the father of a son, he decided to leave the worldly life and become a wandering recluse, living a nomadic life of great austerity and reflection. He is said eventually to have attained complete insight into the world and into how suffering can be overcome. As the Enlightened One he was henceforth known as the Buddha. He returned to Benares where he gave his first sermon and gathered disciples around him, and thereafter for forty-five years, until he was eighty, he travelled throughout India teaching his saving doctrine of the Way to Liberation and is said to have made a pilgrimage to Sri Lanka. At his death his followers cremated his body and his relics were kept in various places. His teachings addressed the problem of rebirth and of how to liberate oneself from an unsatisfactory world. Although he practiced austerity, he also learned the art of yogic meditation and believed in combining meditation with understanding in order to cultivate the right orientation towards philosophical and religious questions. His central insight focused on the impermanence and interdependence of everything. He sought the causes of events, especially in human life, and advocated training in self awareness so as to perceive and understand the nature of events that take place inside us. He believed that we are free to reshape our destinies even though we inherit from previous lives tendencies which, if uncontrolled, can lead us to other destinies conditioned by suffering. Since nothing is permanent, no satisfaction can last for ever and its disappearance is painful – hence human suffering. The Eightfold Path, which develops the implications of trust, ethical conduct and meditation, tries to avoid the extremes of self-indulgence and self-mortification, and of believing that either the soul is eternal or cut off at death, aims at a moderate faith and at a form of present life lived out with complete insight and serenity. The monastic life offers the best hope of salvation in a spiritual and contemplative community with appropriate periods for solitude. The practical aspect of this teaching is yoga which aims at attaining purer levels of consciousness, though reaching *nirvana* and sainthood transcends all faith and meditation and self-training. (*Nirvana* is believed to be a state in which the person no longer desires anything and is able to discern what lies beneath the appearance of things. This is thought to result in total peace and inward freedom where the mind experiences purity and stability.) Followers should refrain from taking life and what is not given, from wrongful sex or speech and from drugs which obstruct self-awareness. The good person is one who is full of friendliness, compassion, sympathy and equanimity.

From the first century AD onwards, Buddhism spread into China and eventually into Korea and Japan and this is the era of classical Buddhism. From the seventh century, the development of Buddhism sometimes involved certain magical and sacramental rites in which spiritual effects were thought to flow from the recitation of sacred formulae or mantras. This was gradually assimilated into Hindu practices of the period and resulted in the almost complete disappearance of Buddhism from the Indian subcontinent. However, it became the dominant form of Buddhism in Nepal and Tibet. Finally, in the modern period, in the south of Asia and in Asia generally, Buddhism was affected by new political forces, such as colonialism and Marxist Communist developments. At the same time, a growing number of Westerners, especially in the twentieth century, have sought serenity and peace of mind in Buddhist practices and religious beliefs, though some of these have been adapted and changed by its new adherents.

See **Hinduism, Ninian Smart**

Further reading: Conze (1959); Leaman (1999); Smart (1971, 1989)

Bultmann, Rudolf (1884–1976): German New Testament scholar and theologian who was influenced by the early philosophy of Martin Heidegger and who attempted to demythologise the New Testament framework by translating its message using existentialist concepts.

See **The Bible, Christianity, Existentialism**

Cambridge Platonists, The: a group of predominantly Puritan English philosophical theologians, centred in Cambridge who wrote and preached in the late seventeenth century and among whom are listed Ralph Cudworth, Henry More and Joseph Glanville. Their writings are a mixture of the thinking of Plato and Neoplatonism, religious and mystical elements and ancient and modern philosophy. They aimed at liberating theology from the polemics of the Reformation and of the early seventeenth century, and restoring the emphasis on religion as a way of life with primacy being given to religious and sometimes mystical experience.

See **Neoplatonism, Plato**

Camus, Albert (1913–60): French-Algerian novelist, essayist and philosopher who received the Nobel Prize for Literature in 1957 and whose concept of the absurd informs many of his writings. This theme is illustrated in his famous novel *L'Etranger* (*The Outsider*) and philosophically explored in *The Myth of Sisyphus* which identifies suicide as the fundamental philosophical option, given that human life can seem so pointless at times and presents us as it does with an apparently endless set of obstacles to be overcome. The disjunction between our hopes and expectations, on the one hand, and life's very difficult challenges, on the other, highlights the absurdity of reality for Camus. However, he rejects the option of suicide and argues that the very struggle to overcome life's difficulties and seeming irrationality is itself the meaning of what constitutes our existence. This Nietzschean type of solution seemed to satisfy Camus who continued in his later book, *The Rebel*, to explore in further detail the difficulties of the human condition and who, throughout his fiction, sought to depict the personification of these difficulties in his fictional characters. His novels and especially his philosophical treatment of absurdity, suicide and rebellion, provide a rich field for investigating some of the central problems posed by religious thought.

See **The Absurd, God, Nietzsche, Reason, Sartre**
Further reading: Camus (1960, 1973, 1983)

Caputo, John (1940–): Thomas J. Watson Professor of Religion and Humanities, Syracuse University, New York, many of whose writings are concerned with the philosophy of religion. His interest in this area is shaped since the latter years of the twentieth century by his understanding of Derrida's philosophical and theological views. It is interesting in this context, for example, to compare the latter's deconstructionist approach with traditional treatments of *via negativa*. Caputo's book, *On Religion* (2001), which explores the concept of love as a major theme of theological importance, argues that what is central is the existential activity of loving God rather than the semantic analysis of theological language. Echoing Derrida's treatment of religion as responsibility in *The Gift of Death* (1995), Caputo concludes that God is not simply a name but 'an injunction, an invitation, a solicitation, to commend, to let all things be commended to God.'

See **Belief, Christianity, Derrida, Faith, God, Religion**
Further reading: Caputo (2001), Derrida (1995)

Causality: a fundamental metaphysical principle of reality according to Aristotle which subsequently becomes important in the writings of thinkers such as Aquinas for signifying the ultimate agency and existence of God as the source of all that is. Hence many proofs for the existence of God, those of Averroes, Aquinas and Leibniz, for example revolve around divine causality.

See **St Thomas Aquinas, Arguments for the Existence of God, Leibniz**

Change: Aristotle argued that change or motion could only be satisfactorily explained by the ultimate agency of an Unmoved Mover, which, though essentially immobile, attracted other things to itself, and was thus responsible for motion. This argument was later used by Aquinas in the first of his five ways for establishing that God exists.

See **Arguments for the Existence of God, Aristotle**
Further reading: Ackrill (1981)

Chesterton, G. K. (1874–1936): an extremely popular and prolific writer of fiction and non-fiction, the author of the well-known Father Brown stories and a determined Christian apologist. He studied at The Slade School of Art, London but did not complete his studies in art and instead became a journalist and a successful writer and essayist. In his early life he was very preoccupied with the problem of evil and for a time became a sceptic. He suffered from depression for a period but his spiritual and psychological crises seem to have been resolved after meeting his future wife, Frances Blogg, whom he married in 1901. He converted to Roman Catholicism from Anglicanism in 1922 and many of his publications from this time onwards are marked by a strong theological tone. Among his best known publications are *Orthodoxy, Heretics, The Everlasting Man, The Man Who Was Thursday* and his books on St Thomas Aquinas and St Francis of Assisi. Chesterton's writings on Christianity and religion, although rather datedly rhetorical in style, are nevertheless of considerable worth to those interested in these subjects, not least because he points out that religious truth is often presented in a paradoxical manner which is difficult to accept if one expects a straightforward rational and logical presentation. The paradoxical nature of religious truth, according to Chesterton, lies in its essentially mysterious divine origins. The ways of God are often obscure to intellectuals and rationalists but can be appreciated if accepted in humility, as is the case with those who have little in life and who are marginalised and often outcasts as a result.

See **Christianity, Faith, God**

Further reading: Chesterton (2001)

Christianity: The religion of Christians, that is those who believe in the divinity of Jesus of Nazareth as Messiah and God made man, that he suffered, died and was resurrected from the dead by the power of God thereby constituted as divine redeemer of all humankind from sinfulness, and the way towards salvation. The story of the life, suffering, crucifixion by death and resurrection and heavenly ascension of Jesus, his preaching and miracles is described in the New Testament. The explanation and theological and philosophical analysis of Christian revelation and teachings began early on in the history of the Church, because of the influx of Hellenic converts who were educated or expert in Greek philosophical thought, especially that of Platonism. Some Christian thinkers such as St Augustine argued that Platonic philosophy was closely aligned to Christianity, while others, such as Aquinas, preferred the Aristotelian approach. There were early divisions among Christians, notably between East and West for political and theological reasons deriving from the political and cultural differences in the east and west of the Roman Empire and the theological differences about the nature of procession from God of the Holy Spirit. The latter issue concerned whether or not the Holy Spirit proceeded from God the Father and Son or from the Son (The Incarnate Word) alone. The Western Church also favoured the pre-eminence of the bishop of Rome over other bishops whereas the Eastern Churches were more in favour of an episcopal collegiality of equals. With the Christian Reformation inaugurated by the scriptural scholar and theologian Martin Luther, who paid particular regard to the writings of St Paul, and later forwarded under the English Reformation begun by King Henry VIII, Western Christianity divided into a number of different Christian churches with varying degrees of theological closeness to the Church of Rome; various religio-political wars resulted from this further theological fragmentation. The Reformers were in the main initially unsympathetic to, even hostile towards and certainly suspicious of, the effectiveness of a philosophical analysis of religion. They perceived it as being potentially and indeed actually capable of distorting Christian faith, an issue which had arisen much earlier in Islam. More importantly, the Reformers believed in the sole primacy of scripture (*sola Scriptura*). As a result, philosophical approaches to religion became increasingly influenced by the view that belief in God and religion itself were totally beyond any adequate reasonable analysis and that philosophical investigations of faith and theology were therefore unsuitable in providing an explanation of Christian teachings. Kant was an important source for this view although his *Religion Within the Limits of Reason Alone* does indicate some significant points of contact between Christian faith and human reason. In the Roman Catholic tradition, the importance of Aquinas's philosophical and theological theories were increasingly favoured by the Church, initially in what came to be known as the Counter Reformation culminating with the Council of Trent (1545–63), and later in 1879 with the Encyclical of Pope Leo XIII which recommended that Aquinas's works should be widely studied by Catholics and especially by theologians and priests and seminarians for the priesthood and by those in religious orders. Thomism thus received a considerable boost and what came to be known as Neothomism flourished widely in Roman Catholic circles for some time. Eventually, and especially from the days of the Second Vatican Council (1962–5), the status of Thomistic theology and philosophy diminished, at least for some Catholic theologians since many of them, particularly those theological experts (*periti*) like Karl Rahner, Edward Schillebecks and Hans Kung, who were advisors to the Council, came from philosophical backgrounds which were shaped by non-Thomistic philosophical approaches such as phenomenology and other forms of twentieth-century thinking.

See **St Thomas Aquinas, The Bible, Jesus, God, Kant, Luther, The Reformation**

Further reading: The Jerusalem Bible, Eusabius (1965), Kant (1960), MacCulloch (2003)

Confucianism: the doctrine of the Chinese philosopher and teacher of ethics, Confucius (551–479 BC) whose teachings were compiled after his death by his disciples in the *Analects of Confucius*. His ethical system emphasised the moral order, the humanity and virtue of ancient Chinese rulers and the education of gentlemen and underlined the importance of human benevolence and propriety in a hierarchical society where individual roles were very strictly determined. According to Confucius, the benevolent person is superior and aristocratic and is obliged to act according to his social rank just as others fulfil their duties in the context of where they are socially located in the community. Doing one's duty to others as one would want done to oneself is determined by one's social rank and others should do likewise. Achieving the right balance between one's own personal interests and the interests of society pleases heaven and deepens our self-knowledge. A gentleman is not necessarily someone of high birth but is rather anyone who acts nobly, unselfishly, kindly and with justice, all of which provides an example to others to do likewise. Propriety is a mixture of morality and etiquette and human beings should constantly strive to develop themselves further in terms of excellence as individuals in the society in which they live. Mencius and Xunzi developed these teachings. The former claimed that there was a human disposition to behave in an ethically controlled manner and that the state should create an environment which facilitated the expression of one's good disposition by an appropriate form of political rule and ruler, and that violence should always be avoided. Xunzi thought that nature and society may be in conflict at times and claimed that propriety and music can sustain and deepen the royal rule. In other thinkers, loyalty to the ruler was given a theological emphasis where it was equated with loyalty to heaven.

See **Ninian Smart**

Further reading: Confucius (1979)

Contemplation: from the Latin *contemplare* 'to gaze at', 'to view attentively', 'to behold'. In philosophy, it can mean the life of thinking for the sake of thinking and thereby attaining happiness or bliss (Greek *eudaemonia*); in religion, it signifies the act of attending to God or divine reality, for example in prayer. Contemplation and perfect happiness are often linked in this context as cause and effect and there is a considerable body of literature on the subject with references in the writings of Plato, Aristotle, Plotinus, Porphyry and many other philosophers as well as in the religious literature of many cultures and traditions, for example in the writings of St John of the Cross and St Theresa of Avila, to name just two in the Christian tradition.

See **Meditation, Mysticism**

Contingent: as distinct from necessary. Since contingent being or events depend on prior causes in order to exist or occur, arguments for the existence of God are based on contingency. These include, among others, Aquinas's Third Way and Leibniz's argument from contingent and possible reality to the necessary existence of God.

See **St Thomas Aquinas, Arguments for the Existence of God, Leibniz**

Further reading: Leibniz (1973)

Conversion: from the Latin *converto* 'to turn around', 'to turn back', 'to reverse'. A religious conversion means a change in belief and attitude towards a (or another) religious point of view. Plato's *Republic* 518cd provides an interesting philosophical example of conversion depicted as the need to turn away from the world of change in order to see reality for what it is in the light of what is most truly good. The Cave Narrative in the same dialogue (*Rep.*514a et seq.) which precedes this account of conversion, describes the journey of the released prisoner towards enlightenment as a process of conversion from darkness to light, from the illusory to the truly real. Stories of conversion are typical of religious literature and the *Confessions* of St Augustine dramatically depicts one such classic example in Christian literature though there are many others. Religious conversion represents a personal re-orientation, the cause of which is usually identified as being of supernatural origin, towards what is believed to be most real and ultimately true and worthy of full assent by contrast with a previous way of living which is retrospectively (and perhaps simultaneously) recognised in the conversion process as being mistaken and seriously flawed and in ignorance of the true way of life. The nature and object of religious (and ideological) conversion is a much discussed area and, especially, in the medieval world particularly in the Christian and Islamic traditions, there was considerable debate about the kind of conditions necessary for converting from one faith to another (and indeed within one faith, which became of political significance particularly for Christians after the Reformation). Also intrinsic to many such discussions was the political desirability of converting to the religious faith which met with dominant approval in a society where there was religious diversity. The issue of religious tolerance is obviously relevant in such a context and some philosophers such as the seventeenth-century Jewish philosopher Spinoza thought it necessary to outline how religious differences might be philosophically, theologically and politically accommodated in a multi-religious society. Thomas Hobbes' contribution to this debate was to argue that the solution to the political divisiveness of different and conflicting religious views consisted in the control of religion by political rule, a view that was undoubtedly influenced by political events in England during and after the reign of King Henry VIII.

See **St Augustine, Hobbes, The *Republic*, Spinoza**

Conway, Anne (1631–79): author of *The Principles of the Most Ancient and Modern Philosophy* written in English c. 1670 and published in Latin in 1690 in which language it was read and referred to by Leibniz. Central to the book is the thesis that three kinds of substances exist, each of which is essentially different from each other: there is the wholly immutable substance of God, the substance of the Word, Jesus Christ, the God–man, as both mutable and immutable, and the mutable nature of everything else, that is to say created substances. Anne Conway asserts, however, that according to the laws of the world, because of God's goodness, someone will not change into someone else nor will someone become an animal, nor, of course, is it possible for human beings to change into the divine immutable substance of God nor the mutable–immutable substance of Christ. The latter raises interesting questions about the immutable nature of the human soul in the human being. The substantial nature of Christ also poses theological questions for Christian theology, for example, with regards to how, for example, Christ can be explained as fully human and fully divine. Conway's metaphysical approach clearly reflects her anti-materialism (and is thus contrasted with Hobbes' views) and she is also opposed to Descartes' claim that there are only two substances, mental and physical substances. She likewise differs from Spinoza's perception that the whole of nature is identical with God when seen from a different perspective. Her metaphysical–theological approach favours the traditional Christian theological–philosophical interpretation of Christ as constituting two natures, human and divine, while substantially being one person as The Word become incarnate. Her views on substance are contained, especially in chapters 6 and 7, of her philosophical work.

See **Descartes, God, Leibniz, Metaphysics, Spinoza, Substance**

For further reading: Conway (1996); Warnock (1996)

Cosmology: from the Greek *kosmos* meaning 'world' or 'universe', and *logos* meaning 'the study of'), cosmology signifies the scientific study of the universe as a rational orderly system. Often used today to refer to that section of astronomy which speculates about the structure, characteristics and development of the physical universe based on observation and the scientific method. Traditionally connected with metaphysics as the study of what is most pervasive and basic in how the universe is structured, for example in space, time, matter, change, motion, extension, force, causality and eternity, arguments from cosmology, such as the argument from design and order, led to the conclusion that God exists, although in contemporary cosmology, with some exceptions, there is little scientific interest in the possibility that there is an ultimate theological agency that can satisfactorily account for the existence and nature of the universe. That being said, there are undoubtedly philosophical and theological implications in contemporary cosmological theories.

See **Aristotle, St Thomas Aquinas, Creation, Emanation, Leibniz**

Creation: the belief that God created the world from nothing (*creatio ex nihilo*) subscribed to by all the major theistic religions. The omnipotence of God is demonstrated in this original creative act that maintains the cosmos in existence. Philosophical and scientific difficulties arise in such traditions of belief, for example in the Middle Ages there was considerable debate as to how belief in creation could be reconciled with the Aristotelian claim that matter always existed in some way on the principle that nothing comes from nothing. Ibn Rushd (Averroes) and Aquinas from the Islamic and Christian traditions respectively tried to deal with this problem. Averroes argued that that there can be different interpretations of the same issue which may not necessarily be in conflict with one another. In the case of creation, an Aristotelian scientifically based interpretation of matter as eternal could, he thought, co-exist with the belief that God created the world out of nothing, provided one understood the nature and objective of the different interpretations involved. Averroes' sophisticated theory of interpretation, which he presented in the context of claiming that there was harmony between religion and philosophy (to include science), eventually led, together with other factors, to an imposed exile from Cordoba in Islamic Spain and to his writings being destroyed. St Thomas Aquinas, who also addressed the question of creation, concluded that from a scientific view the Aristotelian theory of matter could not be disproved, but since Christian teaching declared that God created *ex nihilo*, from a Christian point of view, this doctrine is believed by faith. In the Platonic writings, emanation is thought to be the process which allowed the universe to come into being. The creation debate did bring to light the kinds of difficulties that emerge in the dialogue between religion and science which were to become acute with Galileo's views on planetary movement and Darwin's theory of evolution. Contemporary creationists still maintain that evolutionary theory is flawed and propose instead the direct intervention of God as being directly responsible for creating the universe. In addition, there is also the belief (held, for instance by Christians) that the human soul is directly created by God.

See **Aristotle, St Thomas Aquinas, The Bible, Christianity, Darwin, Dawkins, Emanation, Hermeneutics, Islam, Judaism, Paul Ricoeur, Ibn Rushd, Plato**

Cult: from the Latin *cultus* one of whose meanings is: an honouring, reverence, adoration, veneration. The term has variously come to signify, from a religious point of view, (1) a specific system of religious worship especially with reference to its rites and deity, but also and particularly from the twentieth century, (2) a quasi-religious organisation using devious psychological techniques to gain and control its adherents. What constitutes an acceptable religious cult will obviously depend on individual, social and political preferences and perceptions and on the kind of criteria used to determine what is or is not 'pseudo-religious'. There has been much discussion since the latter half of the twentieth century about the kinds of methods used to put pressure on certain kinds of individuals to join those religious cults that are viewed with suspicion by many people. The perception is that intense psychological methods designed to strongly persuade certain kinds of vulnerable people (for example young adults) are applied to potential members and that tight control of a psychological nature is a feature of retaining the loyalties of those who join. Cult methods may include 'love bombing' whereby members are bombarded with constant group and individual emotional affirmations of being greatly valued and loved. The threat for those who waver in their commitment to the cult may involve social community exclusion and strong group disapproval. The idealised model proposed may be that of close family and community life in which the primary emotional and cognitive needs can be fully satisfied. Frequently, members may be expected to commit themselves financially by way of contributions to the relevant organisation. One of the striking differences between what are conventionally regarded as 'conventional' or 'mainline' religious organisations and those defined as 'cults' may lie in the psychological and even physical difficulties encountered by those who try to leave, for whatever reasons. While some philosophers of religion may be interested in the philosophical implications of such religious cults, other professionals such as counsellers, psychologists, sociologists and physicians may also be concerned as regards the emotional and psychological dangers for some who join.

See **Belief, Faith, Religion**

Cupitt, Don (1934–): ordained for the Diocese of Manchester and formerly Dean of Emmanuel College, Cambridge and lecturer in the Philosophy of Religion in the University of Cambridge, he has published extensively in the philosophy of religion. Although Cupitt would initially have been critical of various forms of projection theory in Christian theology (for example, that the Christian God is a projection of the human mind and a desire for some ultimate form of hope conceived as immortal happiness) and concerned to establish the objectivity of faith, he subsequently came to argue that key Christian themes should be restated and reinterpreted in the context of contemporary society. He also rejected belief in the incarnation of Jesus Christ, was very critical of church institutions, dogmas and practices and adopted a *via negativa* theological approach which held that we can only say what God is not. He takes what he describes as a non-realist theological view of Christianity and argues for a humanist form of religion. In this context, he perceives Christianity and religion in general as a human construction whose language and concepts have to be reinterpreted as being metaphorically useful in so far as they help to promote central human values such as love unto death. He is undoubtedly influenced in his views by the 'Death of God' theology of the 1960s and specifically by John Robinson's book, *Honest to God*. The more remote influence is that of Nietzsche. Cupitt's strength lies in his readable style of presentation and in some of his criticisms of Christianity such as the need to make it more relevant and meaningful. However, there can be a certain degree of superficiality about his views, which is perhaps accentuated by a rather uncritical adaptation of the works of other thinkers.

See **Christianity, God, Humanism, Religion**
Further reading: Cupitt (1995, 1997)

daemon: Greek word (sometimes *daimon*) meaning 'deity' or 'divine power', sometimes used interchangeably with *theo* (a god) or *thea* (a goddess). Also means a divinity whose status is somewhere between the traditional gods and human beings, which serves as an intermediary or guardian (see Plotinus's *Ennead* 111.4) between human and divine. Plato's *Symposium* 202e–203a contains Diotima's description of these entities which are said to occupy a place between heaven and earth 'flying upward with our worship and our prayers, and descending with the heavenly answers and commandments' and welding the divine and human together so as to constitute one totality. 'They form the medium of the prophetic arts', are involved in 'priestly rites of sacrifice, initiation and incantation' and in divination and sorcery and enable human beings to relate to divinity which requires such mediation in order to have contact with humans. Love is identified by Diotima as one of these spiritual mediators. There are obviously similarities between the concept of *daemon* and the angelic spirits found, for example, in the Jewish, Christian and Islamic religious traditions. Aquinas places the independent human soul in the same category as angelic intelligences, which allows him to compare the intuitive intelligence of these spirits with human intelligence.

See **Angels, St Thomas Aquinas, Plato, Plotinus, Soul**
Further reading: Hamilton and Cairns (1963)

Dalai Lama: head of the Yellow School of Monks in Tibetan Buddhism. Historically, Tibetan Buddhism gained considerable prominence after the failure of Buddhism in India during the twelfth century AD. Tibetan monks then became the main inheritors of the Indian Buddhist tradition, preserving many ancient documents and practices that were respected by Theravavan Buddhism in the south. Buddhism spread from Tibet to China, Korea and Japan where the Mahayana tradition flourished and produced other schools of Buddhism. In Tibet a theocratic government was established and Tibetan Buddhism, sometimes called Lamaism, spread to the West in the 1950s following the Chinese invasion of Tibet. The present incumbent and fourteenth holder of the office of Dalai Lama was born in 1935 and until 1959 was the chief lama and ruler of Tibet. He successfully sought religious and political refuge in India after the Chinese occupation and received the Nobel Peace Prize in 1989.

See **Buddhism**

Daoism See **Taoism**

Darwin, Charles (1808–82): English scientist and thinker credited with the evolutionary theory, his seminal work, *The Origin of Species* (1859) appears to have presented compelling empirical evidence and arguments for the theory that the mechanism for the evolutionary biological development from lower to higher forms of life consists of chance variations and natural selection involving competition for survival and reproduction. Prior to Darwin, Charles Lyell (1797–1875), whose work influenced Darwin, had speculated on the evolution of land animals (1832) and in 1853 Herbert Spencer had put forward a theory of evolution from lower to higher forms of life and organisation. Darwin's conclusions, which were based on his own observations while on board the HMS *Beagle* on which he worked as a naturalist led to controversy since his views were seen as a blatant attack on Christian beliefs about divine creation. The debate also reflected a much more extensive argument which occurred historically in the Christian world in particular but also in Islam about the relationship between scientific knowledge and religious beliefs. This issue has continued to be debated into the twenty-first century by, for example, Richard Dawkins, Keith Ward and others. Many religious thinkers regard Darwin's theory as being compatible with Christian interpretations of creation although Creationists reject this because of their literal biblical interpretations. Atheists and agnostics are also dismissive or sceptical about any harmony between Darwin's theory and religious beliefs about creation and perceive evolution as another example of science's exposure of the flawed nature of religious thought. Darwinism has also been applied in the fields of economics, psychology and sociology as a way of explaining survival and change for individuals and societies and one form of social Darwinism presents a generalised theory of social action and change that justifies ruthless competition on the basis of natural selection and the survival of the fittest.

See **The Bible, Creation, Richard Dawkins, Faith, Hermeneutics, Scientism**

Further reading: Helm (1999)

Dawkins, Richard (1941–): currently Charles Simonyi Professor of the Public Understanding of Science at Oxford University and author of such well-known books as *The Selfish Gene* (1976), *The Blind Watchmaker* (1976), *The Extended Phenotype* (1982), *The Ancestor's Tale: A Pilgrimage to the Dawn of Evolution* (2004). Dawkins, who began work in the field of ethology (the study of the nature of animal behaviour) and then moved into the related field of evolutionary biology, puts forward scientific evolutionary views that represent a significant contemporary challenge for the philosophy of religion. Echoing earlier empiricist rejections of the validity of religion, Dawkins argues that science and religion are incompatible. The latter, he states, makes false claims about the universe and encourages people to adopt an obscurantist approach to life by believing in God. The scientific view he holds, by contrast, to be true, inspiring and remarkable, uniting many phenomena under one heading. According to Dawkins the fundamental dynamic in reality is that of cultural replication. He has used the term 'meme' (from mimetic or imitative) to identify the cultural replicator that constitutes the fundamental unit of evolution and forms the basis for survival, change and adaptation. The meme is to cultural inheritance what the gene is to biological heredity. Memes like genes can act like parasitic viruses and the supportive environment in which they thrive is also crucial. Dawkins uses the phrase 'the extended phenotype' to identify the total environment in which the meme thrives. Our current state of high technological development, he suggests, plays a dominant supportive role in present human evolutionary development. It is difficult to know at times whether Dawkins is using the term 'meme' as a theoretical paradigm or whether he believes that it represents an existing ontological tendency or reality; for example, he talks about a meme for religious belief. He claims that replication occurs by an insistent form of repetition of whatever is being replicated all of which constitutes part of a cultural process. Questions arise, however, as to the deterministic nature of memes which might suggest that their influence cannot be resisted. However, Dawkins also wants to assert freedom of choice and claims that certain forms of replication (often linked with religious faith) should and can be resisted. He states that it is possible to combat our selfish memes so that we can live less selfishly. Dawkins is explicitly anti-religious in his writing and challenges those positively disposed towards religion both in the content and presentation of his work. However, there are problems relating to freedom and determinism and to his understanding of and criteria for moral action which render a certain lack of coherency to his arguments. Nevertheless, taken as a whole, his scientific theories and conclusions, because they are presented so dogmatically in an explicitly anti-religious vein, do present challenges for those positively disposed towards religion.

See **A. J. Ayer, Christianity, Darwin, Religion, Scientism**

Further reading: Helm (1999)

Death: a much discussed topic in the philosophy of religion from the earliest times. As the permanent end to human life, death still raises questions about its nature and whether or not it can somehow be transcended by some form of personal survival post-mortem. Questions arise such as whether or not it is in fact the final end of human life or somehow or other some kind of passage into another state of existence and, if the latter, just what that might mean. Death also raises questions about how one should conduct one's life before death, however interpreted. Many religions support the possibility of an afterlife where the immortal human soul or spirit is judged worthy to live with God in a state of ineffable bliss in a life after death.

See **The Afterlife, St Thomas Aquinas, Aristotle, The Body, Boethius, Buddhism, Camus, Christianity,** *The Egyptian Book of the Dead, The Tibetan Book of the Dead,* **Existentialism, God, Happiness, Heaven, Hell,**

Immortality, Gabriel Marcel, Near-Death Experiences, Out-of-Body experiences, *Phaedo*, *Psyche*, Psychical Research, Reincarnation, Religion, Saints, Sartre, Socrates, Soul, Spirit, Supernatural, Transcendence, Transmigration

Further reading: Choron (1963)

Deism: from the Latin *deus* 'god' represents the view that reason rather than divine revelation provides us with the truth about God's existence and nature. God is understood to be First Cause and supremely intelligent creator of an ordered universe that obeys the unchangeable divinely ordained laws of reason. God is not immanent in creation but totally different from it, transcending it, and outside what is created. Reason is in harmony with revelation or vice versa and the Bible should be analysed by reason so that its doctrines are demystified. There is also the implication that God has a preordained plan for the universe and all things in it and that the highest human duty is to fulfil the purpose of the natural laws that God has created. Deism's emphasis on reason is an example of theological rationalism and is found, for example, in the writings of some seventeenth-and post-seventeenth-century thinkers in Western philosophy, for example, Leibniz.

See **God, Leibniz, Rationalism, Religion**

Demiurge: from the Greek *demiourgos* 'one who does work for people', 'a skilled workman', 'craftsman', 'a maker', 'a creator', the term is used in Plato's dialogue *Timaeus*, and refers to the principle of creation in the universe. The Demiurge follows the eternal unchanging perfect ideal Forms shaping chaotic and resistant matter into the best possible rational patterns.

See **Creation, Emanation, Plato**
Further reading: Hamilton and Cairns (1963)

demon (see also *daemon*): usually means an evil spirit or devil.
See **Angels, Plato**

Derrida, Jacques (1930–2004): born in Algeria and educated
in Paris at the Ecole Normale Supérieure where he subsequently lectured in philosophy, he is associated with what
is called a deconstructionist approach. One of his principal philosophical concerns relates to what language can
say and whether we are correct in thinking it says what
it appears to say. Derrida suggests that there are many
hidden factors operating in human language including
the psychological and psychoanalytical and his method
of deconstruction analyses what is involved. It shows, for
example, that communication consists of the presence of
dominant 'privileged' terms which suppress or exclude
their opposites on the basis of choices made. Derrida has
also written on religion, and in *The Gift of Death* (1995)
he puts forward and analyses in detail his theory of religion as responsibility.
See **John Caputo, Emmanuel Levinas, Religion**
Further reading: Derrida (1995)

Despair: the existentialist philosophers, Sartre, Camus and
Marcel emphasised the importance of despair from a
philosophical point of view. Sartre argued that we must
live without hope since there is no ultimate meaning to life
and to reality. Human endeavour in the long run is pointless, he claims in *Existentialism and Humanism* and in
Being and Nothingness and human life as a future project
is destined to remain unfinished and incomplete although
life in the short term can be meaningful as regards how we

perceive the choices we make and decide on the courses of action that we wish to pursue. However, there is no ultimately important goal or end towards which people might direct themselves. Camus argues in *The Myth of Sisyphus* that, in the face of the absurd, it is still meaningful to make the effort to engage in life's struggles and he believes that cultivating an attitude of stoical endurance when confronted with adversity is of human value. Marcel, on the other hand, believes in the necessity for hope as creative fidelity to the mystery of life which, for him, is based on the transcendent mysterious presence of God who calls us to trust and hope.

See **Camus, Death, Existentialism, God, Hope, Marcel, Sartre**

Further reading: Camus (1973); Marcel (1948, 1964, 1978); Sartre (1946)

Determinism: the view that every natural event, including human choices, result exclusively from past events due to causal necessity. The determinist claims that the universe is at every future time fixed, given its state at any particular time and the causal laws that govern events in the natural world. Some philosophical approaches, often based on philosophical empiricism, tend to be marked by determinism, for example that of Daniel Dennett although many determinists of the late twentieth and twenty-first centuries come from the world of science, especially evolutionary science, like Richard Dawkins, and believe that the laws of nature and/or the evolutionary process are the determining factors. There is also psychological and sociological determinism – in the writings of B. F. Skinner and Sigmund Freud, for instance – which argues that environmental factors almost wholly determine human choice and action. In passing, it is worth noting that

Gottlob Frege, logician and philosopher, was careful to distinguish the logical from the psychological and to state that whereas logic provides us with truth, psychological explanations for how we arrive at conclusions are not qualified to deal with the truth per se to include the ethical truth of human action. There is also theological determinism where God is said to directly determine events, which again raises questions about human freedom. This latter issue was debated in the Christian context by St Thomas Aquinas, who, in his treatise *On the Teacher*, argued against Augustine that one should distinguish proximate from ultimate causality in the sense that although the ultimate teacher is God, human beings are validly called teachers since they proximately elicit knowledge from their students. Determinism thus presents a number of serious challenges to human freedom of choice and action which philosophers of religion must also address.

See **Darwin, Dawkins**
Further reading: Helm (1999)

Dialogues of Plato, The: Apart from a small selection of letters whose authenticity has been debated, most of Plato's writings are found in the form of dialogues. These consist of philosophical dramas where discussions take place between various characters many of whom are historically based and chief among whom is Socrates, or rather the Platonic Socrates. The latter represents Plato's understanding of Socrates (as distinct from, for example, Xenephon's portrait of Socrates) as the iconic and ideal philosopher, which undoubtedly has a real historical basis. Thus in almost all of these dialogues, Socrates is the central character around whom the various discussions revolve. The topics discussed cover a wide range of subjects including the nature of knowledge, the soul, justice, education, beauty, the ideal society, piety and the creation of the universe. Plato's dialogues make for intriguing reading, not least because of the difficulties of ascertaining Plato's precise position on the subjects discussed. As author, are his views represented, for instance, by what Socrates says or do these discussions represent exchanges between him and his colleagues in the Academy? Plato's dialogues represent the process that is intrinsic to philosophising, that is they demonstrate that philosophy best occurs through the medium of critical conversational exchanges between people in a spirit of friendship and learning which culminates in insights into the nature of reality as such. Some dialogues such as *Euthyphro*, *Phaedo* and especially *Laws* examine religious and theological themes and *Laws* in particular is important for its philosophical analysis of religion. The mode of dialogue is unique as a way of presenting philosophy and Plato perfected it as a way of teaching the process of philosophising through the form of a written text. Other philosophical dialogues have been written, for example by George Berkeley and David Hume among others, though Plato's dialogues remain unique in style, substance and in philosophical and historical value.

See *Phaedo*, **Philosophy, Philosophy of Religion, Plato**
Further reading: Hamilton and Cairns (1963)

Divine: relating to or characterising God or what is God-like or sacred. Theology in the Christian Middle Ages was known as *divina scientia* (divine science) and was regarded as the Queen of the Sciences by the Scholastics, notably Aquinas. The divine right of kings reflected the claim that the right to rule derives from God and that monarchs are answerable for their political actions to God.

See **God, The Holy, Rudolf Otto, Religion, The Sacred, Theology**

Divine Attributes: are qualities, characteristic features or properties traditionally ascribed to God such as goodness, mercy, love and justice. In the philosophy of religion, what can be thought and said about God is important and questions arise about whether and how it is possible to attribute qualities to God and if so, what kind of language is appropriate to use. What, for example, does it really mean to say that God is good/merciful/loving and just as compared with describing a human being in such terms? Religious discourse about the divine attributes can be negative, positive and analogical.

See **Analogy, St Thomas Aquinas, God,** *Via Negativa, Via Positiva*

Durkheim, Emile (1858–1917): French social scientist, one of the founders of modern empirical psychology and pioneer of the sociology of religion. He developed a naturalistic and functionalist approach to religion which regarded beliefs and rituals as providing a set of unifying symbols that represent the core values of society. In his book, *The Elementary Forms of the Religious Life*, he concluded that religion, philosophy and morals can be understood only as products of the social condition of humankind. The source of religion and morality derives, according to Durkheim, from the collective mind of society and is not inherent in the isolated minds of individuals. One criticism made of his view of religion is that it does not sufficiently recognise the force and importance of the universal aspects of the great world religions as transcending the values of any particular society.

See **Feuerbach, Freud, God, Religion, Schleiermacher**
Further reading: Durkheim (1965)

Egyptian Book of the Dead, The: sometimes known as *The Book of the Great Awakening* was written about 1500 BC for Ani, Royal Scribe of Thebes, and contains a ritual to be performed for the dead with detailed instructions for how the disembodied spirit should behave in the Land of the Gods. Some of Plato's dialogues, *Phaedo* for example, and his myths of the underworld could be usefully compared with this text.

See **The Afterlife, Death, The Dialogues of Plato, *Phaedo*, Plato, *Psyche*, Soul, *The Tibetan Book of the Dead***

Further reading: Wallis Budge (1987)

Eliade, Mircea (1907–88): Romanian philosopher and historian of religious thought, he became professor of religious studies at the University of Chicago in the USA in 1956. He was particularly interested in religious mythology and the ways in which similar mythic religious themes emerged in various cultures and many of his writings reflect this including *The Sacred and the Profane,* which provides an account of how the sacred can be distinguished from what is not sacred, for instance in terms of sacred time and sacred space, and *From Primitives to Zen*, in which Eliade provides a comprehensive anthology of the main religious traditions.

See **Myth, Philosophy of Religion, Religion, Ninian Smart**

Further reading: Eliade (1959, 1977)

Emanation: from the Latin *emanare* 'to flow out of' this is the theory that claims that all reality proceeds from a central principle or source of perfect existence which is one (The

One, The Good, God) and eternally present. Just as the sun is the source of light which emanates from it and is dependent on, though not identical with it, the One is the source of all existence and on it everything else depends. The universe is thus an outpouring from the One as the Good and just as the farther away something is from the sun, the less bright it is, the further away something is from the One, the less intelligent and perfect it is. Matter is furthest from the One while intellect and soul are closer to it. The theory of emanation is primarily associated with Plotinus (AD 205–70) although ultimately derived from Plato's writings, it has influenced Christian and Islamic thought and, because these faiths maintain the doctrine of *creatio ex nihilo*, that is the belief that God created the world out of nothing in time, it has posed some problems for them.

See **Al-Kindi, Creation, Ibn Sina, Islam, Plotinus**

Further reading: Dillon (1991); Leaman (1999a); O'Meara (1995)

Empiricism: the theory that, by contrast with rationalism, emphasises the primacy of sensory experience in the acquisition of knowledge. This poses problems in explaining the spiritual, non-physical nature of religious belief and experience. There are different kinds and degrees of empiricism. Aristotle would be regarded as more empirical than Plato in that Plato's writings claim that knowledge originates in innate ideas whereas Aristotle argues that without sensory experience knowledge could not be humanly acquired and consequently that with the dissolution of the human organism and therefore the sensory powers in death, no further knowledge is possible. Aquinas, who, in the main, followed the Aristotelian approach, could also be perceived as an empiricist. However, given his attempts to explain how it is possible for the soul to survive death and to see God in a non-bodily way, St Thomas is obviously not a thoroughgoing empiricist. In the seventeenth and eighteenth centuries, John Locke and David Hume provided a new impetus to empiricism in Britain with both men insisting that sensory experience is a necessary condition for knowledge. Hume, in particular, was a thoroughgoing empiricist who reduced the acquisition and nature of knowledge to a sensory process and content. He concluded that most knowledge is probable rather than certain and that religious knowledge in particular can be explained by and reduced to psychological feelings and emotions. In his most scathing attack on religion and theology, which is contained in his *Enquiry Concerning Human Understanding*, Hume advises that books on metaphysics and theology should be burned because they do not deal with matters of fact or experience and therefore are nothing but sophistry and illusion. The Lockean–Humean form of reductionist empiricism (particularly that of Hume) later became extremely influential in the twentieth-century English-speaking world and is found, for example, in the writings of A. J. Ayer and, in a more modified way, in Anthony Kenny. Empiricism obviously challenges the ways in which religion and theology and the philosophy of religion are understood.

See **A. J. Ayer, David Hume, Bertrand Russell**
Further reading: Hume (1975)

Enlightenment, The: refers to the eighteenth-century intellectual movement in Europe that emphasised the autonomy and power of human reason and questioned the role of traditional authority. The inspiration for this development undoubtedly has its origins in Descartes' claim that if reason is employed in a methodical, logical, mathematical and scientific way, it is possible to find out everything there is to know. Spinoza, Leibniz and others in the rationalist–idealist tradition concurred with this view while Hume from the empirical tradition also subscribed to the Enlightenment. Kant's short essay, *Answer to the Question: What is Enlightenment?* states that the motto of the Enlightenment is to have the courage to use one's intelligence, to dare to understand and thereby free oneself from dependence on the guidance of others. This also applies to religion, he argues, and in his book, *Religion Within the Limits of Reason Alone*, he argues that it is reason that must judge religion. While Hume's critical and empirical analysis of religion contains some points of agreement with Kant, notably about the rational inaccessibility of God, the immortal soul and freedom, it none the less rejects the rational validity of religious thought, and this view is also shared by others in the Enlightenment tradition, notably Rousseau, Tom Paine and Karl Marx.

See **Kant, Leibniz, Rationalism, Religion**
Further reading: Wood (2001)

Enneads, **The:** Plotinus's treatises compiled and arranged by his disciple and editor, Porphyry, into six sets each containing nine treatises – hence the title *Enneads*.
See **Stephen MacKenna, Neoplatonism, Plato, Plotinus**
Further reading: Dillon (1991); O'Meara (1995)

Epic of Gilgamesh, **The:** ancient Sumerian epic of the second millennium BC, preserved on clay tablets and deciphered only in the nineteenth century AD. The cycle of poems centres on the character of Gilgamesh, king of Uruk (in Iraq) whose friend Enkidu dies, leaving Uruk compelled to search for the secret of immortality. It also contains a legend of the flood similar in many respects to the biblical story of Noah. A mixture of adventure, tragedy and morality, the *Epic* contains themes that are of universal human interest about the kinds of difficulties with which we can all identify as they arise from the human condition.

See **The Afterlife, Death, Immortality, Myth,** *Phaedo, Psyche,* **Soul**

Further reading: Sanders (1972)

Epicurus (341–270 BC): born in Samos and exposed to the philosophical approach of Plato and later to that of Aristotle. He became interested in the physical atomic theories of Democritus and eventually set up his own school of philosophy with a close circle of friends in the garden of his house in Athens. He is known for his teaching on the importance of seeking happiness. While he encouraged his disciples to believe that 'god is an indestructible and blessed animal, in accordance with the general conception of god commonly held', he is best known for his view that we must accustom ourselves to death because it is nothing to us and we should not be afraid of death because we will not live to experience it. While we exist, death is not yet present and when death is present, we do not exist and the important thing is to live well and seek out what is most pleasant in life as far as is possible. We should be discriminating about our desires and be aware of what is necessary for happiness and for life itself and for freeing the body from troubles. He teaches that what is important is a healthy body and a soul free from disturbance. This is the goal of life, and pleasure in this context is, according to Epicurus, the starting point for blessedness and he cautions us to be careful about our choice of pleasures. Sometimes it is necessary to accept pain in order to attain greater pleasures, but self-sufficiency is also very important and we should be content with a few things so that we can find greater enjoyment rather than by being indiscriminately extravagant. Epicurus advocates the importance of a simple life style and he condemns what he describes as the pleasures of the profligate and the pleasures of consumption. Instead we should soberly calculate the reasons for every choice and avoid anything that is the source of turmoil for our souls. Although the term Epicureanism often suggests an uncontrolled hedonistic pursuit of every available pleasure in large quantities, Epicurus's own words do not advocate this. His philosophical views seek to help people to avoid unnecessary worry or turbulence in their lives and argue for moderation and simplicity of lifestyle. Freedom from bodily pain and from mental trouble is what he preaches. This, he believes, will result in a human state of equilibrium that can co-exist with a disinterested worship of divinity conceived as exhibiting the ultimate beatitude.

See **Death, God, Religion**
Further reading: Helm (1999)

Erasmus (1466–1536): Dutch humanist and leading scholar of the Renaissance, he was born in Rotterdam, became an Augustinian monk and was then ordained a priest. A biblical and patristic scholar, philologist and textual critic who translated a large number of Greek and Latin manuscripts during his lifetime, he is credited with editing the first critical edition of the Greek New Testament in 1516, which was revised several times in the succeeding years. His most famous text, *In Praise of Folly*, presents a critical disapproval of priests and monks because of their ignorance and lack of scholarship, though he later opposed Luther against whom he argued that disagreement is important and that free will rather than pure necessity determines human attitudes and actions. More importantly, he insists that scriptural interpretation is of central importance in understanding the Bible and, in his text, *On Freewill*, he stated that the co-existence of different interpretations of the same text must be respected. He strongly supports the view that human wisdom has a valid place in religious and theological understanding as opposed to

what, according to Erasmus, is Luther's dogmatic acceptance of faith combined with his rejection of reason. The
Dutchman's measured and balanced trust in the human
reasonableness of Christian faith was an important coun-
terbalance to the Lutheran missionary demand for faith
alone in God and Scripture in the absence of such reason.
    See **Christianity, Faith, Humanism, Luther, The Refor-
mation, The Renaissance**
    Further reading: McConica (1991)

Eternal: of infinite duration and identifying the timeless realm
without beginning or end in which God exists. The soul's
destiny ultimately lies in this realm and, on the basis of
having lived a good life, will flourish fully there after
death in a form of life without end. The contrast between
time and eternity is often noted by spiritual writers and
philosophers among whom are numbered Plato, Plotinus,
St Augustine and St Thomas, and it is also interesting in
this connection to note Henri Bergson's distinction between time as temporal sequence and time as duration.
    See **God**

Evidence: the kind of evidence that supports claims for the
existence or non-existence or unknowability of God is of
great importance to philosophers of religion as is the kind
of criteria used to determine the veracity of such evidence.
In Western contemporary philosophy, it is frequently suggested that such evidence should be scientific in nature or
empirically based. The faith–reason debates in the Middle Ages were marked by such concerns and it is interesting to recall in this context Plato's *Theaetetus* 210a
where Socrates states that knowledge is correct belief, a
claim that was later echoed in the Christian world by
St Augustine and dramatically illustrated in St Anselm's
Proslogian where the principle of *credo ut intelligere*,
or faith seeking understanding, precedes the ontological

argument. This inevitably raises question about how we can know whether our beliefs are correct and by what criteria.

See **St Anselm, Arguments for the Existence of God, Belief, Faith**

Further reading: Cohen (2000); Costello (2003)

Evil: poses a particularly difficult problem for the philosopher of religion. There is natural evil (for example natural disasters), moral evil related to human choices and theological evil concerned with what is perceived to be the ability or willingness of God to deal with evildoing. As a problem (or mystery) evil can seriously challenge one's belief in the existence of God as one who is all-good and all-powerful. How God and evil can co-exist is of central concern to the philosophy of religion. Theists tend to argue that evil is an original condition which is inherited from our first ancestors as a result of their primary disobedience to God. This doctrine of original sin is also mythologically depicted in many ancient cultures and narratives and also features in some of the writings of philosophers like Plato and Plotinus, the latter claiming that evil is a lack (of good) – the absence of what should be present. St Augustine and St Thomas Aquinas, among others, also subscribe to this view while the twentieth-century philosopher Gabriel Marcel regards evil as a mystery of which we also are part.

See **God, Leibniz, Gabriel Marcel, Plotinus**

Existentialism: The philosophical approach that emphasises the primacy of existence over essence. Sartre describes this view as originating in the individual's experience of discovering that one exists first and foremost and then being faced with the responsibility of making something of oneself or creating one's own essence. Existentialism is thus a philosophical and literary approach that gives priority to the individual and to his or her freedom over that of the group or community. It often tends to underline the difficult, traumatic and sad features of life and some, like Sartre and Camus, perceive reality as absurd in that our expectations are ultimately doomed to be unfulfilled. 'Expect the unexpected' is Sartre's advice in so far as he is willing to give any, and for Camus the apparent meaninglessness of life gives rise to the question of suicide. Many of the proponents of existentialism have had their own personal traumas, often in childhood, and frequently in the family context. The death of a parent during infancy or early childhood (as with the fathers of Sartre and Camus and the mother of Gabriel Marcel), parental hypocrisy and authoritarianism (as with Kierkegaard's father) or the threat of imminent death by execution (Dostoievsky) are examples of such painful experiences. Existentialism exhorts its followers to live an authentic human existence according to how one sees life, to rebel against inauthentic social and political demands and to set one's own goals for personal fulfilment. It is thus a philosophy of the self, sometimes almost to the point of narcissistic self-obsession and it can be criticised as an approach which is unable to or disinterested in engaging with the reality of the social constraints and demands made by other people. God and religion are themes with which existentialist writers are concerned as issues that relate to the meaningfulness of human existence. Kierkegaard, who is regarded as the 'father' of existentialism, wanted religion to be less institutionalised and more personally relevant and Nietszche also condemned the institutions of Christianity for controlling human spontaneity and our celebratory instincts. Sartre identified himself as an atheistic existentialist and perceived God's existence as a threat to his own freedom while Camus found it difficult to entertain the existence of God in view of his perception that reality is absurd. Marcel (who converted to Catholicism), the theistic existentialist who described himself as a NeoSocratic, argued that we should appreciate reality as a metaphysical mystery rather than seeing the questions it poses to us as problems that should be capable of solution. He encouraged a reflective (and self-reflective) approach to life that recognised the value of interpersonal presence, the mystery of goodness and love, and the mystery of evil. French existentialism from the 1920s to the 1950s exerted a powerful philosophical influence before, during and immediately after World War II. Some existentialist philosophers were also gifted writers. Sartre wrote novels and plays and Camus won the Nobel Prize for Literature in 1957 as an extremely talented novelist, while 'non-philosophical' authors such as Dostoevsky, Kafka and the Irish writer and playwright Samuel Beckett also portrayed the human condition as one marked by suffering, lack of meaning, a sense of not belonging and the apparent absence of God. The sense of exile, alienation and displacement, so strongly noted by existentialist philosophers and writers indicate the importance of their views for consideration by philosophers of religion.

See **Camus, God, Gabriel Marcel, Nietszche, Sartre**

Further reading: Blackham (1962); Camus (1973); de Beauvoir (1960); Kierkegaard (1989); Marcel (1948); Sartre (1946)

Faith: A strong and unshakeable religious belief and trust in God and/or in what is perceived to be divine. The basis of faith is the subject of much discussion in the philosophy of religion and is explained as a supernatural infused virtue or disposition (grace). Faith is also said to be related to convincing evidence acquired from natural reason and/or psychologically derived from the need for personal and emotional security. In the Christian context of the medieval debate on the relationship between faith and reason, Aquinas stated that faith lies midway between opinion and true knowledge, sharing in the former's quality of uncertain knowledge since what is believed is unprovable but it also contains the quality of the certainty of true knowledge. Aquinas, like Maimonides, claimed that faith is necessary for human beings because its absence would mean that it would be extremely difficult if not impossible for most people to know anything about God, including those things that are naturally accessible to the human mind. Although Aquinas wants to insist in his Five Ways that we can establish God's existence by natural reason, he was also convinced that faith often needs to be present to supplement the mind's natural ability to discover God's existence by reason. Maimonides had earlier made this claim in his *Guide of the Perplexed* where a number of arguments outlining the difficulties of naturally coming to know God without revelation are set out which point to the need for a teaching authority.

See **St Anselm, St Thomas Aquinas, St Augustine, Belief, Hume, Maimonides**

Further reading: Costello (2003); Helm (1999, 2003); Hick (1957); Kenny (1992, 2004); Newman (1979)

Fall, The: the event of primordial disobedience to God which for Jews, Christians and Muslims accounts for what is believed to be an inherited flawed human condition in which people experience the inclination towards wrongdoing. Myths of the Fall are found in many cultures and in the writings of some philosophers, such as in Plato's *Phaedrus* (the winged souls) and in Plotinus.

See **The Bible, Christianity, Hermeneutics, Judaism**
Further reading: The Jerusalem Bible

Feuerbach, Ludwig (1804–72): German philosopher influenced by Hegel. In *The Essence of Christianity* (1841), he puts forward his theory of sublimation (pre-Freud) where he claims that God is a projection of the human mind which ideally personifies all that is aspirationally good and desirable from a human point of view. Religion precedes philosophy, he concludes, and is the earliest indirect form of knowledge and represents the childlike condition of humanity. We see our nature from outside ourselves, so to speak, before managing to find it subjectively within us. We contemplate our nature as if it were other than us, as an external object. Religion (which, for Feuerbach, means Christianity) represents the relationship of the human being to him or herself. God, he says in *The Essence of Christianity* is nothing but 'the human being purified, freed from the limits of the individual man, made objective – i.e. contemplated and revered as another, a distinct being. All the attributes of human nature are, therefore, attributes of human nature.' Atheism is distinguished from religious faith because the former perceives God as having no properties whereas the believer regards God as a positive and real being. Feuerbach concludes that there is no distinction between God as he is in himself and God as he is 'for me'. This humanist view of religion as a notional projection which externally objectifies and reifies human values in what is taken to be a personal divine being, was to influence Marx and Freud and is also an important notion in the writings of Sir James Frazier, all of whom interpret religion in a somewhat similar way.

See **Belief, Faith, Sir James Frazier, Freud, God, Karl Marx, Religion**
Further reading: Helm (1999)

Finitude: refers to the limitations in the natural order. Under-lying many of the arguments for the existence of God is the claim that the finitude of the cosmos and everything in it is indicative of its dependence on an external reason, cause or source of existence, which in Aquinas's words, is what people call God.

See **Arguments for the Existence of God, Eternal, Evidence, God, Infinite**

Fortune Telling: is said to predict the future by looking into a crystal ball, reading hands, tea-leaves and so on. The suggestion here is that some people have a special gift for foretelling future events and knowing some significant past experiences that others have had. Philosophically speaking, there is an issue of determinism here. Fortune telling ranks alongside astrology, prophecy, shamanism and witchcraft and the dimension of the occult as a phe-nomenon that claims to provide knowledge by extraor-dinary means.

See **The Occult, Prophesy, Shamanism, Witchcraft**

Frazier, Sir James (1854–1941): the first professor of social anthropology at the University of Liverpool, from which post he retired to write extensively on anthropological subjects. His classic twelve-volume work, *The Golden Bough: A Study of Magic and Religion* (published orig-inally over a period of years from 1890–1915 but later also in a one-volume abridged version), is based on the accounts of missionaries, travellers and traders who tended to interpret beliefs and practices out of the social and historical contexts in which they were found. His writings, however, have exerted considerable influence on the development of comparative religious studies. Fra-zier concluded that the movement of higher thought came from magic through religion to science. According to him, human beings in the era of magic relied on their own

strength to combat difficulties and dangers and they believed in an established order of nature which they could
manipulate for their own purposes. When they came to realise the difficulties of the latter and their own limitations,
they then came to rely on the mercy of certain invisible super beings to whom they attributed all the powers which
they once believed they themselves humanly possessed.
This was the religious era in which the omnipotence of
vastly superior spiritual phenomena was widely accepted
though subsequently replaced by a scientific understanding of reality which provided more credible explanations
for natural and other events. Religion thus came to be
rejected by the more intelligent who consigned theological
explanations to the realm of magical thinking in favour
of science which was seen to provide the future hope of
moral, intellectual and material progress. Like the primary era of magic, science restored human self-reliance
and shared with magic a belief in order as the underlying principle of all things. Frazier, however, warns against
thinking that science has the last word since, in the final
analysis, he tells us, magic, religion and science are merely
systems of thought and, just like its predecessors, science
can also be superseded by some more perfect hypothesis which looks at phenomena from a different point of
view presently unknown to us. Knowledge, he states, is
always advancing towards some goal that forever recedes,
and what is important is that we have been and are now
provided with ways of interpreting our environment, all
of which are marked by probability and none of which
can be regarded as absolutely and permanently definitive.
In this context, religion, like magic and science, merely
represents one way of seeing the world which is now redundant as a world view of reality. It is interesting to note
that Ludwig Wittgenstein, who became fascinated with
The Golden Bough, may well have developed his theory
of language games from reading this text. Wittgenstein's

second theory of language claims that there is no ideal language (as he had earlier stated in his *Tractatus Logico-Philosophicus*) but rather equivalent though varied ways of communicating.

See **Belief, Faith, Hermeneutics, Myth, Religion, Wittgenstein**

Further reading: Frazier (1993)

Freud, Sigmund (1856–1939): Austrian physician and the founder of psychoanalysis who interpreted religion from what some regard as an exclusively reductionist psychoanalytic perspective. He claimed that belief in God is an illusion that originates in the primary childhood need to find an all-powerful father on whom one can utterly depend and whose goodwill one seeks while also looking for freedom and independence in order to be an autonomous and self-sufficient human being. In essence, Freud dismissed the idea of God as an illusion created by human beings for comfort in their psychological helplessness. Original sin and the sense of guilt that religion engenders in believers were, he claimed, related to the primitive and inherited sense of shame derived from an original act of tribal murder which he describes in his book *Totem and Taboo* as occurring when the sons of the tribe rebelled against the father–leader to gain possession of the women. Yet, although he was dismissive of religion, Freud reluctantly decided that human beings were still unprepared to liberate themselves from religious superstition. They needed, he thought, to worship God and to believe in an absolute and divinely ordained system of values if they were to retain respect for law and order. He seems to have thought that, at least in his time, such respect was impossible in the absence of religious constraints. He also interpreted Moses, the Old Testament Law gives, in the light of the father-figure image and argued that Christians displaced their own hidden hostility towards their fathers by persecuting the Jews, including and up to the German (and Austrian) treatment of the Jewish people in Europe in the 1930s. Freud's interpretation of religious faith through his psychoanalytical model has had considerable impact on society as a powerful critique of religion. However, it is argued that this also typically reflects a form of psychoanalytic hermeneutics in general which is too reductionist and one-sided and thereby fails to take into account the validity of any other interpretations of human life and motives, including the religious. There are similarities between Freud and Ludwig Feuerbach who earlier and similarly argued that God represents a dynamic of sublimation constructed by the human mind aimed at attributing those perfections sought by human beings, to an idealised personified illusion.

See **Belief, Christianity, Faith, Feuerbach, Judaism, Karl Marx, Religion**

Further reading: Helm (1999)

Gnosticism: A religious and philosophical movement that existed in the early centuries of Christianity and declared that a higher form of knowledge (*gnosis*) leading to a deeper understanding of God and salvation occurs by means of a special revelation and esoteric spiritual knowledge. Gnosticism also tended to downplay the importance of the physical world and human bodiliness in favour of the higher world of the spirit. It was regarded as an early Christian heresy in that it declared that privately revealed knowledge was superior to Scripture.

See **Christianity**

Further reading: Hanratty (1997)

God: for many believers the attempt to understand, define or explain what God is seems to border on presumptuous arrogance and, in this context, Moses Maimonides, the Jewish thinker, declared that those who believed that they could define God in positive terms (for example as the supremely good, just and merciful being) had no understanding whatsoever of what God is. Instead, we should acknowledge our profound lack of knowledge of what God is, he states, and this will paradoxically provide us with some understanding of God's being and nature. Thus, negative knowledge, according to Maimonides, constitutes the only theologically appropriate epistemological approach to take when we think or speak about God. This tradition of knowing by not knowing, at least from a philosophical point of view, is associated with the Socratic approach and is interestingly examined in Plato's dialogue, *Parmenides*. In the Jewish tradition, the Book of Exodus 3: 14–15 describes God's self-identification to Moses as: 'I Am Who I Am' and God exhorts Moses to inform the people that 'I AM has sent me to you.' As the God of His chosen people, Yawveh remains transcendent yet historically involved. For Christians, God is also wholly transcendent, while yet being immanent in reality. Christian belief is in a Trinitarian God of Father, Son (the Word or *Logos*) and Holy Spirit in whom, The Word, or Second Person of the Trinity, as the divinely equal and identical expression of the Father, became human in Jesus of Nazareth as Jesus Christ, the Messiah. Thus, understanding what God is for Christians, implies an understanding of what Jesus, God made human, is, which is revealed in the narratives of the gospels and other writings in the New Testament and in the traditional teachings of Christianity. Aquinas explores in his writings the ways in which God can be understood and named, in so far as this is possible. He concluded that the most proper name for God is *Qui Est* or I AM WHO AM since it signifies divine existence as the ever-present essence of God. Aquinas also stated that one's knowledge of God can be negative and positive and analogical based on comparing what is created with what is divine, all of which can be flexibly expressed in analogical language.

In the Islamic tradition, Allah, the transcendent, must be humbly worshipped and not represented in images. Nevertheless, God is also immanent in creation. The difficulty here, as in the other religious traditions (Christianity for example), which hold this view is to philosophically account for how divine immanence and transcendence can co-exist since exclusively emphasising divine transcendence makes it difficult to explain God's activity in the universe whereas too great an emphasis on divine immanence can lead to pantheism. In Indian philosophy, references to God are monotheistic, though not always so, and divinity is conceived in different ways, depending on how divine transcendence, immanence and creative activities are understood. Confucius accepts the notion of divinity in the sense of heaven though this view is disputed by others in the Chinese tradition, while Buddhist thought does not employ the notion of God. In the philosophical tradition, there have been many ways of describing and naming God and, in the Western tradition, Plato is sometimes said to be the one who first used the term 'theology' (from *theos* meaning god and *logos* signifying the knowledge of or the study of something). There are also suggestions in his writings of a monotheistic concept of God. Neoplatonic philosophy, which is often marked by a strong religious motif, is noted for Plotinus's writings on the One and the Good which appear to stand for a transcendent God or Absolute divinity that overflows with goodness, and from which every other reality emanates. Finally, the agnostic point of view, which claims that it is impossible to find evidence for or against the existence of God, represents a position of epistemological and personal uncertainty that can lead to scepticism whereas atheism rejects the possibility of God on the grounds that it does not perceive the implications of the divine attributes (such as omnipotence or love) in the world.

Whatever God is, and indeed whether or not God exists at all, remains central to many discussions in the philosophy of religion which, interestingly, can often demonstrate the difficulties of retaining a neutral stance on the issue which in turn may suggest that personal attitudes usually inform to a significant degree the ways in which we conceive of God.

See **The Afterlife, Agnosticism, St Thomas Aquinas, Arguments for the Existence of God, Atheism, Belief, Buddhism, Faith, Hinduism, Islam, Judaism, Maimonides, Neoplatonism, Plato, Plotinus, Religion, Ninian Smart**

Further reading: Boethius (2002); Buber (1958, 1988); Clark (1998); Gilby (1951); Kenny (1986, 2004); Levinas (1998); McInerney (1998); Maimonides (1963); Quinn (1996)

Good, The: in Plato's *Republic* is said to be 'the end of all endeavour' as that which is ultimately sought by all though difficult to define. It is that which gives the objects of knowledge their truth and the power of knowing to those who know and is the cause of knowledge and truth. Just as the sun makes things visible, the Good, as the transcendent cause of their being and reality and the cause of their intelligibility, is still beyond everything, superior to all in dignity and power. Reality is seen in the light of the Good and it is the latter towards which the mind must be orientated in order to reach 'the brightest region of being'. It is clear from the lyrical language used by the Platonic Socrates that the Good is central to reality and society as that which enlightens and transcends all that is and wise philosophical rule must direct people individually and collectively towards it. There are suggestions of equivalence in the Platonic dialogues between the Good (*Republic*), Beauty (*Symposium*) and God (*Laws*), later developed by subsequent thinkers, notably in the Christian tradition, into conceiving of God as the essence of goodness and beauty.

See **Agathon, Iris Murdoch, Plato, Plotinus**

Further reading: Dillon (1991); Hamilton and Cairns (1963); O'Meara (1995)

Greek Tragedy: the dramatisation of myths and stories, many with a historical basis, which often underline the reality and consequences of human limitation. In the latter context, particularly, the exposure of the consequences of *hubris* or *hybris* meaning an unwarranted and arrogant sense of invulnerable self-sufficiency is often dramatically personified. The message is: be aware of the limitations of the human condition by adopting a realistic and humble appreciation of one's powers and capabilities. The religious tone which is at least implicitly found in Greek tragedy determines the overall nature of dramatic content and the interaction of the characters and constitutes Greek tragedy as a cultic event which is existentially dramatised in terms of human limitation, the recognition of which can give rise to enlightened attitudes and action. The contrast between the Oedipus plays, *Oedipus the King* and *Oedipus at Colonnus*, demonstrates this perhaps most clearly: in the former play, Oedipus begins as a capable intelligent ruler of great power who is nevertheless deeply flawed and the drama ends in personal disaster for him; in the second play, Oedipus appears living in a cave, blind, helpless and in rags, and needing to be led about by his daughter. Yet, from such humble beginnings, Oedipus emerges as one who accepts his limitations as a feature of the human condition generally. Many of these dramas therefore provided useful material for consideration in Greek philosophy generally and are especially relevant to the philosophical analysis of religion.

See **Finitude, God, Myth, Philosophy, Plato, The Dialogues of Plato, Religion, Transcendence, Simone Weil**

Further reading: Lesky (1965); Weil (1957)

Happiness: the state of permanent blissful contentment regarded as supremely worth having. Epicurus understood it as a state of contentment and equilibrium free from turmoil and pain. Plato describes it as that blissful state of *eudaimonia* experienced as a result of the good ethical life, while Aristotle understands it as that total state of unalloyed satisfaction achieved by actualising one's potential. For the religious believer, the attainment of true happiness is linked with the blessedness of God, for example in terms of faithfully obeying God's laws or in seeing God face to face in the beatific vision after death.

See **Beatific Vision**

Further reading: Quinn (1996)

Heaven: believed to be the final locus or state inhabited by those who will reside with God in the afterlife which, for Christians, means seeing God face to face in the beatific vision. Plato and Aquinas describe such a state as one of total blessedness and ineffable happiness. St Thomas declares that the glorified and spiritualised bodies of the beatified in this state are wholly at one with their souls, agile, light and perfect. What is interesting about many descriptions of heaven is how physical they often are, which gives rise to questions about the nature of the state described, especially by those who believe in bodily resurrection.

See **Afterlife, St Thomas Aquinas, God, Happiness, Hell, Plato, *Psyche*, Soul**

Further reading: Quinn (1996)

Hegel, Georg (1770–1831): German philosophical idealist who thought that Mind or Spirit was the ultimate reality. Although he accepted the reality of material objects, he also insisted that only the Absolute is entirely real and that its seemingly distinct parts have reality only in virtue of being part of the whole. His philosophical approach is shaped by the influences of the early Greeks, Spinoza, Kant and the New Testament. Hegel was especially sensitive to the religious, social and political change and turmoil of his time (including the French Revolution) and the fragmentation of society that resulted, to which he responded philosophically with his teachings on freedom of spirit, mystical unity and wholeness. Reality and truth define the entire system in which all propositions are rationally and coherently related and any apparent contradictions can be dialectically resolved within the system. A particular view (thesis) which provokes contradictory claims (anti-thesis) can be reconciled in a new unity by synthesis which in turn represents another thesis to be contradicted and synthesised. This ongoing dynamic, which retains rationality throughout, increases the self-consciousness of mind by giving all the objects of thought their proper rational place in the whole. Thus, all of reality should be understood as the progressive unfolding of an Absolute Mind (God) achieved through the dialectical process in which Mind or Spirit overcomes alienation and negation in a higher unity which will ultimately culminate in a free and complete self-knowledge. Hegel regarded human history as the locus in which the Absolute becomes self-conscious and he saw the modern liberal state as the highest form of Spirit in an ethical community concerned with art, religion and philosophy. In his early writings, Hegel was very critical of the Christian churches, both Protestant and Catholic, and of Jesus, because he found Christianity to be incompatible with reason and human dignity. He later came to think that the positive aspects of Christianity could be incorporated in a world view that eliminated whatever was regarded as incompatible with reason and went on to claim that the value of Christianity was that it recognised God as Spirit. Religious consciousness, according to Hegel, reveals God as he is, immediately present as Spirit and attainable only by speculative knowledge which is thereby demonstrated as knowledge of the revealed religion. The hopes and expectations of the world are pressing forward towards this revelation in order to see what absolute being is, and in doing so, to locate itself in it. It is in immediate self-consciousness that absolute Being is recognised as Spirit. Hegel's philosophical and theological approach argues that reality is in process and incomplete. Thus, what he calls Spirit (which often, though not always, is identifiable with God) is constantly, immanently and progressively being revealed within the world. His views resemble in some significant respects those of Spinoza (and thus can also be criticised as pantheistic) and they undoubtedly give rise to questions as to how God should be understood as Spirit in the world. By his own criteria, Hegel's own claims cannot be taken as the last word on the subject so his philosophical-theology can be seen as 'work in progress'. His theories have had considerable influence on subsequent philosophical thought and on theology (as for instance in process theology and some accounts of the theological implications of the environment). Philosophers such as Marx, Nietzsche and Wittgenstein and hermeneutical theorists, both philosophical and biblical, have responded to his views in different ways.

See **God, Kierkegaard, Marx, Nietszche, Religion**
Further reading: Helm (1999); Hodgson (1984)

Hell: in some cultures and religions hell, described as Hades, is the abode of the dead. In Christianity and other religious traditions, it is believed to be the final state of the damned where the powers of evil are located, a locus of unendingly conscious torment for those who are permanently separated from God in the afterlife. Plato's *Phaedo* describes an analogous state of the tainted and impure *psyche* as the result of the latter's exclusive love and care for the body and physical things accompanied by a corresponding hate of, fear for and avoidance of the invisible and hidden intelligible reality. *Phaedo* tells us that in its journey into Hades the *psyche* will be contaminated by its preference for the physical and will be weighed down and dragged back into the visible world to hover around tombs and graveyards until it is bodily imprisoned once more. If gluttonous or selfish, *psyches* might assume the bodily forms of perverse animals, and if lawless and violent might become wolves, hawks and kites. Aquinas also described the post-resurrected bodies of the damned as being non-spiritually disposed, dark, carnal in their affections, unwieldy, heavy and insupportable to their souls, now permanently turned away from God and thus frustrated and in torment by their unfulfilled desire for happiness from which state they are forever doomed to be excluded. By contrast, the souls and bodies of the beatified are wholly in harmony with and united to a spiritualised form of existence defined as a permanently and perfectly happy state of union with God. This latter account of the beatified post-resurrected state somewhat echoes *Phaedo*'s descriptions of the psychic state of those who live good lives and who therefore after death, in separation from the body and the physical world as we know it, will inhabit an invisible, divine and blissfully happy locus, released from all human evil to spend the rest of eternity with God. As with heaven, one wonders also about the nature of hell which the reunited bodies and souls of the damned inhabit, described as a physical, yet spiritual state of eternal punishment.

See **Beatific Vision, St Thomas Aquinas, God, Heaven, Lucifer, Satan, Soul**

Further reading: Quinn (1996)

Hermeneutics: the theory and practice of interpretation. Although sometimes regarded as being quite recent in origin, interpretation has always been intrinsic to the way we know reality in that subjective interpretation is intrinsic to the acquisition of knowledge. The subjective character of hermeneutics does raise questions about how objective knowledge comes about, if at all, and how this can be explained. The nature and role of interpretative theory and practice, while significant in all fields of study, is regarded as being particularly central to theological, philosophical and mythological literature. How to interpret the holy books of Judaism, Christianity and Islam, for example, has historically given rise to theological, philosophical and scientific debate about how differences between these interpretative traditions can be reconciled, if at all. In the Islamic tradition, ibn Rushd set out to reassure Muslims that religious and philosophical–scientific interpretations are in harmony and not in conflict. He argued that where differences exist between the Qur'anic doctrines and those of philosophy and science (which historically have originated in earlier non-Islamic cultures and traditions) an examination of the nature of the interpretative methods used in each discipline should be undertaken.

This would demonstrate, he claims, that different ways of interpreting reality can be reconciled as compatible providing that one recognises the differing interpretative methods involved and does not seek to impose one exclusive way of interpretation over others as the sole universal authoritative one. The question remains, however, as to whether or not there is one mode of interpretation that is prior to others (for example the scientific or the religious). This issue was also discussed in the context of a perceived harmony between faith and reason in the Christian and Jewish medieval traditions and scholars such as Aquinas and Maimonides also took the view that religious faith and human reason could co-exist as partners (though not as equals) in the search for the knowledge of God. The progress of new scientific thinking from the fifteenth and sixteenth centuries onwards and the clashes that ensued between religion and science (for instance between the Church and Galileo) led to further debates about the exact significance of religious teachings and writings. In the period of the Enlightenment, thinkers such as Kant argued that it is reason which must judge religion and science. There were also developments in the more conscious promotion of hermeneutics as an area of great importance for biblical studies which, in turn, led to an increased interest in recent centuries into how interpretation works as a mode of philosophical and scientific thinking. In this connection, Schleiermacher and Dilthey have been identified as key figures, and in the twentieth century when hermeneutics came to link up philosophically with phenomenology (as influenced by Kant and Hegel), philosophers such as Heidegger, Gadamer and Ricoeur concentrated their major philosophical efforts on emphasising the inescapability of the subjective dimension of the human condition as a major determinant of how reality is perceived and understood. Wittgenstein also emphasised this point in his language game theory and now there seems to be general acceptance that hermeneutical subjectivity shapes the ways in which we view reality as objective. This has also led to an awareness of the hermeneutical dimension of the human sciences and of the hermeneutics of the physical sciences generally (Patrick Heelan is an important figure in the latter field), and there is also a potentially rich field for philosophical investigation in the whole area of law. The centrality of hermeneutics to how we think generally about what we know constitutes an important dimension for contemporary philosophical enquiry, including in the understanding and analysis of religion.

See **Paul Ricoeur, Symbol**

Further reading: Babich (2002); Ricoeur (1995)

Hierarchy of Being: refers to the theory that there is a scale of beings or gradations of reality ranging in ascending order of importance from inanimate or non-living entities through living beings such as plants, animals and humans (the latter as living rational beings), to purely rational beings such as angels and ultimately the divine reality of God. There is also a distinction made between the visible, tangible, physical world and the invisible, intangible, immaterial realm based on the principle that spiritual intelligent beings are superior to physical entities. There is also the view that the more rational and self-sufficient something is, the higher up on the scale of being is its location. In the latter context, God is regarded as the most self-sufficient rational and superior being of all, wholly immaterial and infinite reality and from whom all, things come, either by virtue of divine creation or through a process of emanation. There is also the associated view that the further away something is from the source of being, the more it is composed of matter (and sometimes the more evil it is). The theory of a hierarchy of being is associated with Aristotle and with Neoplatonism. A good summary of the theory is provided by Aquinas in *Summa Contra Gentiles* Book IV Ch. 1.

See **St Thomas Aquinas, Aristotle, Boundary Being, Creation, Pseudo-Dionysius, Emanation, Neoplatonism, Plato, Plotinus**

Further reading: Anderson (1953)

Hinduism: the dominant religious creed of India defined by the authority of the religious writings known as the Vedas and the Upanishads. Hinduism embraces a group of religious traditions rather than consisting of a single religious faith since within Hinduism there are both theistic and monistic views of God and disagreements about such issues as the nature of personal identity. Generally speaking, Hinduism is characterised by an acceptance of the doctrine of the reincarnation and transmigration of the soul and the goal of religion is to free the soul from the cycle of reincarnation.

See **Bhagavad Gita, Buddhism, Plato,** *Psyche*, **Reincarnation, Soul, Transmigration, Upanishads**

Further reading: Mascaro (1965); Smart (1998)

Hobbes, Thomas (1588–1679): English philosopher in the empiricist tradition best known for his political treatise, *Leviathan*, who was convinced that the natural human condition or 'state of nature' was one in which people, if left to their own devices, would behave like aggressive competitive savages who would exploit and possibly murder each other to achieve their individual goals. Political stability demanded that people surrendered some of their freedom and rights to the sovereign ruler(s) and, in this context, religion was to be regarded as a potentially destructive political force that would subvert society unless controlled by political rulers. Hobbes, who lived through a turbulent period in English history, had a culture of support for his views on the state control of religion going back to the time of Henry VIII.

See **Empiricism, Religion**
Further reading: Helm (1999)

The Holy See **The Sacred, Rudolf Otto**
Further reading: Otto (1923)

Hope: the opposite of despair and one of the primary Christian virtues with faith and love, hope is the positive expectation of some future good not yet present where there is uncertainty about when that good can be realised. Gabriel Marcel describes hope as creative fidelity and argues for a metaphysical attitude where hope is essentially appreciated as the availability of the soul that has entered into the experience of communion 'to accomplish in the teeth of will and knowledge the transcendent act'. Marcel describes hope as a recognition of the mystery of reality springing from humanity's awareness of our dependent state. His philosophy of hope is clearly religious in character in its emphasis on the transcendent foundation and direction of the mystery of being.

See **Camus, Existentialism, Gabriel Marcel, Sartre**
Further reading: Marcel (1948, 1964, 1978); Sartre (1946)

Hugel, Baron Friedrich von (1852–1925): born in Florence in Italy of Austrian descent he inherited his father's baronial title and spent most of his life in England. A Roman Catholic, he was the author of a number of books on religion and mysticism and his two volume work, *Essays and Addresses on the Philosophy of Religion* (1921 and

1926) is written explicitly from a Catholic perspective. He exercised considerable influence on the Modernist movement with the Catholic Church and defended the methods of modern biblical scholarship despite growing papal disapproval. He saw divine truth in all religions and disliked the proselytising approach. He regarded the adoration of God by God's creatures as constituting the essence of religion and stressed the values common to both the natural and supernatural life.

See **Modernism, The Philosophy of Religion**

Humanism: the view that attributes a central place and value to human beings, activities and achievements which may, though not necessarily, include rejecting the place of God in human life and human progress. Erasmus was considered a humanist because he emphasised the need to use reason in scriptural exegesis but generally the humanist approach is defined in opposition to the theological. Sartre, for example, described his form of existentialism as humanism in *Existentialism and Humanism* while Habermas in *The Future of Human Nature* (2003), in the context of writing about the moral impact of contemporary genetic developments, concludes that 'the voice of God calling into life communicates within a morally sensitive universe'.

See **Don Cupitt, Erasmus, Sartre**

Further reading: Cupitt (1997); Habermas (2003); Sartre (1946)

Hume, David (1711–77): Scottish philosopher, one of the most important thinkers of the Enlightenment and a major influence in British twentieth-century philosophy in particular. Hume was an empiricist who claimed that knowledge is based on sensory impressions which gives rise to the ideas (or faint impressions) that constitute our knowledge. He provides a powerful critique of causality arguing that establishing noetic relationships between things is often based on custom and habit rather than on certainty. Most knowledge for Hume has therefore a probable status though whatever knowledge is obtained must be sensory-based. These principles also apply to his views on religion. Although Hume is often viewed as adopting a vehemently agnostic or even atheistic approach to God and religion in his writings, the reality is more complex. In his *Enquiry Concerning Human Understanding*, he states that 'the religious hypothesis must be considered only as a particular method of accounting for the visible phenomena of the world'. The religious viewpoint thus represents one way of viewing the world based on strong religious feelings about its dependence on a supreme divine creator. Hume's extensive psychological analysis of belief, including religious belief, has a central role to play in how we view knowledge. The importance of custom or social conditioning which sustains the compelling and intense nature of belief based on strong feelings explains the force of one's belief in God and in miracles. He rejects the possibility of miraculous happenings because they cannot be described as natural events and are often believed in by uneducated and primitive people. Hume argues that there are no sensory impressions of God which means there can be no ideas about and therefore knowledge of God. This principle also applies to knowledge of the soul, the self, the mind and substance. However, Hume, while critical of religion because it operates outside reason and despite his scathing rhetoric about the Catholic Church, can still write movingly at times about the content of religious faith. His position seems to be that of an observer and commentator who, while emphasising the emotional and socially inherited dimension of faith, can also voice approval for those who admit to a faith without reason. Hume thus appears as an intellectual outsider unafraid to comment on how he sees the phenomenon of religion though in doing so, he tries, with some exceptions, to be as objective and fair as he can. His *Treatise of Human Nature*, *The Natural History of Religion* and *Dialogues Concerning Natural Religion* in addition to his *Enquiries* contain his views on religion and God.

See **Belief, Christianity, Faith, Kant, Miracles, Religion**
Further reading: Hume (1975)

I

Ibn Rushd, Abu'l-Walid (1126–98): better known to the Latin world as Averroes, was born at Cordoba in Islamic Spain and devoted himself to the study of jurisprudence, medicine, mathematics, philosophy and theology, and combined the roles of *qadi* or judge in civil affairs with that of being a royal physician. He enjoyed great favour at court under the caliphs, Abu Jacub and his son Jacub al Mansur but when he was seventy, he was banished from Andalus to North Africa with other scholars because of his philosophical views and many of his works in logic and metaphysics were destroyed. Although he was rehabilitated when he returned from exile, his religious orthodoxy remained suspect. His commentaries and expertise on Aristotle's writings earned him the title of 'The Commentator' (which is the term of respect attributed to him by Aquinas), and a version of Averroism later came to influence some Christian thinkers. After al-Ghazzali (1058–1111), Islamic philosophy was on the defensive, facing constant critical scrutiny from Islamic theologians and jurists. Ibn Rushd claimed that there was a harmonious relationship between religious law (*Shari'a*) and philosophy (to include scientific thought) since truth is one and indivisible though capable of different explanations and interpretations. He insisted that philosophers are divinely exhorted and guided by God to investigate creation, the knowledge of which provides us with more perfect knowledge of God. He also defended the use of ancient and non-Islamic philosophy and science from ancient Greek thought against the insistence of some who declared that it is only Islam that provides the exclusive path to truth. Ibn Rushd claimed that if there are conflicts between religious and philosophical truth, what is important to understand is the kind of interpretative methods respectively used. This view makes ibn Rushd a figure of considerable historical significance in the literature of philosophical and theological hermeneutics. However, although he insists that religion and philosophy are in harmony, he ranks philosophical thought as superior to theology since he holds that in the order of understanding of truth, the uneducated majority of people should be presented with truth in the form of narratives and parables, which are then theologically interpreted by the theologians. The philosophers, by contrast, are privileged to understand the truth in the most abstract way possible. Each group (philosophers, theologians and the people) should use whichever interpretative method is appropriate for each thus allowing the truth to be acquired in a way that befits the capabilities of each group. This approach undoubtedly aroused suspicion and hostility in theological circles, giving rise to fears that philosophy was indeed subversive from a theological point of view, a claim that ibn Rushd himself rejected. He insisted, by contrast, that philosophy had a vital role in understanding religious teaching and that philosophical hermeneutics makes it possible to appreciate the nature and value of different approaches to the same reality and to provide solutions to some of the problems that philosophy and science appear to present to religious teachings.

See **Al-Ghazzali, Al-Farabi, St Thomas Aquinas, Aristotle, Hermeneutics, Ibn Sina, Islam, Philosophy, Religion**

Further reading: Averroes (2001); Fakhry (1997); Jamil-Ur-Rehmen (1921); Leaman (1988, 1999a)

Ibn Sina (980–1037): Persian philosopher and physician, known to the Latin world as Avicenna. His autobiography tells us that he mastered the Qur'an by the age of ten together with a great deal of literature, and that he also studied geography and Indian mathematics and had a deep understanding of medicine, Islamic jurisprudence and especially philosophy (to include logic, the scientific study of nature and metaphysics), and in particular, the philosophy of Aristotle as well as Neoplatonism and that of the Stoics. His work in philosophy could be regarded as a synthesis of Aristotelianism, Neoplatonism and Islamic monotheism. One of his most important contributions to metaphysics and theology concerned the relationship between essence and existence. He claimed that whereas in created reality there is a distinction between both, essence and existence are identical in God, a view which influenced Western thinkers, notably Maimonides and Aquinas, for whom this claim is central in their theological metaphysics. Following Aristotle's concept of the eternity of matter, Avicenna rejected the theological claim of creation out of nothing (*creatio ex nihilo*). Instead, influenced by Neoplatonism, he favoured emanation stating that the totality emanates from God, 'through Him and unto Him'. God is the uncaused First Cause and necessary being, the absolute and simple unified supreme being in whom knowledge, will and power are one with the divine essence. Ibn Sina states that the afterlife is a notion received from religious teaching and that while there may be some support for the idea of a hereafter through reason and logical demonstration, its truth can only be established fully from religious dogma and from the sayings of the prophets. Prophetic knowledge is spontaneous and intuitive, he declares, and the speculative mystic, who attains the highest degree of knowledge, reaches an intellectual union with God.

See **St Thomas Aquinas, Aristotle, Ibn Rushd, Islam, Neoplatonism**

Further reading: Arberry (1951); Fakhry (1997); Leaman (1999a)

Immanence: from the Latin *immanare* 'to remain in', in the philosophy of religion, the term signifies that God is indwelling and operating within the world. God's presence in the world is understood to be a function of the original and continuing creative act which brought the world into existence and sustains creation in being. How God can be immanent within creation and yet outside and beyond it as transcendent is discussed in theological metaphysics and in the philosophy of religion. Alternatively, the pantheistic view locates God as being wholly immanent such that God and creation are said to be identical as suggested, for example, by Spinoza and Hegel.

See **creation, God, Hegel, Spinoza, transcendence**

Immortality: not being subject to the dissolution of death and capable of some form of subsequent continued existence often described as personal in nature. This is believed to be possible because of the spiritual, psychic or soul dimension of human life. In Greek philosophy, Plato's writings, notably in his dialogue *Phaedo*, strongly argue for the soul's immortality based on its need for total intelligibility and on the belief that it is predestined to return to its primordial spiritual state. Plato also argues this claim on the grounds of justice which is often impossible to achieve before death. Plato also states that there is psychic pre-existence and that the *psyche* can be reincarnated by transmigrating to different bodies. Such views are also to be found in other philosophical approaches such as Hinduism, and Plotinus, the great Neoplatonist, also put forward the concept of cosmic or world soul based on Plato's *Timaeus*. In this context, Plotinus describes the ensouled universe as 'boiling with life' and suggests that individual souls may have originally split off from Soul itself which implies a duty for each to return to the Soul of the All. The Christian analysis of the soul is undoubtedly influenced by these Greek philosophers, principally by Plato but also by Aristotle, and many Christian thinkers provide descriptions of a Neoplatonic soul. Christians, however, do not believe that individual human souls existed before their bodies but are rather directly created by God to be immortal and thereby to survive death and continue into a form of everlasting existence when they will be reunited with their bodies once more. The beatified souls who are privileged to see God face to face will be eternally happy contemplating this vision together, and all the more completely when reunified with their bodies at the final resurrection. By contrast, in a permanent post-mortem state in which they are frustrated from ever attaining perfect happiness, the souls of the damned are doomed to eternal torment and their embodiment will make this situation all the more painful. However, the philosophical analysis of the soul's immortality is rejected by many because it is believed to be a form of religious teaching that is inaccessible to rational investigation. This is the case with many post-Reformation Christians who rely instead on the authority of scripture or who argue, like Gabriel Marcel, for a form of reflective consideration that will reveal the mystery of human spirituality as part of the mystery of reality as a whole. In the Islamic tradition, philosophers such as ibn Sina have attempted to investigate the nature of the soul, though in general its reality and destiny is accepted as religious teaching. In the Jewish tradition, there seems to be less interest in analysing how God looks after the dead, save that He does, though there are some references to bodily resurrection.

See **The Afterlife, St Thomas Aquinas,** *The Epic of Gilgamesh*, **Plato, Plotinus,** *Psyche*, **Soul**

Further reading: Hamilton and Cairns (1963); Quinn (1996)

Infinite: by contrast with finite being, God is often described as unlimited or infinite.

See **God**

Intuition: immediate and direct insight, apprehension and cognition which does not seem to be dependent on sensory experience or reasoning. Christian thinkers such as Aquinas, claim that angelic intelligence works like this.

See **Angels, Henri Bergson, Plato, Socrates**

Islam: the faith and practice of the followers of Muhammad believed by them to be the final and perfect religion revealed by God to the Prophet and through him to others. Islam recognises such biblical figures as Abraham, Moses and Jesus as prophets. Orthodox Islam is rooted in the observance of weekly communal worship, daily devotions, a month-long fast (Ramadan), payment of a religious tax and at least one pilgrimage to Mecca, an Islamic holy city. Islam also includes the concept of *jihad* meaning religious striving though this has been and is interpreted by some as a warlike defence of Islam whereas others perceive it as an internal personal struggle against sin. Divine law or

Shari'a ideally shapes the society of Islamic believers and in some Islamic countries operates as the law of the state. In others, however, such as Turkey, which is currently perceived to be a secular Islamic state, civil and religious concerns operate mutually.

See **Al-Farabi, Al-Ghazali, Al-Kindi, Ibn Rushd, Ibn Sina, Muhammad**

Further reading: Dawood (2003)

J

Jainism: one of the religions of India, distinguished from Hinduism because of its refusal to accept the Brahmanic Vedas as authoritative. Jainism regards the universe as an everlasting succession of heavens and hells to which all beings are bound by *karma* that is, the means by which a person's fate is determined by past actions, but liberation is achieved through ascetic practices, meditation and non-violence. The soul (*jiva*) is the most important substance, perfect, eternal and undifferentiated. There are an infinite number of selves and these bring the world into being by their actions so there is no need to posit a creator god. Liberation occurs when the soul transcends all involvement with actions, including previous actions, and salvation occurs when the connection between self and its actions is broken. Jainism also emphasises the importance of recognising that there are different points of view which can be applied, and critics of this approach argue that this very principle diminishes the value of Jainism which can thus be seen as representing merely one perspective.

See **Afterlife, Buddhism, Hinduism,** *Psyche,* **Soul**

Further reading: Smart (1998)

James, William (1842–1910): American philosopher and psychologist and one of the founders of philosophical pragmatism which views actions and beliefs in relation to their implications for action. In the philosophy of religion, James argued in *The Will to Believe* that faith can be reasonable even if not supported by sufficient evidence. He also describes the phenomenon of religion in his other classic text, *The Varieties of Religious Experience*. James explains religious faith as being akin to an hypothesis that can be considered as a forced, living and momentous and, therefore, genuine option. It is forced because inescapable – we are either for or against belief in God. Agnosticism is not a meaningful option since its message is that it is better to risk loss of truth (i.e. religious truth) than to chance making a mistake (if religion turns out to be erroneous). According to James, this position is as unrealistic as the man who refuses to marry a woman until he is absolutely certain that she is wholly suitable for him. This kind of postponement is tantamount to a decision by the man to seek another partner instead. Thus religious faith or atheism are the only possible options. What forms our choices, in James's view, are our feelings and emotions, but most importantly our will to believe. We seek truth and try to avoid error and we are looking to be convinced, as it were, about what is essentially best for us. The religious option comes in here in the form of whether it is best for us or not to believe in God and we make our choice accordingly. Our choice of belief will in effect convince us of the truth of what we believe although we should always remember the underlying gamble we take. James invokes Pascal's views of gambling on God since we cannot lose either way – if God exists, so much the better and if God does not exist, we have lost nothing. James underlines the risk dimension of choice and advises us to be strong and have courage, to act and hope for the best and take what comes, and if death is the end these attitudes represent the best way to approach it. Faith then is a forced, momentous, vital and therefore genuine option which itself will convince us about the truth of our choice of option. As a passionate commitment, faith provides us with a strong psychological motivation for persevering in the direction chosen, which for the respective individual seems as far as one can tell to represent the best course of life to take. The content of James's discourse on the will to believe clearly echoes Hume's psychological views with the difference of preference on James's part for the faith option. In addition, Pascal inspires James's analysis of the risk and there are early anticipations in *The Will to Believe* of Sartre's views on the inescapable presence of free choice as being intrinsic to all our decision making and human actions. James's emphasis on the importance of the psychological and risk-taking dimensions of religious belief, if applied to what are nowadays described as religious cults, often conventionally regarded as bizarre, takes on a somewhat different if related character. The disposition of some of those who join such cults has been described by some psychological experts as problematic since such people may demonstrate an excessive need to belong to an accepting social group and may be naïve and ignorant about the exact nature and demands of the organisations involved. Cult techniques of persuasion to join are often associated with 'psychological blackmail', such as 'love bombing' of initiates for example (in which individuals are bombarded with emotional assertions of their value to the group), their isolation from other family members and subtle intimidation to remain in the organisation through fear of alienation and the high levels of anxiety that leaving might provoke on those who are emotionally fragile. There may also be high levels of financial commitment involved. In such a context, the psychological dimension of religious choice and the will to believe can have very unfortunate and long-term personal consequences for well meaning members, an experience that is reported and documented more frequently nowadays by affected families and by psychological experts, some of whom try to 'de-programme' those who want to leave a religious cult or who are suffering obvious emotional and personal trauma. Perhaps all this may indicate some of the weaknesses in James's theory of belief and the limitations of his pragmatic approach. In the USA and in the world at large there are more and more dramatic public examples of those who have pursued, often through violence, strong if mistaken religious beliefs with catastrophic consequences for themselves and others. On a different though perhaps related level there are those with schizoid and psychopathic personalities who have acted criminally out of strong convictions, all of which suggests the need for a reasonable approach to religious faith and not one that is based on the will alone but rather the 'informed' will. James does indeed argue for this link but his emphasis on the psychological and emotional may result in a somewhat unbalanced picture. Having said that, it is difficult to strike the required balance which may sometimes be a matter of instinct and common sense though there are also examples of extreme forms of religious behaviour which somehow remain socially acceptable if not understandable. James's special contribution to the philosophy of religion may well be to highlight the insecure nature of religious expectation as one very significant instance of the unpredictability of life generally.

See **Belief, Cult, Empiricism, Faith, Hume, Anthony Kenny, Reason, Religion**

Further reading: Helm (1999); James (1956)

Jesus: the Jewish founder of Christianity, Jesus, son of Mary, believed by his followers to be God made man, the long awaited Messiah of the Jews and Second Person of the Trinitarian God of Father, Son and Holy Spirit. As The Word and expression of God, equal to God the Father and the Holy Spirit, become incarnate, Jesus is believed by Christians to be the fulfilment of God's promises and covenant made with Abraham and Moses and through them with the Jewish people. Historically and theologically, Christianity grew of out of Judaism. The story of Jesus is found in the four Gospels (Anglo-Saxon for 'the good news') of Matthew, Mark, Luke and John which comprise narratives of testimony to the life and message of Jesus by contemporaneous figures. The Gospels contain accounts of his life, death by crucifixion and resurrection from the dead and ascension to God the Father in heaven. The Christian New Testament also contains the Acts of the Apostles concerning the activities of the early Christian communities after Jesus' death, resurrection and ascension, a number of letters, mainly by St Paul (a Jewish Pharisee who became the principal Christian apostle to the Gentiles (those outside the Jewish faith), some few letters by St Peter (the chief apostle), St James, St John and Jude and the Book of Revelation. Christianity, which was initially perceived as a Jewish sect, and survived after an early period of persecution by the Romans, subsequently became the religion of the Roman empire and spread worldwide. It divided into the Western Roman Church and the Eastern Orthodox Churches initially, and, following the Christian Reformation in the West whose moving figure was the Augustinian monk and priest, theologian Martin Luther, Christianity divided once more into various Christian churches throughout the world, the principal denominations being the Roman Catholic Church, which recognises the primacy of the bishop of Rome, the Lutheran Church (mainly based in Germany and in the Scandinavian countries), the Anglican and Episcopalian Churches in England and the USA and many others such as the Methodist and Presbyterian Churches and the Church of the Latter Day Saints (Mormons), all of whom claim to be the one true church of Jesus Christ.

See **Christianity, Judaism, Faith, Martin Luther, The Reformation**

Further reading: The Jerusalem Bible; Eusabius (1965); Freyne (2004)

Job: The principal character in the Book of Job in the Christian Old Testament. The book describes the apparently undeserved sufferings of a man who considered himself with good reason to be faithful to God and is of considerable importance for the Jewish people and also for Christians. Its significance lies in the difficulties that Job has with accepting his situation, which he regards as being imposed by God. The importance of the story lies in its message that we should not expect God to think and function in the same way that we do. God thinks differently in ways that we cannot fathom and we must respect this as a sign of God's utter transcendence and otherness. Whereas Job applies the human expectation and understanding of justice to his own case, where he regards suffering as being divinely inflicted on those who do wrong (which in his case does not apply), God's ways are not the ways of humankind and should not be construed anthropomorphically. Suffering is inexplicable, part of the human condition and intrinsic to it, a mystery of reality as Gabriel Marcel suggests, and God should not be held accountable for it. Towards the end of the narrative, Job seems to accept this insight. Christians may also perceive Job as pre-figuring Jesus Christ who suffered for the sins of humankind, thereby demonstrating the mystery of divine and messianic redemption which by implication highlights the mystery of evil as an inherited dimension of human life.

See **Boethius, Evil, Faith, God, Emmanuel Levinas, Gabriel Marcel, Mystery**

Further reading: The Jerusalem Bible; Leaman (1995)

Judaism: the religion of the Jewish people whose faith is based on God's revelation in the Hebrew Bible (Christian Old Testament) and who believe that they are specially and divinely chosen by God to be his special people. This was demonstrated, it is claimed, by the covenant of agreement between God and Abraham, the father of the Jewish faith, and renewed with Moses who was divinely assisted to liberate the Jews from their state of slavery in Egypt towards the freedom of the promised land of Israel. The Jewish story of belief in the monotheistic Yawveh and the expectation of the divinely appointed Messiah to come is documented in the Old Testament. With the emergence of Christianity, some Jews became followers of Jesus on the grounds that his message represented God's new covenant with the Jews. Jesus himself was Jewish as were all his apostles. However, Judaism continued as a strong religious faith alongside Christianity and its people have survived, despite almost continuous persecutions throughout the centuries down to the present day, much of it influenced by a Christian view of the Jews as the killers of Jesus Christ. Their suffering culminated in The *Shoah* or Holocaust, the crime against humanity, which took place in the concentration camps of Germany and Nazi occupied countries such as Poland where some six million Jews were systematically murdered in the early 1940s. Such cataclysmic events motivated many Jews to leave Europe and seek a safe homeland elsewhere, large numbers choosing to settle in what became the State of Israel. As a religion, Judaism exists today like others in various forms, Orthodox, Conservative, Reformed and Liberal and so on, each of which interprets biblical authority some what differently. Many Jewish thinkers including Philo, Maimonides, Spinoza, Moses Mendelssohn, Martin Buber, Henri Bergson, Hannah Arendt, Emmanuel Levinas, have contributed substantially to the philosophical analysis of religion.

See **Abraham, The Bible, Martin Buber, Job, Emmanuel Levinas, Maimonides, Moses, Spinoza**

Further reading: The Jerusalem Bible; Leaman (1995)

Just War: this is more a concern of ethics and political philosophy than the philosophy of religion. However, some of the issues that arise do tend to overlap, for example if a religious creed rejects violence as a means to an end, then how can this be reconciled, if at all, with believers of the relevant creed justifying violence? This is often posed as an issue for the credibility of religious faith and is certainly a problem of coherence and consistency. If non-violence is a religious principle, then pacifism and conscientiously objecting to war and violence seem to follow. The Christian theoretical conditions under which a conflict may be termed a just war state that the cause must be just, the war must be waged by a legitimate government, the means used must be moral, the war must be a last resort and there must be some reasonable chance of achieving the goals of the war. Aquinas argued, for example, that in a society where one's faith is threatened, it could be justifiable to defend it by violent means if necessary, although the violence must be judiciously proportionate in the relevant situation. He also thought that it was justifiable to forcefully compel apostates and heretics to return to the faith, this, of course, being the Christian faith. The

Christian Reformation also gave rise to religious wars which in this case were based on different interpretations of Christianity. In the contemporary world, too, similar views are associated with some in the Islamic tradition who construe the principle of *jihad* (or religious striving) to signify violent means if the situation requires it, in order to achieve goals. Neutral observers can become sceptical and hostile to religion as a result and some like Hobbes have argued for the state control of religion while others, especially in recent centuries, have wished to remove religion from political and personal life (sometimes, ironically, by violent means) in order to bring about a more rational and scientific approach for intelligent living. The fundamental religious question here, however, is whether the destructive nature of war can ever be justifiably used from a religious point of view if a primary principle of faith is that of non-violence.

See **St Thomas Aquinas, Christianity, Islam, Religion**

Justice: as a political ideal, justice has been extensively discussed by many philosophers from Socrates and Plato onwards and was traditionally regarded as a virtue. Plato and Aristotle were concerned about the conditions which are necessary for individual and social justice, and theological questions also arise about the nature of divine justice in, for example The Book of Job and in Boethius's *Consolation of Philosophy*.

See **Boethius, Job, Plato, Socrates**

Further reading: Hamilton and Cairns (1963)

Kant, Immanuel (1724–1804): one of the greatest philosophers of the Enlightenment who tried to synthesise idealism and empiricism. He argued that human knowledge was restricted to the phenomenal world of appearance, which we are mentally and physically structured to see and experience in particular ways, such as temporally and spatially. We are not entitled, therefore, to make claims based on human reason about what is not phenomenally accessible, that is, reality in itself, which is unknowable to us. The latter realm consists of such areas as divine existence, the immortal soul and freedom. Kant is very dismissive in his *Critique of Pure Reason* of medieval attempts to prove the existence of God, free will and the immortality of the soul. He was reared in a Pietist Lutheran family in Königsberg, Prussia, and his mother was especially devout. As a form of Lutheranism, Pietism, emphasised the devotional and practical aspects of Christianity in the need for good works and neighbourly charity. It was particularly prevalent in Königsberg where Kant was raised and his father sent him to a Pietist school where there was much emphasis on religious studies as the context for understanding the other subjects taught there. He initially considered studying theology at the university but decided in favour of philosophy instead. Kant's writings on religion are particularly interesting including his short piece on 'What is Enlightenment?' where he argues that while the preacher as preacher is charged with teaching what is believed doctrine, as a theological scholar and investigator, the same individual is free to critically explore the teachings of faith and the relevant theological claims. This is a remarkable text which is well ahead of its own time in preparing the ground for subsequent critical theological and philosophical analyses of religion. What is even more remarkable is that Kant had to be careful of political disapproval in the Prussia of his time for making such claims. In fact, his other even more radical account of the philosophy of religion which is contained in his classic text, *Religion Within the Limits of Reason Alone*, was, after the first volume was published, politically banned from publication in Prussia until a later date. In this text, Kant seems to clearly suggest that it is reason that provides the criteria for evaluating the nature of religion and there are some hints of deism in his general approach, which would not be unexpected in an Enlightenment thinker. What Christianity adds to morality and one's compelling sense of the need to do one's duty is that, according to Kant, it provides a theological context for understanding the basis of such a requirement. It also supplies the divine model for the ethical human being, namely Jesus Christ. What is notable too in this text is his dismissal of Judaism as not representing a true religion. Indeed he appears to suggest that it is not really a religion at all but more a cultural creation, native to the Jewish people. All in all, Kant's important contribution to the philosophy of religion lies in his claim that reason is the arbitrator of religious validity, that Christianity as he understands it represents the religion of reason, that it provides us with the ethical and religious exemplar of Jesus Christ as the model to be followed, and that theological freedom is compatible with orthodoxy.

See **Christianity, The Enlightenment, Hume, Jesus, Judaism, Reason, Religion, Theology**

Further reading: Helm (1999); Kant (1960)

Karma: literally meaning 'action', is believed to be an eternal law of cosmic cause and effect, or acts or deeds, that decide the destiny of individuals. It is usually understood as the means by which someone's fate is determined by past actions. *Karma* is complex and has many levels of meaning; it has been popularised in the West as a way of understanding fate.

See **Hinduism**

Kenny, Anthony (1931–): English philosopher who has written extensively on the philosophy of religion. Honorary Fellow of Balliol College, Oxford and Master of Balliol (1978–89), Pro Vice Chancellor of Oxford University (1984–2004) and President of the British Academy, Sir Anthony Kenny, now an agnostic, was formerly a Catholic priest who studied in Rome and who left the priesthood because of his doubts about faith, especially as regards proving the existence of God. He adopts an analytic approach to philosophy and this is also evident in his writings on the philosophy of religion. One of his most interesting contributions in the latter field is his book, *What is Faith?* which compels attention not least because it is clear that Kenny is honestly and clearly putting forward his own position on this subject. Though not a confessional text, it does sum up the direction of his thinking on such issues as belief and faith, the existence and nature of God and it justifies his agnostic stance while respecting other positions. In *What is Faith?* Kenny distinguishes between (1) belief that there is a God and that God exists, (2) belief in a doctrine on the word of God as revealed by God and, (3) belief in God and trust in and commitment to God. Whereas the first represents a propositional belief (that God exists, for example) with varying degrees of conviction, the second, represents for Kenny belief as faith, the third involves a trustful commitment to and love of God and God's revealed plan for the world and humankind. He argues that the philosophy of religion deals with (1) and (2) and identifies its most important question as whether or not belief in God is rational and worthy of a reasonable human being. Kenny claims that there is a virtue of rationality which aims to avoid either the excessive extreme of credulousness on the one hand, where the person believes everything, and scepticism on the other where the individual believes nothing. Kenny's aim is to understand and apply this kind of rationality to religious belief in the sense of (1) and (2) and he adopts the principle that the intensity of belief will correspond to the strength of the available evidence. The question then is what kind of evidence exists for religious faith and how strong is it, all of which implies selecting criteria that will determine what the evidence is and the degree of its compelling force to bring about a state of unshakeable conviction. He sums up belief as a cognitive, though not affective or emotional, state of mind. Kenny concludes that extensive investigation demonstrates to him that there is no compelling evidence to show him that God exists nor indeed any to indicate that God does not exist which leaves him as a 'contingent agnostic' though he accepts that the public perception of his position might describe him as a sceptic. Kenny's analysis in *What is Faith?* is lucidly probing, sifting through the possible evidence on which belief in God might be justifiably based and always raising the question as to what kind of evidence would convince him of the need to believe in God. By implication, it suggests that faith is a disposition which favours the acceptance of certain kinds of knowledge and represents, as William James suggests, an optimistic and hopeful, though not necessarily credulous, viewpoint. What Kenny's investigations highlight is that faith cannot be acquired solely on the basis of the analysis of evidence unless there is a predisposing conviction, and that without such a predisposing conviction no amount of analysis will succeed in convincing. In *The Unknown God* (2004) Kenny continues with his exploration of faith, though in it he admits to the value of religious discourse as a more apt and flexible medium for depicting religious and theological thought and belief.

See **St Thomas Aquinas, Arguments for the Existence of God, Belief, Faith, God**

Further reading: Kenny (1992, 2004)

Kierkegaard, Søren (1813–55): Danish philosopher, regarded as the father of existentialism, the philosophical approach that emphasised the importance of the human person as an individual and the need to live a meaningful life and choose what we want to make of ourselves. Like many existentialist thinkers, Kierkegaard found life traumatic and oppressive and this was the context from which he struggled to understand how he should conceive of God and respond to the challenge of institutionalised religion. He had an ambivalent relationship with his father who dominated his childhood as he dominated the household generally, demanding absolute obedience, and combining a shrewd business approach with a strong religious commitment to the Lutheran Church and an insistence on duty and self-discipline. There was considerably melancholy in the family that affected Kierkegaard himself who was often in despair while externally appearing to be cheerful and happy. His state of dejection was further accentuated when he terminated his engagement to his fiancée Regine Olson, perhaps because of the family history. He then became a full-time writer on theological and philosophical issues. Kierkegaard was a committed Christian but contemptuous of organised religion and of any teachings that tried to ignore the importance of one's personal existence. He attacked the rational humanism of his time and argued strongly for a 'leap of faith' which could give true meaning and a passionate commitment to the religious dimension in life. He objected to Hegel's philosophical approach because of its abstractions and lack of due respect, as he perceived it, for the individual and the particular. By contrast, Kierkegaard argued that the individual human will and free choice are of primary importance and to regard people as mere elements in an inevitable process is philosophically and morally wrong. He declared that while the religious 'leap of faith' may seem to be irrational, just like Abraham's decision to sacrifice his son which was revoked at the last minute by God, it must be made without reference to the experience or advice of others since it involves a recognition of one's complete separateness and the need to take responsibility for one's own actions. In his book, *Either–Or,* he contrasts the aesthetic dimension with the ethical and both with the religious which transcends the other two. People in the aesthetic phase try to escape boredom and life's struggles by romantically pursuing a range of pleasures which they think will satisfy their needs. However, this fails and is replaced by despair which might lead to an ethical stage of committing oneself to one's duties and obeying the demands of objective morality. However, this too has its limits in that it does not address the need for personal meaning and the validation of one's existence. However, it can be transformed into the religious stage where by choosing to acknowledge one's mortality and state of sinfulness and by recognising the inadequacy of objective ethics to provide personal meaning for oneself, one becomes aware of the dread of total emptiness and decides to make the 'leap of faith' over and over again in order to fulfil all one's needs for completeness. We only exist in faith, according to Kierkegaard, and it is only through faith that we can find the kind of truth which is individually true for each of us and for which we are prepared to die. It is clear that Kierkegaard's philosophical and subjective approach is considerably influenced by his own personal experiences. His subsequent influence in philosophy generally is considerable and those who followed in the existentialist mode of philosophising and writing have found it difficult to ignore the significance of the relationship between God and the individual person, as a result.

See **Christianity, Existentialism, Faith, God, Luther**

Further reading: Helm (1999); Kierkegaard (1985, 1989)

L

Leibniz, Gottfried (1646–1716): German polymath: mathematician, scientist, lawyer, diplomat, engineer, historian and philosopher who claimed that reality consisted of monads which he describes as the atoms of nature and the simple elements of things. He was interested in a rational basis for religion and argued that the reason why anything exists at all is because God as the ultimate and necessary uncaused cause of all contingent existing things constitutes the reason for what exists. The universe is so organised by God that everything fits harmoniously with everything else in the whole system and this is due to the law of pre-established harmony. The latter signifies that God brings potentially existing things which have the urge to exist into real existence in such a way that they fit with what is already in the system. In addition, according to Leibniz, God created for us the best of all possible worlds, regardless of how matters might appear to us to be and if we fail to recognise this, it is because we are focussing on specific and distressing aspects of reality to the exclusion of how these relate to the whole. It gives pleasure, he states, to recognise the order, beauty and perfection in the universe and failure to do so is due to a defect in our understanding. It is the mind that makes us most closely resemble God and enables us to distinctly perceive necessary truths (for instance that there is a reason for everything and specific reasons for specific events). Mental pleasure comes about when we perceive perfection and even evils serve a greater good since mental pain is necessary if one is to reach greater pleasures. There is determinism in Leibniz's account which raises questions about freedom, including God's freedom, which also seems restricted, and about the problem of evil which Leibniz seems to argue is a force for good, if looked at from the right point of view.

Though a Cartesian, Leibniz remains in the tradition of classical metaphysics which goes back to Aristotle and the medieval world.

See **Arguments for the Existence of God, Aristotle, St Anselm, St Thomas Aquinas, St Augustine, The Enlightenment, The Ontological Argument, Rationalism, Reason**

Further reading: Leibniz (1973)

Levinas, Emmanuel (1906–95): Jewish philosopher born in Lithuania who studied with Heidegger and spent most of his life in France, he is the author of a number of philosophical and theological works, including *Totality and Infinity*. Perhaps the best and clearest introduction to his thought is *Ethics and Infinity* which consists of transcriptions of a series of radio interviews broadcast by Radio France-Culture in February/March 1981. Levinas identified metaphysics with ethics which he regarded as 'first' philosophy'. He claims that responsibility is the essential primary and fundamental structure of subjectivity expressed as responsibility for the Other: 'since the Other looks at me, I am responsible for him, without even having *taken* on responsibilities in his regard; his responsibility is *incumbent on me*. It is responsibility that goes beyond what I do.' (Levinas 1985, p. 96). This ontological disposition of responsibility is figuratively depicted in Levinas's concept of 'the Face' (Levinas 1985, pp. 85–92). Access to the Face of the other is straightaway ethical, he states, with regard to its upright naked exposure and its essential poverty which people try to mask by putting on various poses. The Face, however, is exposed and menaced as if inviting us to an act of violence and yet forbidding us to kill. Face and discourse are linked together, he states, because the Face speaks and therefore initiates all discourse as a response or responsibility which marks the authentic relationship with the other. The Face of the other is the beginning of all love, according to Levinas, and represents one's encounter with God. His understanding of metaphysics as ethics is theologically grounded in his Jewish faith especially with respect to the transcendent otherness of God, caring for the stranger, the poor and those who suffer.

See **Martin Buber, God, Judaism**
Further reading: Levinas (1985, 1998)

Liberation Theology: a theological movement that initially emerged in Latin America in the 1960s which claimed that Christianity and the Gospels should be understood as containing a preferential option for the poor and the marginalised in society. Catholic priests and bishops such as Gustavo Guttierez and Helder Camara were to the forefront in providing Scriptural justification for this approach which argued for political liberation from oppression and injustice, the result of discrimination and unjust economic, social and political structures and policies. Controversially, Marxist principles were adopted in order to provide a philosophical framework for the theory and practice intrinsic to liberation theology in the belief that Marxism and Christianity could be regarded as compatible in the search for social justice for the poor.

See **The Bible, Christianity, Marx**
Further reading: Marx (1977)

Logos: from the Greek, meaning 'speech', 'discourse', 'word', 'study of', in philosophy, the role of *Logos* as discourse becomes important in twentieth-century hermeneutics, for example in the writings of Paul Ricouer, especially in the context of his views on religious discourse.

Theologically, *Logos* is used at the beginning of St John's Gospel to identify the Second Divine Person, the Word Incarnate, Jesus Christ.

See **Hermeneutics, Paul Ricoeur**

Lonergan, Bernard (1904–84): Canadian Jesuit philosopher–theologian whose book, *Insight*, contains a very detailed study of the nature and acquisition of knowledge. Many of his other philosophical writings are found in a number of *Collections* and, in addition, he wrote extensively on theology, for example in *Method in Theology*. His approach was influenced by his reading of St Thomas Aquinas, though Lonergan is identified as a transcendental Thomist whose philosophical approach is primarily epistemological in focus. His analysis of the relationship between philosophy and religion is therefore Thomistic in approach. He argues that while human beings have a detached, disinterested, unrestricted and natural desire to know (which ultimately aims to know God), this desire can only and paradoxically be fulfilled supernaturally through the grace of God. This claim underlies much of his thinking on how philosophy and religion interact.

See **St Thomas Aquinas, God, Thomism**
Further reading: Crowe (1985)

Lucifer: from the Latin, 'lightbearing', otherwise known as Satan, and personifying the power of evil. St Jerome, one of the early Christian writers explained the reference in Isaiah 14:12–15 (Christian Old Testament) as naming the principal fallen angel who was condemned to permanently suffer the loss of his original state of brilliant glory. This view has prevailed in the Christian tradition where it is claimed that Lucifer, the most intelligent of all the angels, was motivated by excessive pride and the desire to be God's equal to lead a rebellion against God with some of the angels. The result was that Lucifer and his followers were permanently banished from heaven and the vision of God to an ultimate state of eternal punishment in hell.

See **Angels, God, Heaven, Hell**

Luther, Martin (1483–1546): the Augustinian monk, priest and theologian responsible for what came to be known as the Reformation. Luther was motivated by the urge to expose serious defects and scandals in the Church and in how the Church was ruled. He regarded such activities as the selling of indulgences, which implied buying one's way out of having to suffer for sins in the afterlife, as an affront to God. His public confrontations with the ecclesiastical hierarchy led to a considerable number of Christians who were similarly disenchanted following his lead, and these included some in political office who undoubtedly had political as well as theological agendas. This resulted in the fragmentation of Western Christianity in terms of beliefs and practice. Luther's theological approach emphasised the need to have faith alone (*sola fide*) through divine grace alone (*sola gratia*) and through Scripture alone (*sola Scriptura*). Salvation, he claimed, is attained by one's personal relationship with God in faith and God's supernatural response of assistance to us through our reading the word of God in Scripture. As a theologian and preacher, Luther was very familiar with Scripture, especially the Book of Psalms in the Old Testament and the New Testament Letters of St Paul to the Romans and Galatians, and he argued that the Bible should be translated into German. He was perceived as a theological and charismatic leader who could be depended upon to reform Christianity. Historically, the political consequences of Luther's stance were internecine Christian conflict and war and political as well as theological fragmentation that facilitated the emergence of nation states on the basis of religious adherence. The Reformation thus represents a watershed in Christianity from a theological, historical and political perspective and, taken together with the Renaissance and the new scientific developments that emphasised the physical nature of the universe as being of central scientific concern, combined to create modern Europe and crucially shaped Western thinking. The need for independent thought and action liberated from religious concerns, the growing marginalisation of religion as a political force and the exclusion in many cases of philosophical analysis from religious concerns are just some of the effects of Luther's revolt. Lutheranism initially became the religion of many northern European states and this remains the situation even today. Later there was a Counter Reformation, which was Roman Catholic in nature, that attempted to address the Reformers' theological and pastoral concerns but which failed to stem the tide of the religious and political changes that had taken place.

See **St Augustine, The Bible, Christianity, Erasmus, The Papacy, The Reformation**

Further reading: MacCulloch (2003)

MacKenna, Stephen (1872–1934): born of Irish descent in Liverpool. After a varied and adventurous life as a journalist, he spent more than twenty years translating Plotinus's *Enneads* into English. He was attracted to the mystical, aesthetic and religious aspects of Plotinian thought which led him to develop his own personal views about the nature of spirituality and what constituted the essence of religion. In later life, he became more agnostic and, like Iris Murdoch, he concluded that acknowledging the wonder, beauty and goodness of this world was what really counted in the end.

See **Aesthetic, Agnostic, Awe, Beauty, The** *Enneads*, **God, The Good, Immanence, Iris Murdoch, Mysticism, The One, Philosophy, Plotinus,** *Psyche*, **Religion, Soul, Spirituality, Transcendence**

Further reading: Cheney and Hendrix (2004); Dillon (1991); Dodds (1936)

Maimonides, Moses (1134–1204): or Moses ben Maimon, born in Cordoba in Islamic Spain, the most eminent of the medieval Jewish thinkers who tried to synthesise Aristotelian philosophical and scientific thought with Judaism. One of his difficulties, which also arises with Christian and Islamic thinkers (Aquinas and Averroes for instance) centres on how the doctrine of divine creation could possibly be reconciled with Aristotle's scientific conclusion that the world is eternal and had no beginning. Maimonides' Aristotelian approach was influenced by such Islamic philosophers as ibn Sina and ibn Rushd and, in turn, his views were to influence St Thomas Aquinas and Spinoza, among others, especially through his most celebrated work, *Guide of the Perplexed*. Here Maimonides argued that philosophy and religion are quite different, though complementary in nature, and it is the task of philosophy to apply rational analysis to religious truths in order to support them philosophically and, on the other hand, to disprove doctrines that seemed contrary to revelation. In the *Guide* (Bk 1 Chs 31–5), he sets out the difficulties that hinder the search for divine truth and identifies a number of obstacles in the way of seeking it. These include the obscure nature of truth, which makes it difficult to grasp, the influence of one's upbringing and habitual way of thinking and living, the human need to dominate others and cause strife which can distort the truth, the immaturity of young people who seek truth but are easily swayed by their emotions, the absence of the right conditions for truth seeking such as an atmosphere of tranquillity and quiet, a lack of learning and education, the time constraints that operate because of family responsibilities, a morally dubious life style and a greater interest in the superficial things of life. What is needed, he argues, is an extensive period of education in the study of such subjects as astronomy, general cosmology, psychology, mathematics and the sciences and logic prior to studying theology for which the right kind of mental training and moral disposition is necessary. Maimonides concludes that very few people would acquire the truth about God if left to themselves. Hence the need for a teaching authority, divine revelation and tradition so that divine truth can be presented to people in such a way that they can understand it, for example through parables and stories. This hermeneutical approach anticipates later developments in hermeneutical theology and philosophy which took place in the nineteenth and twentieth centuries. Maimonides also took the view that it is only when we become aware of our lack of knowledge about God that the most profound understanding of God can become possible. Thus we should reflect on the 'negative' divine attributes and be aware, conversely, that to assume that we can attribute any positive qualities to God is wrong. This agnostic theological stance on the part of Maimonides undoubtedly aims to respect divine transcendence and unknowability (and therefore divine unnameability) and this is supported by God's naming of himself in the Hebrew Bible (Christian Old Testament) as: I AM WHO AM (YaHVeH) thereby declaring that the divine essence is to be. Maimonides carefully analysed this doctrine in considerable detail in the *Guide* and influenced Aquinas's treatment of the subject, and more generally, the latter's view of the relationship between philosophy and religion, particularly in the context of how reason and faith interact.

See **Agnosticism, St Thomas Aquinas, Judaism,** *Via Negativa*

Further reading: Maimonides (1963)

Marcel, Gabriel (1889–1973): French philosopher and playwright, he was particularly interested in metaphysics and ontology which he perceived as the guide to what is transcendent. He has been described as a Neosocratic Christian existentialist. His writings, which include a number of philosophical diaries, emphasise the need for constant reflection and wonder about reality as a mystery of which we are part, which is expressed in terms of presence (especially as interpersonal co-presence), love, death, goodness and evil. There is a strong religious motif permeating all of his philosophical writings and it is no coincidence that his particularly self-reflective method of philosophising led to his conversion to Roman Catholicism. His writings include *Metaphysical Journal* (1927), *Being and Having* (1949), *The Mystery of Being* 2 vols (1950–51), *Homo Viator: Introduction to a Metaphysics of Hope* (1951) and *Creative Fidelity* (1964).

See **Belief, Christianity, Death, Despair, Evil, Existentialism, Faith, Hope, Metaphysics, Mystery, Philosophy, Sartre, Socrates, Transcendence**

Further reading: Marcel (1948, 1950–51, 1964, 1978)

Marx, Karl (1818–83): German political philosopher whose thinking and writings have had enormous influence world wide, especially in the twentieth century, on European politics, and particularly in Russia and in other countries in Eastern Europe, in Asia, especially China, Vietnam and Cambodia, in Latin America, notably in Cuba and in the African continent. More than any other nineteenth-century philosopher, Karl Marx's thinking was to bring about global cataclysmic social and political change, the general need for which he had enunciated in his famous observation that philosophers have only interpreted the world whereas the point is to change it.

His parents were Rhineland Jews who had converted to Protestantism, the faith into which Marx was baptised, and his father was a lawyer who communicated his interest in the ideas of Voltaire, Rousseau and other eighteenth-century rationalists to his son, whom they clearly influenced. After being unsuccessful in his attempt to secure an academic post following the completion of his doctoral thesis on Democritus and Epicurus, Karl Marx became a journalist, writing highly critical political articles on Prussian censorship. He then moved to Paris, Brussels, and back to Germany from where, when he was expelled for his political activities, he returned to Paris, but in 1849 was also expelled from there and finally settled in London where he spent the remainder of his life with his wife and family, researching and writing in the British Museum. From 1844 onwards, he collaborated with Engels in working out a joint approach in the philosophical and political analysis of societies' economic structures in order to understand how economic and social justice and equality might be implemented for the good of all. The philosophical basis of Marxist philosophy is materialism. It is from this that human consciousness dialectically derives and interacts in the human relationships of production that constitute the economic structure of society. It is the mode of production of material life that conditions the social, political and intellectual life processes in general. Marx insists that it is not the consciousness of human beings that determines human existence but rather their social existence that determines their consciousness. Social revolution and change result from the conflict between the material productive forces of society and the property relations within which they have hitherto operated. It is within this context of materialism that Marx employs an adapted Hegelian concept of the dialectical process together with Feuerbach's theory of the nature of religion to further his own approach with its practical emphasis on the material basis of human life in society. Central to Marx's analysis and political philosophy is his critique of the role and function of religion and he concludes that the criticism of religion is the premise of all criticism. Following Feuerbach, he states that human beings make religion and he claims that people who look for the superhuman being in heaven simply find a reflection of themselves. It is only man who constitutes the world of man, the state and society and the human essence has no reality. Marx does admit that religious distress is an expression and a protest of real distress but it is of oppressed human beings who exist at 'the heart of a heartless world'. In his best known claim, religion, declares Marx, constitutes 'the opium of the people', a pacifying drug to keep people happy in their chains. Real happiness, by contrast, is only achieved by abolishing religion as an expression of illusory happiness and so the criticism of religion represents '*in embryo the criticism of the vale of woe*, the *halo* of which is religion'. The task of history is to establish the truth of this world, and philosophy, as the servant of history, has the immediate task of unmasking alienation in what Marx calls 'unholy forms'. Therefore the criticism of heaven, religion and theology are transformed respectively into critiques of the earth, of the right and of politics. There is no reality outside humankind and nature so history is reducible to human activity in pursuit of human goals. Progress towards human fulfilment involves overcoming the experience of being alienated by the perception and experience of other human beings and products as alien hostile objects. Such alienation can result from religion and the lack of economic power with the difference that religious estrangement occurs only in the field of consciousness whereas economic estrangement is a function of real life. The religious world is only a reflection of the real world and conceives of human beings in an abstract way by contrast with a concrete acceptance of the practical and intelligible human relationships that pertain to social life and to the interaction with nature. The social principles of Christianity, states Marx dismissively, justified ancient slavery, glorified medieval serfdom, defended the oppression of the proletariat while always preaching the necessity for the existence of a ruling class and an oppressed class. The resolution of what Marx describes as 'the Jewish question' lies in the free states of North America since it is only there, according to him, that the theological significance of the Jews can assume a purely secular character. Human beings, he states, must free themselves politically from religion by expelling it from the sphere of public law and by confining it within the private legal domain. It fragments society rather than unifying it, he claims, because it differentiates people from one another. It is the atheistic state that is truly democratic and relegates religion to its proper place as simply one element among others in society. The Christian state (and presumably any other religious state) is the imperfect state by contrast with the real democratic state which does not need religion for its political development. Political democracy is only acceptable as Christian when everyone, and not merely one man, is considered to be a sovereign supreme being.

See **Christianity, Feuerbach, Hegel, Materialism, Liberation Theology, Religion**

Further reading: Helm (1999); Marx (1977)

Materialism: The belief that nothing but matter and material objects exist and that everything can be explained in terms of matter, including human behaviour. There are thus no non-material entities (for instance souls, minds, God) or states of existence, and the universe and all within it function in a purely material way. Science is often invoked by materialists as providing the justification for their theories and there are various degrees of materialism ranging from the very extreme to more modified forms, which, in some cases, imply that matter and material beings can be understood to operate intelligently. As a philosophical theory, materialism is obviously unsympathetic to the existence of God and, while sometimes tolerant of religion and religious activities, fundamentally seems to regard the religious way as immature, primitive, unscientific and redundant in today's world with little to offer as a valid interpretation and explanation of reality.

See **Agnosticism, Atheism, Empiricism, Epicurus, David Hume, Karl Marx**

Meditation: is the state of thinking about something deeply, including one's spiritual beliefs and concerns, such as God and how one relates to God. Meditation can also involves a very profound contemplation of God in so far as this is possible and there are religious meditative practices, such as forms of prayer in an atmosphere of silence and quiet tranquillity which are believed to assist the development and cultivation of the appropriate disposition for contemplating God and divine reality. In the philosophical field, Plato and Aristotle, wrote about the state of contemplation, the former with regard to seeing the vision of reality in the ineffable light of goodness whereas for Aristotle, the highest form of happiness is achieved by meditatively considering what is intrinsically worth while for its own sake. In the religious and theological field, *visio Dei* or the beatific vision of God, is said by some to constitute the goal of human life, which, when attained, according to Aquinas, brings perfect happiness. Meditation and contemplation have been extensively written about and advocated as identifying a way of life which will help us to encounter what is most real. Mystical experiences may sometimes result from religious and philosophical contemplation and Socrates and Plotinus are said to have personally had some such experiences. Plotinus, for example, describes his own out of body state. in *Ennead* IV. 8.1 while St Thomas Aquinas in *De Veritate* Q.13 and *Summa Theologica* II-II.Q.175 provides a fascinating analysis of what he takes to be a self-description of such an experience by St Paul in 2 Corinthians 12:1–6. Aquinas claims that for Paul's state of religious ecstasy to have occurred, it was necessary for his sensory powers to have been temporally suspended in order to free up his intellect to see God. Intense prayer and other forms of worship and religious practices (including certain kinds of dances, as in Sufi or Islamic mysticism) are regarded as usually, though not always, preparatory to mystical experiences.

See **Beatific Vision, Contemplation, God, Mysticism, Socrates, Plotinus**

Further reading: Quinn (1996)

Metaphor: from the Greek 'to bring beyond', 'to carry over', 'to transfer'. In Aristotle's *Rhetoric*, where he discusses persuasive speech and the kind of discourse that can arouse emotions, *metaphora* means 'a word used in a changed sense'. As a figure of speech, it refers to a word, phrase or statement that denotes the way one thing is applied to something else so as to suggest some likeness between them. Aristotle argued that what is being communicated assumes a special vitality when the right proportionality exists in the attribution of a likeness between one thing and another and this makes the hearers (and presumably readers of a text) 'see' things which they might not otherwise perceive. It is not surprising that metaphors are frequently used in religious language to serve as descriptions of the likeness between divine and created reality. The use of descriptive language, it is argued, suits the religious worldview because it provides flexible ways of portraying religious truth, especially for the less well-educated. St Augustine, St Thomas Aquinas, Moses Maimonides and ibn Rushd, and more recently Paul Ricoeur remark on the very positive aspects of metaphor in religious discourse and point to the fact that divine revelation is itself communicated in imaginative form in the foundational sacred texts of faith.

See **Hermeneutics, Paul Ricoeur, Ibn Rushd**

Further reading: Ricoeur (1995)

Metaphysics: from the Greek '*meta ta physika*' meaning 'after or beyond *physikos* or physics (the scientific study of nature)'. Metaphysics is that part of philosophy which aims to study the most fundamental aspects of reality, which is to say being as being. For Aristotle and those in the Aristotelian tradition such as Maimonides, ibn Rushd and Aquinas, metaphysics was regarded as the scientific study of being *qua* being although in the post-Cartesian world this was to change in that the empirically based physical sciences using mathematics as a methodological procedure, replaced metaphysic's role in analysing the nature of reality. This also led to the marginalisation of the theological dimension of metaphysics with regards to reality's implications for the existence of God, which was no longer generally perceived in the post-Cartesian and post-Reformation Western world as a fit subject for scientific investigation. Kant's critique of scholastic metaphysics and his own attempts to reposition this discipline as an enquiry into the phenomenal world, gave rise to a new kind of metaphysics. In the twentieth century, especially from the time of Heidegger onwards, metaphysics focused on what could be fundamentally said about the human condition in relation to *our* way of being in the world. From another point of view, the absence or rejection of metaphysical thought has had consequences for the philosophy of religion in that metaphysics seems to philosophically ground and 'firm up' the analysis of religious thought in the absence of which theological discourse appears to be intellectually 'thin'.

See **Aquinas, Aristotle, Leibniz**

Further reading: Ackrill (1981); Anderson (1953)

Metempsychosis See **Transmigration**

Miracles: events believed to be caused by a special act of God. Some say that a miracle is an exception to the laws of nature or involves some event that exceeds the natural powers or capacities of natural things. Others claim that a miracle is primarily recognisable by its power to reveal something about God or God's purposes and that such events do not have to be scientifically inexplicable. David Hume stated that since a miracle is defined as a violation of the laws of nature, the proof against a miracle is just as compelling as the reasons given for it and there will be as many people providing evidence against the possibility of miracles as there will be those who will provide proof of miraculous happenings. There is always some doubt as regards such a happening and people should function on the basis that evidence for any conclusion should be proportionate. However, sometimes people are gullible and credulous and the more absurd and miraculous something is said to be, the more people believe in it. The basis may be emotional since the feelings of wonder and surprise that these apparently extraordinary miraculous events arouse, delight those who experience them and lead to the conviction that a miraculous event has indeed occurred. When this is taken in the context of the attitudes and behaviour of those who are more favourably disposed to take a religious view of the world, their belief in miracles will be all the stronger. Hume also claims that barbarous and ignorant societies are much more inclined to accept supernatural and miraculous happenings, which should indeed caution us about accepting miracles as being true. His discussion of miracles in *An Enquiry Concerning Human Understanding* concludes with Hume claiming that the Christian religion is based on faith, not on reason, which makes it inevitable for people to look for support for their beliefs in what are taken to be extraordinary manifestations of divine power. Hume's critique of miracles as irrational has led to considerable debate about their status in the context of religion by contrast with the traditional view which claimed that miracles confirm the presence of a genuine prophet or apostle sent by God. It should also be said that evidence of miracles is not confined to Christianity but is attested to in the traditions of Judaism and Islam and in other religious traditions past and present. Indeed, it might be argued that the extraordinary nature of miraculous events seems to function in religion as a basic foundation that constitutes the relevant religious tradition as such.

See **Christianity, Faith, David Hume, Jesus**
Further reading: Hume (1975)

Modernism: emerged in Europe in the late nineteenth and early twentieth centuries as a movement aimed at modifying Christianity by emphasising the importance of science and the need to incorporate social and political teachings into Christian teaching. The intention was to make the Christian faith more relevant and acceptable to people in the contemporary world. Modernism was found particularly among Roman Catholics and often seen by the hierarchy as a threat to the faith in that it was perceived as encouraging more secularisation. Catholic theologians and Roman Catholics generally were therefore warned against modernism and those who studied for the priesthood in pontifical Roman colleges and universities had to take an oath against it before being conferred with degrees or licentiates in theology.

See **Christianity, Baron von Hügel**

Monotheism: from the Greek *monos* 'one', 'single', 'alone', 'one and only', and *theos* meaning 'God', monotheism states that there is only one God.

See **Polytheism**

Moses: the Hebrew leader and prophet chosen by God to lead the Israelites from slavery in Egypt to the Promised Land and who gave them the Ten Commandments received from God. In the Old Testament or Hebrew Bible, the story of Moses is told in the books of Exodus, Leviticus, Numbers and Deuteronomy.

See **Abraham, Judaism**

Further reading: The Jerusalem Bible

Mosque: a Muslim place of worship, usually having one or more minarets and often decorated with elaborate tracery and texts from the Qur'an.

See **Islam**

Muhammad (AD 570?–632): The Prophet and founder of Islam believed by Muslims to be the channel for the final unfolding of God's revelation. He began to teach in Mecca in 610 but persecution forced him to flee with his followers to Medina in 622. After several battles he conquered Mecca in 630 and established the principles of Islam, as contained in the Qur'an, in Arabia. Islam has subsequently spread worldwide and in some countries is the fastest growing religion.

See **Islam**

Further reading: Dawood (2003)

Murdoch, Iris (1919–99): was born in Dublin but spent most of her life in England and died in Oxford in 1999. She studied classics, ancient history and philosophy at Somerville College, Oxford and later undertook a post-graduate studentship in philosophy under Wittgenstein. In 1948 she was elected a fellow of St Anne's College Oxford where she worked as a tutor until 1963, following which she devoted herself completely to writing although she lectured for a time at the Royal College of Art between 1963 and 1967. She published extensively in the field of philosophy, including her collection of essays entitled *The Sovereignty of the Good* (1970) and *Metaphysics as a Guide to Morals* (1992). She was also a best selling novelist whose fiction contains many philosophical themes. Although her main philosophical interests are aesthetics and morality, she emphasises their connections with belief in God and religious behaviour, particularly, though not exclusively, in the context of Christianity. Her special interest in Plato and his account of the Good is central to much of this. In her article, 'On "God" and "Good"', she states that God is or was taken to be 'a single transcendent non-representable and necessarily real object of attention' who is worshipped in a prayerful loving attentiveness. Focusing on God in this way is as natural, she claims, as loving another person and reflects a unifying experience in addition to revealing the transcendent nature of that towards which one's attention is directed. Furthermore, it leads to behaviour that is informed and shaped by the object of one's attention. Focusing on a work of art is somewhat similar to this kind of religious attentiveness and implies discovering its value as a good to be appreciated. Iris Murdoch observes that because of the contemporary decline of interest in God and in religion, especially among the young, appreciating what is good and beautiful may provide an adequate substitute for the foundational grounding now required for morality, which was formerly supplied by one's religious beliefs. She also acknowledges the consolatory powers of faith in God as sinners hoping for redemption and for the representative aesthetic power of works of art inspired by the religious vision, especially by Christianity. She ultimately appears to be looking for another way of recovering the values associated with religious faith which she suggests might be possible through art. Belief in and love of God gives spiritual and emotional energy because of faith in divine goodness, and likewise, the Good, like beauty, can be clearly seen 'in our ordinary unmysterious experience of transcendence'. The latter occurs in the encounter with the quality of 'beyondness'. This illuminates and inspires action, giving us a positive experience of truth which can be stronger or weaker depending on circumstances. In times of moral difficulty, Murdoch concludes, we should try to become more conscious of our general awareness of good or goodness which accompanies us all the time, like the sense of God being present that accompanies the religious believer. What we need, she suggests, is a form of theology as moral philosophy which can continue to exist without God.

See **Aesthetics, Christianity, Faith, God, Stephen MacKenna, Plato, Religion**

Further reading: Murdoch (1992, 1997)

Mystery: an unexplained or apparently inexplicable event or phenomenon which, in the philosophy of religion, demonstrates the inability of human reason, or of any finite intellect, to understand the divine, or God's nature and attributes, however conceived of. The Platonic tradition emphasises the mystery of otherness in what is transcendent (while yet being somehow immanent), like the Good in Plato's *Republic* and Beauty in *Symposium*. For Plotinus, it is the ineffable One (which from another perspective is also the Good) who is this ultimate mystery, and equated in the Jewish, Christian and Islamic traditions with God, who for Christians is also incarnated in the mystery of Jesus Christ, the God–man. Divinity in most cultures, East and West, is mythologically and theologically depicted somewhat similarly in either monotheistic, polytheistic or pantheistic form. For Otto, the Holy constitutes the ultimate mystery while the French philosopher Gabriel Marcel distinguished a mystery from a problem in that he claims that whereas the latter has a solution, mystery is what we are part of, being inside the frame, so to speak. Mystery, according to Marcel, thus refers to what most profoundly real, there to be appreciated rather than problematised. The mystery of being, title of one of Marcel's works, is what we are part of, and this mystery shows itself in different ways, for example, as presence and co-presence, in good and evil. The problem-solving approach, by contrast, reduces the real to manageable empirical proportions, thereby losing sight of what it is. Wittgenstein too writes somewhat along these lines in his *Tractatus Logico-Philosophicus* when he describes the things that cannot be said but rather show themselves as the mystical. Like Marcel, Wittgenstein claims that we cannot be outside reality as observers of it; instead, we exist within reality as part of what constitutes it. Theologically, divine truth is revealed in the mysteries of faith which transcend, while not being contrary to, reason.

See **God, Jesus, Gabriel Marcel, Miracles, Transcendence**

Further reading: Marcel (1948, 1950–51)

Mystery Religions: the title given to a number of religious cults of ancient origin and syncretistic tendencies and practices that existed from the eighth century BC to the fourth century AD. Secret initiation rites were involved and some of the more popular mystery religions during the Graeco-Roman era included the Eleusinian, Dionysiac and Mithraic mysteries and those of Iris and Osiris. There are suggestions that Plato may have been familiar with one or more of these and there have been enquiries into the relationship between these cults and Christianity since they appear to have been popular during the early centuries AD and share some religious practices and vocabulary in common with it, according to some late nineteenth and early twentieth century German theologians, including Rudolf Bultman. It is suggested, for example, that early Christology may have been shaped by a pre-Christian Gnostic 'primal man' and there are precedents for Christian baptism in the mystery religions.
See **Gnosticism, Plato, Religion**
Further reading: Hanratty (1997)

Mysticism: term describing a tradition within a religion direct and immediate encounter with or experience of God or divinity, however conceived, or experiencing a state regarded as transcending human reason and sensory experience. In religious traditions, such as, for example, in Judaism, Christianity, Islam and Hinduism, the mystic claims some form of direct awareness of God or ultimate reality, sometimes as a result of certain kinds of experiences or practices, perhaps ascetic in nature. Theists interpret such claims as signifying a special intimacy with God or divinity, though there may be, in addition to believing in the reality of such claims, some other forms of verification or criteria applied to adjudicate on the validity of experiences that are subjectively declared to be mystical. Mystics are found in most religious traditions, including those that are explicitly shaped by philosophical considerations. It is suggested, for example, in some of Plato's dialogues that Socrates may have had some mystical experiences. There is also the classic description given by Plotinus in *Ennead* IV.8.1 of his out of body experiences, while his biographer Porphyry, his disciple and arranger of The *Enneads*, also admits to mystical experiences in his *Life of Plotinus*. In the Christian tradition, there is a considerable body of literature on mysticism and by mystics themselves, for example Julian of Norwich, St John of the Cross, St Theresa of Avila, St Therese the Little Flower and many others. St Thomas Aquinas himself is reported as having mystical experiences and his interesting philosophical analysis of what he took to be a description by St Paul of his own mystical experiences in 2 Corinthians 12:1–6 is quite intriguing. In *De Veritate* Q.13 and in *Summa Theologica* II–IIQ.175, St Thomas sets out to explain how this temporary vision of God before death might be possible. He argues that what happens between the intellect and sensory powers is that the latter are suspended from operating and this frees the mind up to see God. However, he was also aware that other factors can result in states that are similar in ways to religious ecstasy and brought about by certain kinds of hallucinatory herbs, extreme fatigue or illness or stress, even the power of evil, not to mention activities that can self induce out of body experiences. However, he argues that authentically religious mystical states are unique in that they cannot be self induced but result often suddenly and unexpectedly through the supernatural power of God. They are authentically self-authoritative, he claims, in the sense that the human subject is certain about the religious nature of the event. However, this can also be a problem since schizoid and psychotic states can be equally convincing to a deranged person and there is abundant testimony, professional and otherwise, to this. Thus mysticism is difficult to investigate in that those who have had mystical experiences will claim that they have had encounters with what is ineffable and transcendent, and therefore beyond any adequate description or comprehension.

See **Plotinus**

Further reading: Dillon (1991); Quinn (1996)

Myth: from the Greek *mythos* meaning 'fable', 'legend', the term can be interpreted in different ways, for instance as a widely held fallacy, a narrative about imaginary beings and fantasy worlds and so forth. A working definition of a myth might be that it is an imaginative narrative about superhuman beings that were often believed by members of a pre-literate societies to actually exist. Many myths have religious and philosophical implications in that they imaginatively express beliefs about the nature and activities of supernatural beings which explain why the world is the way it is and what rationale underlies the rules by which people live together in a given society. There are, for example, myths of origin (such as creation myths), myths of the Fall, myths of salvation, and myths about what is regarded for a whole variety of reasons as the sacred or divine. Myths can also be understood as providing truth about deeper aspects of reality than history or science can reveal because these narratives may facilitate a flexible metaphysical understanding, in metaphorical form of what reality amounts to and what its significance is for human beings. The famous Babylonian mythic narrative, *The Epic of Gilgamesh*, one of whose central themes is the search for immortality, and the Homeric and the biblical myths can be rightly said to represent foundational narrative sources for Western civilisation. Homer's stories served as the educational foundation for the subsequent development of Greek religion, drama, science and philosophy, while the Bible is the sacred book for the Jewish and Christian traditions – in the latter case, added to with narratives about the life and mission of Jesus and the early documents about the extraordinary happenings in the first Christian communities. Plato's philosophical use of myths are noted for their imaginative and pedagogical nature and for their relevance to the central themes in his dialogues. Ibn Rushd also identified the importance of imaginative stories in terms of their accessibility for the simple and uneducated Muslim faithful. Much earlier still, in the Indian tradition of sacred writings such as the Bhagavad Gita and the Upanishads, mythic narrative was also central to the religious and philosophical thought depicted in these texts. The same is true on the broader cultural stage and still true today in that myths are understood to portray beings and situations in ways that stimulate people to think imaginatively about what life really means and what its limits imply for human endeavour. A myth is thus a story with the culturally formative power to direct and inform the lives and thoughts of people individually and collectively in any given society.

See **Mircea Eliade,** *The Epic of Gilgamesh,* **Sir James Frazier, Hermeneutics, Plato**

For further reading: Eliade (1977); Hamilton and Cairns (1963); Sanders (1972)

Near-Death Experiences: Experiences of people, quite widely reported and documented, on the verge of or being close to death (for example those whose hearts may have stopped beating) who claim to have been out of their bodies and aware of this as well as conscious of the general situation (such as the room, operating theatre or hospital ward) in which they and their bodies are. Such people have reported finding themselves out of their bodies up in one corner of the ceiling looking down on their bodies in the room and seeing and hearing clearly what was going on around them, for instance medical staff trying to revive them by trying to restart their heartbeats, what the doctors and nurses were saying and so forth. There are also reports of people who felt they were experiencing themselves being drawn into a tunnel at the end of which there was brilliant light, and subsequently having to return, often reluctantly, from this state 'back' into their bodies again. Most of the cases reported confirm that those who claim to have had such experiences often regard the near-death episode as being very significant for how they viewed their lives thereafter. Not all such experiences were positive, however. Questions obviously arise as to whether the individual (as mind or soul?) has actually experienced the beginnings of immortality or whether the sensations or feelings or state of mind in near-death is organically and physically induced by how the bodily constituents of human life are effected by the trauma which triggers the event. Some regard it as a proof of the soul's or mind's immortality and become convinced that there is an afterlife of tranquillity and state of perfect bliss (or alternatively a state of darkness and fear) which can be validly interpreted from a religious point of view.

See **The Afterlife, Death, Immortality, Out of Body Experiences**

Further reading: Choron (1963)

Negative Theology: a tradition that emphasises God's transcendence by focusing on what God is not, that is on the dissimilarities between God and everything else. In this approach, God is described or defined as not having any of the properties of created and finite reality, for example God is not bodily, not temporal and not limited in power or in knowledge. This negative theological approach is linked with the mystical way of negation (*via negativa*) which is characteristic of some forms of mysticism, where it is claimed that knowing God by unknowing, disposes human beings towards recognising the ineffable and transcendent nature of divinity. In terms of philosophy this has Socratic connotations, and writers and thinkers such as Plato (in the dialogue *Parmenides*), Plotinus, Pseudo-Dionysius and Maimonides to name but some, argue that the negative way provides the best form of knowledge of what is essentially absolutely simple.

See **Mysticism,** *Via Negativa, Via Positiva*
Further reading: Quinn (1996)

Neoplatonism: a term used in recent centuries describing Platonists or followers in the tradition of Plato, especially from the third to the sixth centuries AD. Although Plotinus (AD 205–270) is usually regarded as the founder of Neoplatonism, Platonism continued immediately after Plato's death with philosophers such as Speusippus (c.407–339 BC) who succeeded Plato as the head of the Academy, Xenocrates (396–314 BC) who headed the Academy after Speusippus and Polemon (c.350–267 BC), who succeeded Xenocrates, New developments in Platonism began with Antiochus of Ascalon (130–68 BC) and then there were the Alexandrians, Eudorus and Philo of Alexandria, followed by Ammonius and Plutarch of Chareonia, the second century AD Athenian school and the school of Gaius and the Neopythagoreans. Neoplatonism, as it came to be called much later, consisted of Platonic philosophy combined with elements of Aristotelianism, Stoicism and Pythagoreanism and came to assume a spiritual and religious framework. It taught belief in a supreme principle (or deity), the One, wholly transcendent above being, undifferentiated, unknowable and simple and also that from which everything else emanates. This constitutes it as the Good, whose overflowing disposition, makes it the source of being. Next to the One, there is Intelligence and then Soul, followed by sensory based reality in time and space and, finally, there is matter, which sometimes carries connotations of badness or evil. There are also hints in Plotinus's writings, for example, of a primal separation of individual (and subsequently incarnated) souls from Soul itself. In addition, there is the cosmic or world soul and the overall objective is to restore the individual soul and world soul to Soul itself. Two other prominent representatives of Neoplatonism are Porphyry (AD 234–c.305) who was Plotinus's disciple and biographer and who arranged the order of Plotinus's writings in the text known as *Enneads* and Iamblichus who died c. AD 330. Among Porphyry's writings is an excellent introduction to teachings of Neoplatonism, a work on Aristotle's Categories and his polemic, *Against the Christians*, where he argued against the credibility of the sources of Christianity as regards, for example, Scriptural authorship. Iamblichus expounded what he considered to be Pythagorean doctrines and his *Egyptian Mysteries* is a philosophical–allegorical interpretation of Egypt's rites and religious teachings. Among the later representatives of Neoplatonism, Proclus (AD 410–485) stands out, especially as regards his comprehensive and systematic account of Neoplatonism in his *Elements of Theology*, and a Latin summary of this work under the title *Liber De Causis* was a considerable influence on Aquinas's thought, especially on his concept of the human soul and on his understanding of the hierarchy of being. What is also interesting about Neoplatonism is that because of its religious and theological tendencies, and despite the hostility of some of its adherents towards Christianity, it came to substantially influence, and indeed dominate in many respects, Christian thought right up to the Middle Ages, and thereafter had an impact on Renaissance thinking and later on those known as the Cambridge Platonists. In addition, Neoplatonism was also significant for the philosophical and scientific views of Islamic thinkers, notably ibn Sina.

See **Al-Kindi, St Augustine, The Cambridge Platonists, Christianity, Ibn Sina, Islam, Plato, Plotinus, Porphyry, Proclus**

Further reading: Alexandrakis (2002); Cheney and Hendrix (2004); Dillon (1977, 1991); Leaman (1999a); Wallis (1972)

Newman, John Henry (1801–90): English theologian, educationalist and philosopher, with a special interest in the nature of belief, particularly religious belief, the latter constituting the central concern of his classic work on the dynamics of belief, *A Grammar of Assent* (1870). As a young man, Newman was a leader of the Oxford or Tractarian movement which inspired the subsequent tradition of High Church or Catholic Anglicanism. In 1845 he was converted to Roman Catholicism and subsequently ordained a priest to be later made cardinal. A prolific writer who famously justified his conversion to Catholicism in his *Apologia Pro Vita Sua*, he published extensively in theology as well as on education, for example, *The Idea of a University* (1852) and *University Sketches* (1856). He founded the Catholic University in Dublin, later to become the National University of Ireland University College Dublin. *A Grammar of Assent*, written between 1850 and 1870, sets out to explore what is involved in the belief process, especially as regards the convictions of certainty that seem central to the nature of religious belief in the content of the relevant faith regarded as being true. For Newman, the structure of personal religious faith reflects the structure of personal knowledge as regards any subject matter and, in this context, the imagination also has a significant role to play. The contrast between faith and reason for him is a contrast between two different modes of rationality and he argues that unbelief is just as opposed to reason as it is to belief. Thus faith is simply another way of reasoning about reality and religious truth is found and accepted as being certain by knowledge attained from a confluence of factors, not merely by exercising one's intellect, but also through conscience, one's sense of duty and observance of the moral law, among others. His analysis of how knowledge (including knowledge of religious truth) is acquired depicts it as a process that is constantly developing by being added to from various experiences noetically digested. This leads to convictions and a sense of personal certainty that x is indubitably true. Newman claimed that his *Grammar* was essentially concerned with the reasons that someone of goodwill has for believing as distinct from a sceptic's reasons for doubting. He argued in effect that we do have certainty about all kinds of issues, including religious matters, and that the noetic process involved is quite similar in all instances. Having belief in God is basic, which for him as a Christian means believing in Christ's revelation of God, and shares many features in common with the structure of our common sense knowledge of empirical reality generally which includes engagement with what it is that we are trying to know, experientially and pre-reflectively and most importantly, through the use of imagination. Although he concedes that it is difficult to imagine certain mental facts that are unknown to us, it is not impossible either, so the question is how one can rise to the required imaginative level to apprehend God. This can be put into the form of 'Can I believe as if I saw?' The phenomenon of conscience is important here, according to Newman, since it provides the most authoritative channels of communication between God and human beings. By reflecting on our own experience, we can become aware of the difference between 'notional' and real belief and assent and this is where the role of the imagination also plays its part in the belief process. Proof of the certainty of one's belief comes through what Newman describes as the Illative Sense which represents the power of judging and concluding at its most perfect, and this reasoning faculty, when exercised by gifted or educated or otherwise well-prepared minds, permeates the noetic process that culminates in convictions of faith, though always in the context of a developing and continuing process marked by the ongoing confluence of factors that map human life itself. Thus, rather than involving a 'leap of faith', we grow into our convictions of faith as it were, according to Newman, just as more generally we grown into our convictions and certainties about other aspects of life.

See **Belief, Christianity, Faith, God**

Further reading: Newman (1959, 1979)

Nietzsche, Friedrich (1844–1900): Born near Leipzig in Germany, his parents were Lutheran and his father was a Lutheran pastor. At the age of twenty-five, before he had completed his doctorate, he became professor of philology at Basle University, Switzerland. He retired from this post in 1879 for health reasons and devoted himself entirely to writing. He eventually suffered a complete physical and mental breakdown in 1889 and remained insane until his death. His first book, *The Birth of Tragedy* (1872), drew attention to what he regarded as the two essentially opposite themes in Greek tragedy, namely, the Dionysian spirit of frenzied and excessive abandon, on the one hand, and the Apollonian restraint, order and harmony, on the other. This suggests a constant tension and conflict between the human tendencies towards chaotic abandon, and the inhibiting and controlling organisational power of political rule and its correspondingly religious organisational restraint. Nietzsche argued that it is we who have constructed the world in which we live and rejects the possibility of any underlying and fixed reality. Our beliefs about causality, necessity and substantiality are simply useful devices to enable us to communicate with and understand each other but tell us nothing of what reality fundamentally is. We construct values since in order to continue to function, we need new ideals and new values while simultaneously rejecting existing conventional wisdom and accepted truth. By exerting a 'will to power' one can accept suffering as a way of acquiring richer and more authentic experiences that fulfil the yearnings of the human heart rather than fitting in with the dictates of reason. Although Nietzsche regarded the work of reason and the acquisition of scientific knowledge as a means towards creating new perspectives and values, he also advises us to understand how accepted values come to exist, for example how and why the practices of fasting and celibacy assumed such importance in Christianity. In time, people will realise, he believed, that all values are humanly constructed and maintained and that there is no divine basis for them, because there is no God. This will lead humankind to affirm their own existence and to accept every pain and pleasure as part of the human condition. Nietzsche put forward the doctrine of eternal recurrence which means that happenings will keep repeating themselves infinitely and it is in this context that he claims that this life is the only one each person has. His concept of the *Übermensch* – poorly translated as the Superman, in fact it is the Overman – permeates much of his work. This is the ideal of human life for men and women, namely someone who is rigorously self-disciplined and who voluntarily exposes him or herself to suffering in order to exercise the will to power. This attitude of courageously bracing oneself against the adversities and vicissitudes of life defines the authentic human being by contrast with those who are submissive and mediocre and who lack the courage to take themselves in hand and face life in just this way. The will to power constitutes the essence of human existence and the source of all our strivings. As exercised by the *Übermensch*, the will to power is not simply about pitting oneself against the pain and bitterness of life for reasons of self-preservation, but is primarily an effort to master all adversity and in doing so become more self-creative. For Nietzsche, God is dead so there are unlimited opportunities for humankind. This means following one's highest ideals and acting on them at every given opportunity. His anti-Christian polemics, which became more central to his writings as time went on, are informed by his conviction that Christianity demands not just the control of but the annihilation of human passions and emotions. Associated with this are Christian attempts to denigrate the sexual impulse as being unclean. Although Christianity does express the will to power this has to be identified as that of the weak and frustrated whose resentment is translated into forms of perverse hostility towards physical and intellectual excellence, a preference for those who are mediocre and lower in status, a hatred of sex, a depreciation of the body in favour of the soul and of this world in favour of another fictitious one. In *The Antichrist*, he becomes strident and shrill in his critique of Christianity on such issues, although he also recognises in this work that exceptional human beings will, out of a sense of duty as well as politeness, care for those he describes as mediocre. Nietzsche also argued that belief in another world is psychologically based. In his views on morality he claims that the rationale behind moral codes can be understood in terms of rulers or the ruled, where the former's moral activity originates in self-affirmation, whereas the latter's perception of morality is perceived as being based on resentment. As a philosopher, Nietzsche has exerted enormous influence on subsequent thinkers, notably on the existentialists, and though his religious critiques in part at least are somewhat similar to those of Schleiermacher and Feuerbach and even contain resonances of the views of Marx and Freud on religion, and his thinking is undoubtedly influenced by Hegel, Nietzsche's lucid and often trenchant prose and clarity of style made his views widely known, especially after his death. His approach to religion in particular, though often strident, is notable for the challenges it poses to the rationale that underlies the conception of the divine–human relationship.

See **Camus, Christianity, Existentialism, Feuerbach, Freud, Karl Marx, Schleiermacher**

Further reading: Blackham (1962); Nietzsche (1956)

Occult, The: meaning 'that which is hidden' refers to magic rituals and various forms of spiritualism.

See **Shamanism, Witchcraft**

Omnipotence: being all powerful – a divine attribute. The question of evil challenges the possibility of divine omnipotence in that it raises the question as to how God and evil can co-exist.

See **God**

Omnipresence: being present everywhere – a divine attribute, God being transcendent and immanent. The philosophical problem is to explain how this might be possible.

See **God**

Omniscience: being all knowing – a divine attribute in that God is believed to know everything. This poses the philosophical problem of free will with regards to how people can be free to act since God already knows what they are going to do. One answer proposed is that God's knowledge is always in the present, not in the past nor future, so it as if God is seeing what is happening as it happens rather than, as it were, seeing into the future and thereby predicting what people will do then.

See **God, Sartre**

One, The: Plotinus's name for the Absolute – that which is beyond everything and from which everything emanates. The One is unknowable, transcendent, unnamable.

See **The *Enneads*, Stephen MacKenna, Neoplatonism, Plotinus**

Further reading: Dillon (1991); O'Meara (1995)

Ontology: The study of being, that is to say of what is, what exists.

See **St Thomas Aquinas, Gabriel Marcel, Metaphysics**

Further reading: Anderson (1953)

Other, The: that or whoever is over against me, sometimes perceived as constituting the mystery of being, as with Buber and Levinas, or alternatively regarded as a potential threat to one's own personal freedom and subjectivity, as in the case of Sartre.

See **Martin Buber, Levinas, Rudolf Otto, Sartre**

Further reading: Buber (1958), Levinas (1985)

Otto, Rudolf (1869–1937): German theologian who is regarded as a pioneer in promoting the phenomenology of religion and was particularly interested in the nature of religious experience. His book, *The Idea of the Holy*, first published in 1923 and revised in 1929, argues that religion is essentially the apprehension of the numinous or wholly other which human beings can grasp by religious insight. Just as one can speak of feeling the beauty of a landscape in the sense, not only of an emotion that is evoked, but as a recognition of something in the objective situation awaiting discovery and acknowledgement, so too, the 'numinous feeling' or perhaps 'the feeling of the numinous' indicates not just the relevant psychological process but its object, the Holy. Thus, although Otto does accept that the rational and the moral constitute an essential part of what is meant by the holy or the sacred, he also insists that there is what he describes as a 'non-rational' (as distinct from irrational) dimension involved with the added qualification that this non-rational aspect is neither counter to reason nor above reason either. In setting out this view, Otto seems to be looking for a more rounded human experience of God, who is both mysterious, on the one hand, yet somehow humanly accessible on the other. In doing so, Otto wants to avoid two extremes, (1) that of subjecting everything, including religion, to reason which would result in religion losing its mystery and supernatural character and (2) putting forward a view of religion that offends the principles of reason, which would make it appear that religious faith is absurd and ridiculous. The Holy, as *Mysterium Tremendum*, is the transcendent otherness of God, and the religious recognition of this is a function of three elements: (1) the interplay between one's predisposition and the stimuli involved, (2) a searching recognition, favourably predisposed, in specific sections of history, for the manifestation of the Holy and (3) fellowship with the Holy through knowing, feeling and willing, brought about on the basis of (1) and (2). Otto's exploration of the nature of religious experience was broadly defined and included, not only the Christian, but other religious viewpoints with which he himself became personally familiar, especially in the course of his travels in the East during 1910 to 1911.

See **God, Religion, The Sacred**

Further reading: Otto (1923)

Out of Body Experiences: describes a state where some people are convinced that they have experienced themselves being, or had the sensation of being, outside their bodies. Extraordinary religious ecstatic or mystical states have been described in this way as have near-death experiences.

See **Mysticism, Near-Death Experiences**

Further reading: Quinn (1996)

P

Panentheism: combines insights of pantheism and deism by claiming that the world is included in God's being. All things are in God which means that God is more than all there is and constitutes the highest unity possible.

See **Deism, Pantheism**

Panpsychism: from the Greek *pan* ('all') and *psyche* ('soul'). The belief that God is a psychic force and/or mind, consciousness, spirit, soul, and is completely immanent in everything in the universe.

See **God, Panentheism, Pantheism**

Pantheism: from the Greek *pan* meaning 'all' and *theos* meaning 'god', the belief that God and nature are identical where nature is taken to mean the universe and the totality of all that is; alternatively that God is all and that all is

God, that God is identical with the universe. This doctrine holds that all beings are modes, attributes or appearances of a single, unified reality or being. Hence, nature and God are believed to be identical. Baruch Spinoza's philosophical views, as set down in his *Ethics* were regarded by many as being pantheistic.

See **God, Religion, Spinoza, Theism**

Papacy, The: the office or term of a Pope and the office of government in the Roman Catholic Church where the Pope as bishop of Rome is believed by Catholics to be the head of the Catholic Church on the grounds that, historically, Jesus instituted Peter as the leader of the apostles. Peter subsequently became bishop of Rome and later was probably martyred there. Hence the primacy of Peter and those subsequently elected bishops of Rome as the ruling bishops of the Christian Church. Following the Reformation, the bishop of Rome remained, as the principal bishop, the head of the Roman Catholic Church (the Church of Rome), though there was considerable debate about this issue during the Second Vatican Council (1962–5) where it was strongly argued and supported by the then Pope John XXXIII, that there should be more equality among bishops in that each should exercise greater independence and freedom in the Church's decision making processes and at local pastoral level. Meanwhile in the Christian Orthodox tradition, the Greek Orthodox patriarch of Alexandria is also sometimes called Pope, and this also can apply in Coptic Christianity.

See **Christianity, Luther, The Reformation**
Further reading: Eusabius (1965)

Parables: are simple stories aimed at conveying some spiritual or religious truth or moral lessons by using examples from everyday life. The Bible has many such stories both in the Old Testament or Hebrew Bible and in the

Christian New Testament Gospel stories which contain many parables told by Jesus. Parables are also found in the Islamic tradition and in many other religious cultures. Ibn Rushd claimed that parables help the general body of believers, especially those who are uneducated, in that graphic and illustrated accounts are provided which can relate to the narrative needs of those who might otherwise find it difficult to believe if they have to use more abstract methods. St Thomas Aquinas also recognised the value and accessibility of the parables of Jesus as narratives of faith.

See **Ibn Rushd, Jesus**

Paradox: from the Greek *paradoxon* 'contrary to' and *doxa* 'opinion', a paradox is an apparent contradiction which seems to be opposed to accepted opinion. A paradoxical statement therefore on the surface, may seem absurd or self-contradictory but in fact may be true. There are paradoxical aspects to God's choice of Abraham and Sarah in old age to become the progenitors of the chosen people of Israel as there is the foundational paradox in Christianity of God becoming humanly incarnate in Jesus of Nazareth who controversially claimed that it is the poor in spirit and in possessions, the oppressed and those on the margins of society who will inherit the kingdom of God. Bernard Lonergan also identifies as a central paradox the natural desire to know God which can only be supernaturally fulfilled, while G. K. Chesterton constantly emphasised the paradoxical dimension to Christianity. Indeed, the content of religious belief of whatever kind, often seems defined by paradox. As a consequence, the philosophical analysis of religion can find itself addressing paradox as a feature of religious belief, doctrine and behaviour.

See **G. K. Chesterton, Christianity, Bernard Lonergan**
Further reading: Chesterton (2001)

Phaedo: Plato's classic dialogue set in the death cell of
   Socrates where he speaks to his friends about death and
   the afterlife before drinking the cup of hemlock that will
   kill him. The discussion deals with the significance of human mortality, the soul's immortal status, and the nature of the afterlife. Socrates also insists that philosophers should welcome death rather than fear it since it
   liberates us from bodily existence, thereby providing the
   opportunity to live in a purely psychic state of being in
   the eternal unchanging divine world beyond. Plato's compelling analysis of these issues in this dialogue went on to
   shape future discussions and philosophical debates down
   through the centuries and was particularly influential for
   Christian philosopher–theologians such as St Augustine
   and St Thomas Aquinas.
      See **Afterlife, Death, Immortality, Plato,** *Psyche,* **Soul**
      Further reading: Hamilton and Cairns (1963)

Philosophical Theology See **Philosophy of Religion**

Philosophy: taken from the Greek *philos* ('love') or *philia*
   ('affinity for' or 'attraction towards') and *sophia* ('wisdom', 'knowledge'), philosophy has many meanings, one
   of which is the love or lover of wisdom, as Plato and the
   Platonic Socrates claim. They and others, such as Epicurus and Plotinus, regarded philosophy as a way of life. For
   Aristotle, philosophical life meant that of a philosopher–
   scientist in the pursuit of knowledge, at the highest level
   for its own sake. St Augustine thought of Christianity
   as the true philosophy, while other medieval Christian
   thinkers regarded philosophy as a useful tool for theological investigation and a means of rationally teasing
   out the intellectual dimensions of Christian faith. This
   was also true in other faith traditions such as Judaism,
   although ibn Rushd in the Islamic tradition seems to suggest that philosophy is superior to theology. Historically,

there has existed, for quite a long time, a close and often overlapping relationship between philosophy, theology and religion. In the Western European post-Reformation and post-Cartesian world, the latter shaped by new developments in the physical and mathematical sciences, strong attempts were made to break this connection on the grounds that philosophical analysis was not, for various reasons, welcome into the theological arena. This did have repercussions in that some explicit and implicit restrictions were placed on philosophy with regards to its terms of reference for its content of investigation. However, the links between philosophy and religion survived almost out of necessity in that, even for philosophers such as Kant who restricted philosophical enquiries to the phenomenological world of appearance, it seemed to be unavoidable not to proceed at times with excursions into the religious and theological arena, something that continues to this day under the form of what is now known as the philosophy of religion. In the contemporary world, philosophy is also seen as a way of analysing reality, usually in specific ways, for example with regards to investigating the nature, extent and certainty of knowledge, the kind of relationship that exists between mind and senses, the nature and principles underlying the application of philosophical and religious principles to what is believed to constitute moral behaviour, and, more rarely nowadays, philosophical investigations into the nature of reality itself. The latter is philosophical metaphysics, dramatically resurrected in the twentieth century by Martin Heidegger, especially in his classic work, *Being and Time* (*Sein und Zeit*). There is also the philosophy of beauty or aesthetics, the philosophy of science and the human sciences (psychology, sociology, anthropology for example), the philosophy of the human person or philosophical anthropology (sometimes known as philosophical psychology), the philosophy of language and hermeneutics (interpretation), the philosophy of logic and mathematics, the philosophy of education, political philosophy and the philosophy of law. Indeed, philosophy, as a particular kind of analytic method, can be applied to virtually every area of human life, thought and experience and to the world at large, since everything seems to implicitly contain at least some material with possibilities for philosophical enquiry. Paradoxically, the more experience one has in this field whether through study, research, teaching or writing, the more problematic it is to explain just what kind of subject philosophy is and what it is that philosophical investigation amounts to. This is why the history of philosophy can be instructive for those who seek a definite answer since it contains varied accounts of what it is that philosophers do. For Schopenhauer (1788–1860) it meant thinking critically for oneself. This was also the view of Wittgenstein who claimed that philosophy's task was to elucidate, if possible, what was otherwise unclear and obscure. This involved working on oneself, on one's own interpretation of events, and, most importantly, on one's own way of seeing things. For Wittgenstein, philosophy meant looking at things 'this way' rather like a poetic work that depicts one panorama in which the world and one's place in it with others can be seen for what it is, in so far as this is ever possible.

See **The Dialogues of Plato, Plato, Socrates, Wittgenstein**

Further reading: Gadamer (2000); Nagel (1987)

Philosophy of Religion: the branch of philosophy that tries to understand and evaluate the beliefs and practices of religions. Topics include the nature of religion and belief, religious faith as a form of belief and the nature of religious experience, the existence of God, how subjectivity and objectivity function in philosophy's analysis of religion, life after death as conceived by various religious traditions and other related issues. Sometimes the phrase 'philosophical theology' is used, though some would see a distinction between both, where philosophical theology is perceived to enquire into key theological concepts and beliefs and is regarded as not just being concerned with arguments for the existence of God, but also with the divine attributes, for instance omniscience, omnipotence, goodness and so on and with examining the coherence of theological doctrines, in Christianity, for example, God as a Trinity of Persons, the Incarnation, Resurrection and so on. However, the distinction between the philosophy of religion and philosophical theology is somewhat artificial.

See **Arguments for the Existence of God, Evidence, God, Philosophy, Philosophical Theology, Religion, Theology**

Further reading: Burrell (2004); Davies (2004); Helm (1999)

Plato (427–347 BC): probably the single greatest philosophical writer in Western thought in that his writings encompass almost all of the topics that are of importance to philosophers. These include political philosophy, ethics, the significance of death and immortality for bodily and spiritual life, love and beauty, the origins of the universe, education and language, the nature of knowledge and the philosophy of religion. These are discussed in his dialogues, usually with each dialogue devoted to at least one main topic, and are handled very astutely in that the dialogues constitute philosophical dramas which depict the process of philosophising through conversational exchanges usually between Socrates, or rather the Platonic Socrates, and other interested persons, many of the latter being based on actual historical individuals. The aim of these dialogues is to provoke insight often through the perception of contradictions in how the relevant subject matter is discussed.

Born in the city state of Athens, Plato was a disciple of Socrates and Aristotle's teacher. He founded the Academy, a school of research and teaching, in Athens, and his thought is available to us mainly in the form of the dialogues and some letters and in what is reported and written about him by his followers, including Aristotle. Many of Plato's writings are concerned at some point with religious and theological issues, and his presentation of discussions about and analyses of the *psyche* or soul, goodness, virtue, the ideal society, the meaning of human life and death, the afterlife, theology and religion, constitute him as a writer and thinker who is of perennial interest. Such dialogues as *Euthyphro*, *Phaedo*, the *Republic* and especially *Laws* contain accounts of human activities and social behaviour that have significant implications for philosophical enquiries into religion and theology. There are frequent references to the significance of a divine dimension to reality and in the *Apology*, for example, Socrates, the central character in most dialogues, is portrayed as being divinely commanded to pursue his enquiries and questions as a divinely mandated task. This gives a special status to philosophy as the pursuit of wisdom since it implies that obligations of a religious nature are at work when we philosophise and that ethical and political consequences follow as a result. At the end of the dialogue *Crito* where Socrates decides to face his fate (of execution) rather than to escape it, Socrates declares: 'God points the way' (54e) and the Platonic writings continually emphasise this divine directedness as being intrinsic to the Socratic project. In *Phaedo* the confidence of Socrates 'on his way to the other world . . . under the providence of God' (58e–59a) helps him to welcome death as an entry into a purer form of psychic existence in the divine realm of reality where the search for justice will finally be rewarded. In the dialogue *Euthyphro*, which is set on the steps of the court where Socrates is due to be tried for corrupting the young and being an atheist, there is a theological discussion about whether or not something is pious because the gods will it or whether the gods will something because it is pious. *Euthyphro* also raises questions about how the gods perceive human activity and whether or not there is conflict between them as the Homeric narratives suggest. In the dialogues *Symposium* and *Phaedrus*, the nature of beauty and the love of beauty is examined respectively. In a remarkable passage (*Symposium*, 211ab), Socrates is told that Beauty in itself does not 'take the form of a face, or of hands, or of anything that is of the flesh ... but (subsists) of itself and by itself in an eternal oneness' while in *Phaedrus* 246d et seq., the divine realm is described as ineffably transcendent, which is reminiscent of the form of the Good, the source of life and knowledge, in Plato's *Republic*. The divine creative role and, specifically, divine responsibility for the relationship between soul and body is discussed in Plato's *Timaeus*, though it is in what was probably his last dialogue, *Laws*, that more extensive and explicit emphasis on the centrality of God is clearly stated. God is described here as ' "the measure of things", much more truly than, as they say "man" ' (716c). This is undoubtedly a criticism of Protagoras and the Sophists who are said to have regarded the human being as the measure of all meaning. In *Laws*, the implications for a God-centred society are set out as follows:

Now he who would be loved by such a being (God) must himself become such to the utmost of his might and so by this argument, he that is temperate among us is loved by God, for he is like God, whereas he that is not temperate is unlike God and at variance with him; so also it is with the unjust and the same holds in all else. (*Laws* 716cd)

In Book x of this dialogue, where the role of religion is examined, a number of arguments are put forward in support of the existence of the gods and of their divine concern for human life and the world, and also in support of the importance of piety. It is stated that the lack of respect that people, especially the young, have for sacred objects and sacred property and the damage done to the latter is deplorable, together with the lack of respect for and violence towards parents. This deterioration in public and private life is attributed to a lack of respect for the sacred and an agnostic attitude towards the gods, who are perceived to be, even if they should exist, unconcerned for human beings. Alternatively, it is thought that the gods, if they are worshipped, can be persuaded to overlook morally unacceptable activities. The dialogue asserts that divinity is neither an artificial concept nor a legal fiction but reflects what is truly real. The soul is essential for the perception of the divine and justice is crucial to human action as criterion and sanction. No one will escape justice and the message is that although life can be difficult, we do get divine help to cope with its vicissitudes. Perhaps more than any other dialogue, *Laws* demonstrates Plato's concern for religious values and indicates their centrality to political and private life. It is not surprising either that Platonism became so influential for Christian thought and subsequently for some thinkers in the Islamic philosophical tradition.

See **The Afterlife, Agathon, Aristotle, Death, Demiurge, The Dialogues of Plato, The Good, Neoplatonism,** *Phaedo,* **Plotinus,** *Psyche,* **Religion, The** *Republic,* **Socrates, Soul**

Further reading: Hamilton and Cairns (1963)

Plotinus (AD 205–70): said to have been born in Egypt, he came to Alexandria to study philosophy under the only teacher who could satisfy him, Ammonius Saccas, who was a self-taught philosopher and who, like Socrates, left no written text but whose influence on Plotinus was considerable. In AD 243 Plotinus left with the emperor Gordian's expedition for the East hoping to learn about Persian and Indian philosophy, but when Gordian was murdered in Mesopotamia Plotinus went to Antioch and from there to Rome where he spent the rest of his life teaching philosophy and gaining great respect from, among others, the emperor Gallienus and his wife Salonina. It was in Rome that he wrote the philosophical treatises collected under the title *Enneads*, which were edited into six sets of nine treatises by his disciple and friend Porphyry who also wrote *The Life of Plotinus and the Order of his Works*. Plotinus's primary aim was to teach those capable of understanding it how to return to the source from which they and everything else came, namely the One or the Good. This return journey, often described in terms of mysticism by Plotinus, requires moral purity and intellectual effort. The One or the Good, as the first principle of reality, is ineffable, indescribable, unknowable and ultimate, beyond any determination or limitation, transcending all discursive thought and human language. The One as the Good which overflows into reality and the source from which all being emanates gives rise to Intelligence (or the Intellectual Principle) which contains all intelligent forms and thought itself, indeed is thought thinking itself. From Intellect comes Soul, which, at its highest level, is fully illuminated and formed by Intellect and raised to its level, while at a lower level it constitutes the animating principle of natural reality as World Soul and the souls of individual human beings. All levels of soul from the lowest to the highest are permanently present in us and we can opt to remain at the level of the lower soul, immersed in bodily concerns, or tune in to the consciousness of the higher realities present in us. The physical universe is conceived as a living organic whole, while matter, though it proceeds from the Good, is the principle of evil because of its deficient lack of being which marks the material end of the descent from the Good through the various successive levels of reality. However, despite its material potential for evil, the physical universe is also regarded by Plotinus as beautiful, 'boiling with life' as he states, as the work of the Soul. This ambivalent attitude towards bodiliness and the physical universe reflects some of the difficulties in trying to identify a coherent approach in Plotinus' views about matter and the physical universe. The lack of clarity that immediately strikes any reader of the *Enneads* may also be due to the mystical elements in his thinking. In *Ennead* iv.8.1 Plotinus gives an account of a frequently occurring mystical experience in an out of body state which causes him to wonder why it is that he came to be in the body and Porphry, his disciple, significantly begins his *Life of Plotinus* by stating that his state of embodiment was often a source of shame to Plotinus. In his dying words as reported by Porphyry he gives back what is divine in himself to 'the Divine in the All'.

See **St Augustine, Christianity, The *Enneads*, Stephan MacKenna, Neoplatonism, Plato, Porphyry**

Further reading: Dillon (1991); O'Meara (1995)

Polanyi, Michael (1891–1976): born in Hungary, he first studied medicine but subsequently devoted himself to research in chemistry. Polanyi worked in Germany until Hitler expelled the Jews from public positions in 1933 and then and went to the University of Manchester as Professor of Physical Chemistry 1933–8. From 1948–58, he held the Chair of Social Studies there. During this period and in subsequent years he examined the nature and basis of knowledge and belief, particularly scientific beliefs, and came to identify the importance of what he describes as 'tacit knowledge' in every noetic (knowledge) process, including the scientific. Polanyi argued that apart from what he called 'focal awareness' meaning the conscious attentiveness to whatever is under scrutiny, there is also an unacknowledged form of 'subsidiary awareness' which constitutes the personal – contextual backdrop to our focal knowledge. This subsidiary awareness consisted of one's implicit world view and beliefs about how the world is, all of which combine to influence everyone's noetic approach (whether scientific or not) in relation to whatever it is that one is trying to understand. Polanyi argues that the scientific notion of pure objectivity must be questioned since one's participation in knowledge, both in its discovery and validation, is indispensable to the scientific process itself. Even in the most exact sciences, knowing is an art in that the skill of the knower, who is inevitably guided by a passionate sense of increasing contact with reality, forms a logically necessary part of the scientific investigation. An important aspect of this is belief, states Polanyi, firstly because we all have beliefs and this applies as much to scientists as to everyone else, and, secondly, the scientific process like other forms of knowledge, rests on a set of scientific beliefs. To be conscious of what these are and to make them more explicit, is necessary in science, argues Polanyi, since there is always some vision of a hidden reality that guides scientific work. In his book, *Personal Knowledge* (1958), Polanyi claims that belief is the basis of all knowledge and that 'no intelligence, however critical or original, can operate outside a fiduciary framework' that is constituted by 'tacit assent and intellectual passions, the sharing of an idiom and of a cultural heritage, (and) affiliation to a like minded community'

(Polanyi 1958, p. 60), all of which shapes our vision of how things are and grounds our ways of controlling reality. Although Polanyi is not explicitly investigating the nature of religious belief one can take it from what he says (and he does point to examples of religious belief in *Personal Knowledge*) that religious belief is itself a form of belief in general. Since belief supplies the foundation of all knowledge this constitutes religious belief as an inescapable condition that is appropriate for the rationale of one's theological creed, whatever that may be. Polanyi is thus drawing attention to the nature of the epistemological and hermeneutical predispositions in the acquisition of all kinds of knowledge, including religious knowledge, by identifying the indispensable role of belief as a necessary precondition for further noetic acquisition. One might detect in his treatment some echoes of Socrates' statement in Plato's *Theaetetus* that 'knowledge is correct belief' and there are some similarities too with Newman's account of belief in *A Grammar of Assent*.

See **Belief, Faith, Hermeneutics, John Henry Newman**
Further reading: Polanyi (1958, 1967)

Polytheism: the belief in the existence of many gods.
See **God, Monotheism**

Porphyry (AD 232–309): born in Tyre in the Lebanon, he studied in Athens under Longinus, then spent some six years with Plotinus in Rome, then went to Sicily and late in life married Marcella, the widow of a friend. He owed his great learning to Longinus and also the critical scholarship which is evident in some of his own writings. Most famous for writing the biography of Plotinus and for organising and editing the latter's writings, The *Enneads*. He seems to have had some interest in mysticism and may have had mystical experiences. In his own right, he is well known for his attack in *Against the Christians* which criticised the Christians of his own day as being ignorant people whose doctrines he set out to undermine on philosophical and exegetical grounds. He also commented on Aristotle's *Categories*, provided a basic study of Neoplatonism and his Consolatory Epistle to Marcella, his wife, is extremely readable. His attack on the Christians and his interest in the moral and ascetic aspect of Neoplatonism and his concern for religious forms demonstrate his spiritual interests and his suitability for undertaking the translation of Plotinus's religious philosophy.

See **Plotinus, Proclus**

Further reading: Dillon (1991); Wallis (1995)

Pragmatism: the philosophical view, developed in the USA by Charles Sanders Peirce, William James, F. C. S. Schiller and John Dewey, that regards ideas and beliefs in the context of their implications for action. Peirce defined pragmatism as 'the theory that a conception, meaning the rational import of a word or other expression, lies exclusively in its conceivable bearing upon the conduct of life'. Since, according to Peirce, it is only whatever results from the experimental that has a direct bearing on conduct, this means that it is only when one can accurately define all the conceivable experimental phenomena which are implied in an affirmation or denial of a concept, that one can then have a complete definition of the concept in question. William James developed this theory in his text, *Pragmatism*, to mean that ideas become true in so far 'as they help us to get into satisfactory relations with other parts of our experience' and that 'the true is the name of whatever proves itself to be good in the way of belief'. The connection with the view of Peirce is that once an idea or belief is granted to be true, it makes a concrete difference to one's life or, put another way, that the true is what has good experimental consequences. Underlying this approach to truth is the conviction of James that everything must be understood in the light of human purpose including thought itself which constitutes thoughts as tools used by human beings to achieve their goals. Thoughts are thus judged by how effectively they serve these goals and beliefs are tools for dealing with experience and must be similarly judged as such.

See **William James**

Further reading: Helm (1999); James (1956)

Preternatural: from the Latin *praeter* 'beyond' and *natura* 'nature' and refers to that which is beyond and/or different from (in the sense of the irregular or abnormal) what is natural, ordinary and explicable but which is not supernatural or miraculous.

See **Ghosts, The Occult, Spiritualism, Supernatural, Witchcraft**

Priesthood: the institution of those ordained or specially charged with acting as mediators between God or divinity and human beings. The priest leads religious ceremonies and services of divine worship, she or he blesses and provides spiritual guidance to the faithful, and, in Christianity (where Jesus Christ is regarded as the divine high priest), the ordained priest preaches and administers the sacraments (for example baptism, matrimony.) considered as the outward signs of inward divine grace. Priests can be male or female, though in some religious traditions, for example Roman Catholicism, where only a male priesthood is acceptable at present, considerable debate surrounds the gender qualifications for priestly office.

See **Christianity, God, Jesus, Judaism, Religion**

Process Theology: an approach to theology inspired by the philosophical approach of A. N. Whitehead and Charles

Hartshorne with Shubert Ogden as one of its main proponents. Process theology rejects the classical view of God as immutable and transcendent in favour of a God who is partly evolving with and in relation to, and therefore affected by, the created world. The dominant emphasis is therefore on divine immanence and there are also, not unexpectedly, some hints here of pantheism.

See **A. N. Whitehead**

Further reading: Whitehead (1925)

Proclus (AD 410–85): one of the most influential of the Neoplatonic followers of Plotinus, Proclus presented a very systematic and comprehensive account of Neoplatonism in his *Elements of Theology* and *The Theology of Plato*. Like Plotinus, he claims that everything is derived from the One alone, simple and ineffable. However, Proclus also writes about all reality being derived from two principles, the Limit and the Unlimited, which are somehow present in the One. In addition, he seems to assume the existence of Ones (immediately following the One), identifying these with gods and he also claims that matter derives from the One. Proclus enunciates a triadic principle according to which everything remains, in one way – in that from which it emanates; in another way it is turned away from its source, and, in a third way, it turns back to its source. A number of Proclus' hymns also constitute remarkable records of the religious ethos of Neoplatonism. As a thinker, Proclus represents a significant link between ancient and medieval thought, especially through *The Elements of Theology*. A purely academic and theoretical theological work, it introduces in a structured almost geometrical way the general metaphysical themes with which Neoplatonism was concerned: unity and plurality, causality, the unmoved, self-moved and passively mobile, transcendence and immanence, continuity, procession and reversion, eternity and time, limit and infinitude, being, life and thought, and the hierarchy of being: divinity, intelligences and souls. Proclus, like Aquinas in the Christian tradition, was a systematiser who influenced Christian thought through such figures as Pseudo-Dionysius (particularly), Eriugena, Albertus Magnus and St Thomas Aquinas. In the Middle Ages, the text, *Liber de Causis*, which passed in medieval times for the work of Aristotle but was in fact a summary of Proclus' *Elements of Theology* (as St Thomas Aquinas recognised), was also highly influential. Aquinas's own thinking about the interfacing nature of the human soul perceived to exist between the physical temporal domain and the eternal metaphysical realm was, at least in part, influenced by it. The *Elements* retained its significant influence into the Renaissance period.

See **Plato, Plotinus, Pseudo-Dionysius,** *Psyche,* **Soul**
Further reading: Dodds (1963); Wallis (1972)

Prophecy: the act of revelation whereby a prophet mediates an inspired communication from God or divinity, however conceived, to humankind. Usually prophecy is linked to foretelling future events though it can also include messages of inspiration or admonishment or warnings about how the will of God applies to a particular society of people or to an individual. Philosophers of religion are sometimes interested in trying to understanding how prophecy can be authenticated and how it occurs in terms of the human dynamics involved in the cognitive acquisition of prophetic knowledge.

Protestantism: the religion or religious system of any of the Churches of Western Christendom that are separated from the Roman Catholic Church and that subscribe to the theological doctrine and principles of the reformers such as Luther, Calvin, John Knox, John Wesley and other significant leaders in Reformed Christianity.

See **Luther, The Reformation**

Further reading: MacCulloch (2003)

Pseudo-Dionysius: variously known as Pseudo-Denys/Denis, Dionysius the Areopagite, c. the fifth century AD. He claimed to be a convert of St Paul and to have been present at the death of the Virgin Mary, but was later unmasked in the nineteenth century as someone whose writings, which exerted great influence on the early and medieval Christian world, could only have appeared around the middle of the fifth century AD. In fact we know almost nothing about Pseudo-Dionysius, not even his name. In his Introduction to his translation of *Proclus The Elements of Theology*, Eric Dodds describes him as 'the unknown eccentric who within a generation of Proclus' death conceived the idea of dressing [Proclus's] philosophy in Christian draperies and passing it off as the work of a convert of St Paul' (pp. xxvi–xxvii). This deception or fraud succeeded in becoming sufficiently important because of the privileged status, based on the author's supposed apostolic connections, that was conferred on Dionyius's texts, *On the Divine Names, On the Celestial Hierarchy, On the Ecclesiastical Hierarchy* and *On Mystical Theology* together with some ten letters. The result was that the texts were highly respected, translated and extensively discussed and commented on by a whole range of Christian thinkers in the West such as Maximus the Confessor, Erigena, Hugh of St Victor, Robert Grosseteste, Albertus Magnus and St Thomas Aquinas and also by theologian–philosophers in the Eastern Church, such as St John Damascene, especially concerning the negative theology and the hierarchical schematism outlined in these writings. It was only in the late nineteenth century that the theological primacy of

Dionysius was effectively challenged by scholarly study that revealed the very questionable authenticity of the Pseudo-Dionysian claims to represent the early Christian apostolic era. Dionysius puts great emphasis on the essential inaccessibility of God to human reason and the senses – hence his stress on negative theology. He also insists on positive theological attributes by means of super-attribution, for example God as supremely just, good, beautiful and the like. God manifests divinity through created reality which emanates from God and flows back to its source and therefore knowing creation provides us with ways of knowing God in order to return to God. Knowing God, He Who Is, takes us above all affirmation and negation, in that we know that God cannot be known and this constitutes the mystical ignorance in which the supreme degree of theological knowledge is to be found. St Thomas Aquinas, in particular, was very taken by the writings of Pseudo-Dionysius, notably with regard to the naming of God, the treatment of divine beauty, the hierarchy of being and the angelic intellect, and there is no doubt but that Aquinas's Platonism is due in no small way to the influence of the Dionysian writings. Finally, it should be said that despite the questionable provenance of the texts, Dionysius' style of writing is very literary and lyrical and suitably expressive and appropriately deferential to the ineffable character of the subjects discussed.

See **St Thomas Aquinas, Neoplatonism, Proclus**
Further reading: Dodds (1963); Helm (1999)

Psyche See **Soul**

Psychical Research: investigations into the paranormal such as the phenomena of spiritualism for example in seances, ghostly appearances of those who have died, or of unknown spirits and the like. These enquiries frequently aim to prove that the dead can be contacted from this world or 'cross over' from 'the other side'. There has always been some debate about the credibility of such occurrences. In Western society some well known people such as Sir Arthur Conan Doyle and G. K. Chesterton (very briefly) have been involved in this area, and in other traditions, such as those of tribal societies where witchcraft, shamanism or voodoo practices have been or are still prevalent, contacting the dead and similar paranormal activities are regarded as being *de facto* possible.

See **The Occult, Spiritualism**

Punishment: as a sanction for evildoing or sin is closely associated with obeying God's or divinity's commands. All religious traditions seem to hold that it is necessary in justice to punish those deemed to be wicked, though there is some disagreement as to whether or not and why such punishment should be partial or permanent. There is also the view that, since suffering is a part of the human condition, we will all suffer anyway to a greater or lesser degree, even those who are regarded as being wholly innocent among us, for example children, targets of racism or gender bias. The biblical story of Job represents an intriguing account of innocent suffering which seems to challenge God's criteria for imposing suffering as a punishment. In the Jewish tradition, the story of Job has been interpreted as signifying the difference between the way God thinks and the way we do and therefore the lesson of the story is to realise this and acknowledge the incomprehensibility to the human mind of divine actions, while also preserving an attitude of loving regard for God, rather than seeing God as sadistic and/or uncaring. Punishment is also an issue in philosophical literature from Plato onwards (in Plato's writings, it is linked with justice) right through to twentieth and twenty-first-century thought where the issues of absurdity and irrationality arise in relation to the imposition of punishment and suffering. Another significant text that deals with unfairly imposed punishment is *The Consolation of Philosophy* by Boethius, who gives a wide-ranging and accessible treatment of punishment, which is regarded in this text, as in the Book of Job, as a serious challenge to the rationale behind the imposition of punitive sanctions that seem to have little rationale behind them.

See **The Afterlife, Boethius, Hell, Job, Purgatory, Religion**

Further reading: Boethius (2002); Leaman (1995)

Purgatory: from the Latin *purgatorium* literally 'a place of cleansing' and *purgare* 'to purge'. Purgatory is a place or condition of suffering or torment, usually temporary in nature. In Roman Catholicism it refers to a state or place in which the souls of those who have died in the state of grace are believed to undergo a limited amount of suffering to expiate their venial sins and become purified from the remaining effects of more serious and grave sin, that is to say mortal sin.

See **Heaven, Hell**

Rationalism: the philosophical movement associated with Descartes, Leibniz and others who believed that reason functioning according to the objective laws of logic, of mathematics and geometry independent of human feelings and the emotions, represented the only way to truth and, according to Descartes, enabled us in principle to find out everything there is to know. Leibniz conceived of the cosmos as an ordered whole designed by God while Kant argued that Christianity represented the religion of reason.

See **Belief, Faith, Leibniz, Myth, Reason**
Further reading: Descartes (1968); Leibniz (1973);
Wood (2001)

Reason: the ability to understand, abstract, reflect, discern
and create causal relationships between various entities
and notions, and infer similarities and differences. The
power that human beings have to think and deliberate and
to see the connections between propositions and draw
proper inferences defines reason for many philosophers
and others. Aristotle's definition of the human being as a
rational or reasoning animal implies that the faculty or
power of reason can be understood in the broadest sense
as that which frames all human life at the socio-political
and the individual level. Thus he can argue that our biological and emotional way of functioning is not separate
from our rationality but is structured by it in terms of how
we experience reality such that our emotions, feelings and
sensations always supply us with potentially cognitive
material. In the narrower sense, reason has been thought
of as opposed to sensations and emotions. This char-
acterises Descartes' approach which defines the human
being as a mind or a thinking substance, essentially distinct from one's bodily substance. The Enlightenment,
from the seventeenth century onwards, gave priority to
the particular conception of reason that is associated with
Descartes and which argues that the application of our
reason in a mathematical–logical way allows us in principle to know everything there is to know and to, for
example, organise society and individuals in the best and
most effective way according to the logic of this kind
of rationality. This led to debates and disputes about
the priority and value of reason over sensory experience
which caused a split in Western philosophical thought
that has continued in different forms into the twenty-first

century. The empiricists give priority to experience, and the rationalist–idealists emphasise the value of the mathematical mode of reasoning. In more recent times, there is emphasis on intelligences such as emotional and artistic as they are described by psychologists like Howard Gardner who want to restore value to other forms of reasoning. As regards the faith versus reason debates which still characterise the philosophical analysis of religion at the beginning of the twenty first century, the direction of such discussions has resulted, at least in part, in opening up ways of understanding the role of faith and beliefs in terms of how we acquire knowledge. While views still exist about the exclusive irrationality and emotional and psychological aspects of belief and religious faith, the concept of reason has also been opened up to conceptual changes that avoid an exclusive reductionist approach that gives unqualified approval to the mathematical mode of reasoning associated with the Cartesian era.

See **Belief, Faith, Myth**

Further reading: Ackrill (1981); Descartes (1968); Kant (1960); Leibniz (1973); Wood (2001)

Redemption: deliverance from sin or evil by atonement. In the Christian tradition, Jesus Christ is believed to have redeemed humankind from sin by his sufferings and death. The nature of this deliverance is theologically conceived as humankind being purchased from the slavery of sin by the redemptive power of Christ's sufferings and death.

See **Christianity, Jesus, Sin**

Reformation, The: the religious and political movement in sixteenth-century Europe that began as an attempt to reform the Roman Catholic Church and ended in the establishment of the Protestant Churches. There was a Counter Reformation by the Roman Catholic Church in the sixteenth and seventeenth centuries to reform the Church, but the split was there to stay. That said, one of the main objectives of ecumenism, which gained particular strength during the Second Vatican Council (1962–5), is to restore unity among the Christian churches on the grounds that disunity among the followers of Christ creates a continual scandal.

See **Christianity, Martin Luther, Protestantism**

Further reading: MacCulloch (2003)

Reincarnation: the belief that after death the soul transmigrates into or is born again in another body. Plato's dialogues contain this view, a belief which is also widely held by the religions that originated in India, especially Hinduism and Buddhism and their various forms. In Plato's writings and in these religions, the soul is depicted in successive reincarnations, the quality of which is often determined by one's past actions (or *karma* in Hinduism and Buddhism) until final purification is attained, at which stage, the wheel of reincarnation is transcended.

See **Buddhism, Hinduism, Plato**

Further reading: Mascaro (1962, 1965)

Relativism: the theory that values may differ from one society to another since each is uniquely conditioned by the particular circumstances of the society in which values arise. This also implies that there can be no universal absolute set of values or value systems for human beings. In this connection, an important principle of anthropological investigation is that the anthropologist should maintain an unbiased, value-free and non-judgemental approach towards different cultures, rather than seeking to judge them by criteria linked to her or his own cultural and religious values and society. The philosophical and logical problem that arises with relativism relates to how relativism itself can be a credible account since, by its own criterion, it must be regarded in a relativistic and not absolute way.

See **Religion, Ninian Smart**

Religion: derives from the Latin *religio* meaning 'to bind' and signifies belief in or obedience and sensitivity to the sacred, which is conceived to consist of a supernatural power or set of powers regarded as divine and having control over human destiny. Religion also means the formal or institutionalised expression of such beliefs and the practice of sacred ritual observances as well as the attitude and feelings of those who believe in transcendent divine power. As a cultural and social phenomenon, religion seems to be universally found in all early societies and historically and globally, it has defined many, if not most, societies and traditions. It still remains significant today for many people as the guideline to what is ultimately significant for human life, individually and socially, and is also regarded by many as providing the ultimate foundation for moral behaviour. Historically, there have always been some close links between religion and philosophy, hence the analysis of religion from a philosophical point of view.

See **Belief, Divine, God, Mircea Eliade, Faith, The Holy, Ibn Rushd, Mysticism, Myths, Rudolf Otto, Philosophy, Philosophy of Religion, The Sacred, Supernatural, Theology, Transcendence**

Further reading: Smart (1971, 1998)

Religious Language: people talk and write about God in all kinds of ways, in narrative and poetic descriptions, in analytic and scientific and theological language, and many religions are based on sacred texts that are believed to contain divinely inspired revealed truth. Many philosophers have examined the kind of language used in religion and in religious texts and fundamental to their enquiries is the question of how human language can effectively communicate the reality of God, if at all. For example, if God is transcendent, then how can God be described and with what validity? Some have argued that God can only be depicted linguistically in a negative way while others claim that we can make positive statements about God by extrapolating from what is good in the world around us and attributing such qualities to God. Judaism and Christianity have devoted much time to investigating how God can be named (and therefore meaningfully spoken of) and for these two religions the most significant divine name is one that is believed to be revealed by God himself to Moses as described in the Book of Exodus 3:14–15: I AM WHO AM, and I AM. This names the unnamable God who liberates his people from oppression. For Christians, Jesus Christ expresses the incarnate reality of God, as the Word made flesh, in his human life, death and resurrection and in his continuing presence in a unique way in the Eucharistic meal. Prominent from the traditions that are concerned with how to name God are figures like Maimonides the Jewish philosopher–theologian who emphasised the importance of negative theological language while St Thomas Aquinas, influenced in part by Pseudo-Dionysius, proposed his analogical theory of religious language which he believed respected the negative and positive naming of God. Analogy allows a comparison of sorts between God and human beings, negatively and positively, according to Aquinas, although he insists like Maimonides that God's self-description in Exodus represents the most appropriate divine name. In the Islamic tradition, ibn Rushd's theory of interpretation argued that the ways in which God is depicted will vary according to (1) whether it is in the form of descriptive and imaginative language and parables for the vast majority of the faithful, or (2) in theological language as used by theologians or (3) in philosophical and scientific language. In the twentieth century, A. J. Ayer, in *Language, Truth and Logic*, claimed that theological statements are literally nonsensical and meaningless since the existence of what they refer to cannot be empirically established. He argued that such theological references are more akin to poetry, designed to evoke emotions and feelings but not to be regarded as factual in nature. Wittgenstein, by contrast, supported the need for religious descriptive language and stated that since religion encourages us to think and act in certain ways, it follows that such rules of life are linguistically and validly conveyed in descriptions. In his *Tractatus Logico-Philosophicus*, he was also careful to say that language has its limits and that there are some things that cannot be said. These constitute what he calls 'the mystical'. Later, in *Philosophical Investigations*, he argued that there is no one ideal form of language like the logical model which he had hitherto described in the *Tractatus*. Instead, there are equivalent linguistic forms that map life in a variety of ways, all of which can be valid. Philosophers concerned with hermeneutics put forward a somewhat similar view of religious language, for example, Paul Ricoeur, who states that whatever the ultimate nature of religious experience, it is necessarily articulated in language. However, religious discourse is saying something that other kinds of discourse are not saying and by its nature this implies a mode of discourse that is always concerned in some way with God and divine reality. Religious texts, like other texts, represent a medium of interpretation, including self-interpretation, and some texts are foundational in the sense that they constitute the authoritative basis of a particular faith. Religious texts, draw us into 'the world of the text' and their revelatory and religious character enables us to appreciate something of God's nature and relationship with us. God is variously revealed to us, for example, in the Hebrew Bible or Christian Old Testament as a liberating, caring and compassionate, as a Father angry with the chosen people, and so forth and according to Ricoeur, these descriptions name God more effectively than philosophical terms such as omnipotent and omniscient. The New Testament also reveals God to Christians in similar ways in the life, death and resurrection of Jesus Christ and provides a divine exemplar made human who constantly points out the way to salvation, indicating that he is the Way. The hermeneutical approach is inevitable when dealing with religious texts and discourse, according to Ricoeur, who insists that a particular 'listening' disposition is necessary to get 'inside' such discourse, oral and textual, in order to appreciate what is being communicated.

See **Analogy, St Thomas Aquinas, A. J. Ayer, the Bible, Hermeneutics, Ibn Rushd, Philosophy of Religion, Religion, Paul Ricoeur, Wittgenstein**

Further reading: Arberry (1951); Ayer (1936); Ricoeur (1995)

Renaissance, The: describes that period of European history that marked the waning of the Middle Ages and the rise of the modern world, usually considered to have begun in Italy in the fourteenth century. The spirit, culture, literature, art and science of this period was defined by a new tone of independent discovery (or rediscovery, for example, of the value of ancient classical texts) and freedom which emphasised the importance of humanism through the cultivation of individual human potentialities and creativity in the context of a growing emphasis on the active secular aspects of experience over religious and contemplative life. Characteristics of the Renaissance involved intensified classical scholarship and scientific and geographical discoveries along with a renewed independent re-evaluation of the significance of the secular and of the religious as aspects of life and the relationships that exist between them. In the long term, the Renaissance movement, together with the Reformation and the growing emergence and influence of the physical sciences perceived as the secular pursuit of scientific knowledge, resulted in the creation of a new European and modern world view, more secular and less religious in nature, and concerned to promote the freedom of the individual in society. This inevitably had consequences for philosophy and religion in Western society.

See **Erasmus, The Reformation**

Republic, **The:** Plato's best known dialogue in ten books which begins by examining the nature of justice, then moves into a discussion of the ideal society in which justice can flourish. This leads to a discussion on the centrality of knowledge in society, institutionalised in the *Republic*'s programme of education, and on the necessity for the ideal ruler of society to be highly educated and philosophically wise. Book VII presents the famous Cave Narrative in which one of a group of prisoners is released from his chained position in a dark cave where he and his fellow prisoners have taken for real the reflected shadows on the cave wall which faces them. After the released prisoner comes out of the cave and sees reality as it is in the light of the sun, he realises that he had formerly taken as real what were in fact merely reflections of reality. Now that he has seen reality, he feels obliged to return to tell the good news to the others, although Socrates, who is telling this story, suggests that the released prisoner may be ridiculed as a result, even injured or killed. The Cave Narrative is an allegory of enlightenment, depicting the process and journey of knowledge, which liberates us from the captivity and darkness of ignorance or mere opinion and leads us into the freedom and brilliance of knowledge of reality as it is, in the light of goodness. Plato's *Republic* can be variously interpreted as constituting a discussion document on the ideal society, or perhaps a proposed model of the just and civilised state, or even a political aspiration at which to aim. The author's anonymity functions effectively to allow us to interpret the significance of the *Republic* as we see fit, thereby participating in the process of philosophising which leads to insight. There is some evidence from Plato's Letter VII that the *Republic*'s model of state was considered by Plato as a serious possibility in view of his sojourn in Sicily, where he was invited to put his political theory into practice. Unfortunately, the choice of ruler, Dionysius, was unsuitable as the human model to direct Plato's ideal society. After considerable difficulty, having been prevented from doing so, Plato himself left Sicily for home. The bitterness he felt as a result of the lack of success in his political project is documented in Letter VII. Plato's *Republic* is thus a seminal text on political philosophy which has had theological applications, for example in ibn Rushd's conception of the Islamic theocratic state.

See **The Dialogues of Plato, Plato**

Further reading: Hamilton and Cairns (1963)

Ricoeur, Paul (1913–): French philosopher, born in Valence, principally renowned for his contribution to the developments in hermeneutics (the philosophy of interpretation). His classic piece, *Reading a Text: Explanation or Understanding?*, argues that the relationship between people in a conversation and that which pertains between the author and reader of a text must be clearly distinguished. In a conversation we can check with one another what we say. The question is: should the reader of a text aim to understand what the author intends to say by trying, for instance, 'to get into the mind' of the writer? Is this even possible? Ricoeur argues that whereas the author's intention is to say something in a text, the reader is entitled to interpret what is said and will do so anyway in terms of his or her own world view shaped by the cluster of factors which individuate each person, in this case, the reader. Even when the author reads his or her own text, the position assumed is different from that of writing the text. Ricoeur argues that it is the reader who brings the text to life as a text by reading it in a necessarily interpretative way. On a wider scale, one can see the world and reality as a text to be interpreted and digested accordingly. However, there is a question of how one is to conceive of subjectivity and objectivity as they apply here, and indeed whether or not there can be any objective account of what a text means, and if so how this might be possible. Ricoeur claims that the text as discourse is the realisation of language as discourse and as a work of discourse, it creates its own world – the world of the text. The text also represents a medium through which we come to understand ourselves. Ricoeur applies this approach to religious discourse, which, for him, includes the foundational religious texts considered as the word of God. As a Christian, the basic text for him is the Christian Bible which, according to him, uniquely contains God's Word. Ricoeur claims that hermeneutics teaches us that 'biblical faith cannot be separated from the movement of interpretation that elevates it into language'. Thus, constantly renewed interpretations of significant events such as the exodus in the Old Testament and the resurrection of Jesus in the New Testament as events of deliverance, open and disclose to each of us the utmost possibilities of our freedom and thus become for us the word of

God. Ricoeur identifies this as the properly hermeneutical constitution of faith. The philosophy of religion aims to show how the religious fact can be accounted for in philosophical discourse. The positions of atheistic humanism and of onto-theology (defined by Ricoeur as 'the conjunction of ontology and theology in a new type of discourse) constitute the subject matter for investigation. At one extreme are the philosophical approaches which try to account by reason for the religious affirmation of God as the absolute and, at the other end, are those philosophies for which religious statements have no meaning or do not, according their criteria, satisfy the logical and/or epistemological standards that apply for all scientific discourse. In between these extremes writers have positioned themselves in a variety of relations towards the poles and have thereby adopted a complex relationship to the religious fact, as Ricoeur describes it. Philosophers of religion deal in one way or another with all three categories and indeed represent them in the approaches they themselves adopt. What should always be kept in mind, according to Ricoeur, is that the religious attitude and experience will inevitably be subject to hermeneutics since there is no human experience that is not interpreted and this is what constitutes the philosophical interpretation of religion as a particularly compelling form of enquiry, especially if we subscribe to the view that the religious fact is somehow intrinsic to human life and the human condition.

See **Hermeneutics**

Further reading: Ricoeur (1995)

Rushdie, Salman (1947–): born in India and educated at Rugby school in England from the age of fourteen. He spent some time working in television in Pakistan, and later worked in England as an actor and advertising copywriter before, becoming a full-time writer and novelist drawing on material from fantasy, mythology, religion and certain oral traditions. He is best known worldwide for his book, *The Satanic Verses* (1988). The book was regarded as blasphemous by many Muslims as a result of which he was forced into hiding in 1989 when the Ayatollah Khomeini called for his death by *fatwah* or religious edict. By 1998, when the first indications were made that it might be safe for him to lead a more public life, he had been living in hiding for years. His case brings into sharp focus how the relationship between literature and religion is viewed by various cultures and religious traditions and what rights and sanctions can apply and according to what criteria and laws and by whom.

See **Ibn Rushd, Islam**

Russell, Bertrand (1872–1970): well-known English philosopher and mathematician who studied at Trinity College Cambridge with a scholarship in mathematics but soon moved into the field of philosophy and in 1895 obtained a Fellowship at Trinity. In July 1900 at a Philosophy Congress in Paris he exchanged ideas with the Italian logician Peano about the possible connections between mathematics and logic. He subsequently collaborated with Alfred North Whitehead on *Principia Mathematica* which aimed to show how mathematics can be derived from logic. Russell was also a social activist and a pacifist who was a conscientious objector during the two world wars and later one of the founders of the Campaign for Nuclear Disarmament (CND). He was also an agnostic and a champion of women's suffrage in the early 1900s, and was responsible for inviting to Cambridge Ludwig Wittgenstein to whom he became a supportive influence until the 1920s. Russell was also instrumental in gaining recognition for the logical work of Gottlob Frege. Though he initially took an interest in philosophical idealism under the influence of Hegel and Bradley, he soon propounded a realist and atomic view of reality and regarded science as providing the paradigm for human knowledge. He also rejected religion and traditional views of human sexuality. On the question of religion, Russell seems to have retained an almost life-long interest and admits that from his teenage years he was absorbed in exploring such theological issues as belief in God, immortality and freewill. He came to reject any belief in God's existence or in immortality on scientific grounds and because he claimed that arguments for such beliefs are often based on emotional factors. He also came to see moral doctrines as impositions, especially by the Catholic Church, and he concluded that religion is fundamentally based upon fear, including fear of the unknown. He argues that fear gives rise to cruelty – hence the cruelties practiced by religious creeds, notably Christianity, to defend religious views and impose them on others. Science is a greater teacher than religion, he states, since it makes us look to our own efforts to make this world a fit place to live in. Our motto should be to stand on our own feet, look fair and square at the world, see it as it is and not be afraid of it. Sometimes Russell seems to equate agnosticism with atheism, at one point indeed claiming that an agnostic does not believe in God. In an article entitled, 'What is an Agnostic?' contained in his collection of writings in *Bertrand Russell on God and Religion* Russell sets out his agnostic (in fact, atheistic) views including his disbelief in the soul's existence and in God's existence. Life in general has no purpose, he states: 'It just happened'. Russell reserves his harshest criticisms for the Catholic Church's treatment of Galileo, and in his book, *Religion and Science* (1935), he sees religion and science in conflict because of their different points of departure. He contrasts a religious creed with a scientific theory stating that the former claims to embody eternal and absolute truths whereas science is always tentative, expecting to have to modify its theories in the light of future developments and always aware that the scientific method is logically incapable of arriving at a complete and final solution. However, scientific theories are serviceable and their application can be seen and tested, and, moreover, science discourages any search for an absolute, whereas religious teachings assume a dogmatic form and are not essentially subject to change. They are forever and always absolutely true, demanding credal acceptance. Russell's analysis of the differences between these very different ways of thinking in *Religion and Science* makes for compelling reading, even if it does seem nowadays somewhat dated in part. Much of what he writes about religion does seem to dismiss it as a non-scientific, somewhat emotional, even primitive and certainly mistaken approach to reality which he implies is now redundant. However, his fascination with the subject remained a life-time one, hinting perhaps at some regret at being unable to subscribe to at least some religious teachings that might positively indicate a more meaningful dimension to reality than the material world can supply.

See **Christianity, Empiricism, Faith, Hume, Religion**
Further reading: Russell (1980); Seckel (1986)

S

Sacred, The: refers to what is holy and divine, consecrated, worthy of reverence, awe and respect for the divine however conceived. As two important aspects of the sacred, sacred space and sacred time represent two significant features of the sacralised world. Sacred space applies to places and locations that have a specific religious significance, such as a church, synagogue, mosque or temple. Entering many of these buildings from, say, a busy street, is a movement for the believer into sacred space since it is a place which the divine inhabits in a special way. From a profane point of view, space is neutral and does not carry in itself any special significance other than a natural or humanly designed area. Time also manifests itself for the religious human being as sacral in character. For the religious individual profane temporal duration can be arrested and transformed through ritual and sacred activities, and for certain religions historical time itself is specifically sanctified. In Judaism, God enters into history for the Jewish people, and for Christians, historical time assumes a transcendent and sacred aspect through the divine incarnation in the person of Jesus Christ. Sacred time thus renews in various ways original events and experiences through ritual and religious celebrations that may in different forms express beginnings, fall, redemption and salvation. The links between natural events and religious rites and festivals have very long traditions that are still retained in various ways in the social and individual lives of many people. Thus the religious response to the experience of reality is a very deep-seated one on the part of many cultures and individuals for whom the domain of the sacred maps human life itself as a major interpretative perspective on reality and on human forms of thought and activity.

See **Mircea Eliade, God, Rudolf Otto, Religion**

Further reading: Eliade (1959); Otto (1923); Smart (1971, 1998)

Saints: are persons of exceptional holiness and goodness. In the Christian tradition, especially in the Roman Catholic Church, saints are those who after death are formally recognised as having attained through holy actions and behaviour a specially exalted place in heaven and worthy of special veneration as those who constitute the Communion of Saints. From a biblical point of view, saints represent the collective body of those who are righteous in God's sight (and hence the Church of the Latter Day Saints or the Mormons). In the Roman Catholic Church, the Communion of Saints refers to the unity between the faithful on earth, the souls in purgatory being cleansed of their sins and the saints in heaven.

See **The Afterlife, God, Heaven, Religion**

Sartre, Jean-Paul (1905–80): French philosopher, novelist and playwright, Sartre was a leading exponent of French existentialism. He categorised himself as an atheistic, as distinct from a theistic, existentialist (like Gabriel Marcel), and, as did other representatives of this philosophical approach, Sartre emphasised the priority of existence over essence. We find ourselves existing and then we are faced with what we want to make of ourselves. One of Sartre's reasons for rejecting the existence of God lies in his concept of freedom. If God exists, then we are not free to create ourselves since God has a predetermined model of what our essence is in much the same way as the inventor of a prototype (Sartre gives the example of a knife or letter opener) determines the essence of all the copies that will then be produced. Similarly, if God exists as the creator of humankind, each human being is essentially determined by God, which means that we are not free to create ourselves essentially to be what we choose to be. Thus, according to Sartre's logic, if God exists then I am not free: but God does not exist since I experience myself to be free, all of which culminates in Sartre's definition that to be human is to be free and wholly responsible for ourselves and what we choose to make of ourselves. However, freedom is a paradox in that we are not free not to be free: we cannot choose not to choose. Even if we

like to think that we can decide not to choose, this itself
is a choice. Thus we are condemned to be free in a world
without God where we must constantly choose and make
decisions all of which contribute to the construction of
what we essentially are. Like painters painting our own
portraits, our life of decision making constitutes us as
'work in progress' until death cuts us off from all our future possibilities. Human life is a project aimed towards
the future whose point of departure lies in our present,
that is shaped by our past. How I choose to see my place
in life, my past, my environment, my fellow human beings and my death, in relation to what is fixed for me
(for example my place of birth and my always being in
a place) and how I respond to this 'fixity' or facticity as
Sartre calls it, demonstrates my freedom to myself and to
others. Authenticity is what counts – being true to myself
in so far as I can. One's experience of this world also indicates that our expectations and hope for an ultimately
positive outcome in life are doomed to failure. Life is
absurd, he states: 'It is absurd that we are born, it is absurd that we die'. Sartre advocates that we should live
without hope and accept responsibility for what we are
and for what we do, despite being unable to know the
ultimate outcome of any of our actions down the line.
Angst, a sense of abandonment and despair, are attitudes
which will always be part of our consciousness. Death is
the ultimate absurdity and dehumanising event for each
human being since it takes away all our subjectivity and
constitutes us wholly as an object for others – 'a prey'
for others as he says. Sartre's atheistic existentialism is
thus starkly challenging and still relevant in terms of his
analysis of choice, although in later years it does seem
as if his views somewhat softened, at least if one is to
believe his partner Simone de Beauvoir's account of his
final months in her book *Adieux*. Despite his claim that

we create our own values by our actions and by what we choose to do, Sartre's very individualistic philosophical stance of becoming engaged and involved (which he did try to accommodate to Marxism), did assume a strongly social and political dimension when it came to his own involvement with some of the major political issues of his times such as the French occupation of Indo-China and Algeria, the United States' role in Vietnam, the French student and trade union protests in France in 1968 and even the British presence in the North of Ireland. Sartre was one of the great philosophers of the twentieth century and his challenges to the apparent meaninglessness of life at times and his critique of God retain their interest into the twenty first century for those concerned with human freedom, choice and responsibility and the context of human commitment that we find ourselves inhabiting.

See **Camus, Existentialism, God, Kierkegaard, Gabriel Marcel, Nietzsche**

Further reading: Blackham (1962); Sartre (1946)

Satan See **Lucifer**

Schleiermacher, Friedrich (1768–1834): born in Breslau, Prussia into a family of Reformed Calvinist ministers during the Enlightenment which was defined by a deep confidence in the power of reason and the willingness to discuss religion in the broadest context possible. His philosophical studies at the University of Halle widened his intellectual horizons in that he encountered the critical theological approach of Wolf and Kant's philosophy among other significant influences. A scholar–pastor, he argued that religion represents a way of thinking that results in contemplating the world from a particular point of view, a way of faith and a way of acting, desiring and loving, that results in a special kind of conduct and character. In his book *On Religion: Speeches to its Cultural Despisers* (1799), Schleiermacher claims that metaphysics, morals and religion all have the same object, 'namely the universe and the relationship of humanity to it'. This, he suggests, has led to the invasion of religion by metaphysics and morals and much of what belongs to the domain of religion has been hidden in the other two under 'an unseemly form'. Therefore, he concludes, religion has to be differentiated from metaphysics and morality in some way since its method of dealing with people's relationship with the universe will be unique to it. He then goes on to claim that metaphysics classifies the universe according to the various entities in it, looks for the reasons for what exists and then deduces the necessary aspects of reality. Morality, for its part, develops a system of duties that are implied by human nature and our relationship with the universe, and also commands and forbids certain actions with what he describes as 'unlimited authority'. Religion, by contrast with both of these, deals with intuition and feeling: 'It wishes to intuit the universe, wishes devoutly to hear the universe's own manifestations and actions. Longs to be grasped and filled by the universe's immediate influences in childlike passivity'. Religion lives out its whole life in nature, considered as a totality, and addresses everything, including human life, within it and is thus not concerned, as metaphysics is, with speculation nor, as morality is, with praxis (theory in action). Schleiermacher also took the ecumenical view that faith can unite people in spite of doctrinal differences. Faith is also communal rather than being the faith of isolated individuals and theology should reflect the experience of a specific community. Described by many modern Protestant theologians as 'the father of modern protestant theology', Schleiermacher's influence is considerable. His concept of religion as intuited and felt experience while interesting nevertheless poses questions about religious subjectivity and the role of reason in religious attitudes and activities.

See **Christianity, Faith, Feuerbach, Kant, Karl Marx, Protestantism, The Reformation**

Further reading: Helm (1999)

Scholasticism: the Christian medieval philosophical and theological tradition in which Greek philosophy was synthesised with Scripture and the teachings of the Church and those of the Church Fathers. Leading figures in this movement included St Augustine, St Anselm, St Albert the Great, St Thomas Aquinas, John Duns Scotus and William of Ockham. There is some difference about the period involved, one view identifying this era starting with St Augustine in the fifth century AD and lasting until the mid seventeenth century while another view understands it more narrowly to refer the period from about 1000 AD around the time of St Anselm to about 1300 AD shortly after the time of St Thomas Aquinas. The Scholastics set out to apply reason and logic to issues of philosophical and theological concern and Scholasticism developed particularly during the Middle Ages because it was during this time that new translations of Greek texts, especially those of Plato and Aristotle, became available, the latter mainly introduced from Arabic sources.

See **St Anselm, St Thomas Aquinas, Christianity**

Further reading: Hyman and Walsh (1973)

Scientism: the belief that scientific knowledge, especially as derived from the physical sciences, is the highest, even only form of true knowledge. Scientism therefore doubts that ultimate truth can be derived from religious, moral and aesthetic beliefs or experiences and it rejects the claim that truth can be arrived at on the basis of any special revelation, such as the Jewish, Christian, Islamic or other revelatory-based religions.

See **Dawkins, Empiricism, Hume**
Further reading: Dawkins (1989)

Scientology: a controversial religious movement founded by L. Ron Hubbard (1911–76) which aims to apply religious philosophy to recover spirituality and increase personal ability. Hubbard was a science fiction writer who proceeded, in 1955, to found his own scientific religion (Scientology) for which his book, *Dianetics: The Modern Science of Mental Health* (1951), provided the basis while his science fiction novels supplied him with a mythological dimension for his religious thought. Dianetics claims that psychological and other problems result from 'engrams' or bad impressions in subconscious awareness so it is necessary to eliminate negative engrams in order to allow individuals to realise their natural and spiritual potential. Scientology, or Dianetics as it was originally called, states that the human mind can resolve all problems when humans become their own saviours and free their inner spiritual being. There are resonances here of a modern form of gnosticism or self-enlightenment and Scientology also promotes a Westernised version of a yogic religious approach that is mythologically supported by the fictional content of Hubbard's science fiction novels. Some see Hubbard as a kind of modern shaman while others regard Scientology as another manipulative modern cult that appeals doctrinally to vulnerable people through its eclectic borrowings from aspects of actual religions.

See **Cult, Gnosticism, Religion**

Secularisation: describes a process and a state of mind defined by a lack of concern for or an indifference to and perhaps hostility towards religion and religious beliefs and the role of religion in human life, individually and socially. A growing phenomenon, especially in the West, secularisation is regarded as a serious challenge to religious faith. Its roots are often located in eighteenth-century Enlightenment thinking and more recently in twentieth- and twenty-first-century attitudes that favour materialism in its many forms.

See **A. J. Ayer, Hume, Kant, Marx**
Further reading: Habermas (2003)

Shamanism: an indigenous religion of northern Eurasia of which a central feature is trance and the belief that spirits can be controlled by exceptional individuals or a shaman, understood as a medicine man or priest of this religion who has the power to mediate and negotiate between this world and the spirit world. Shamanism is found among hunting peoples who believe in a multiplicity of spirits and in the survival of the soul after death. This religion now seems almost extinct though there has been renewed interest in the role of the shaman in some new religious movements of the twentieth–twenty-first century.

See **Religion, Soul, Spirit, Supernatural, Witchcraft**
Further reading: Smart (1998)

Shintoism: the traditional religion of Japan and central to Japanese culture and identity, the way of *Kami*, or the gods, is based on prehistoric religious practices, a priesthood and household rites. In modern Shinto, until the end of World War ii, both the emperor and the geographical territory of Japan were thought to be divine. The status of the emperor today is somewhat unclear and there are questions as to whether the deification of the emperor is an integral part of the religion or a development that occurred in more recent times.

See **Religion**
Further reading: Smart (1998)

Sin: any serious offence against a religious or moral principle. In the major religions a transgression against what is believed to be required by the divine will, however conceived. The result of sin is a state of estrangement from what is believed to be divine that can only be rectified by repentance for the transgressions and subsequent reliance on divine forgiveness and mercy. Christians believe that Jesus Christ as the God–man made reparation for sin through his sufferings, death and resurrection.

See **Christianity, Evil, The Fall, God, Jesus**

Smart, Ninian (1927–2001): born in Scotland, an Episcopalian, and expert on world religions, he was responsible for introducing religious studies into British universities and pioneered the teaching of world religions in English schools. Whereas the study of theology aims at the analysis of religious beliefs and doctrines, the study of religions and their belief systems together with the kinds of societies and socio-historical cultures which contextualised them can contribute to a growing awareness of religious faiths and the need to respect religious differences. Smart's scholarly and extensive publications in religious studies, which include *The Religious Experience of Mankind* (1971) and *The World's Religions* (2nd edn, 1998), are therefore of considerable importance in the field of religion. In an interview given in 1999, he observed the personal impact on those who study world religions, himself included, and noted that this can lead to the knowledge that no one religion can contain the whole truth but that we can learn from all of them. Smart had great interest in Buddhism and discerned in it, with its detection of humankind's chief problems of greed, hatred and delusion, a clearer and more systematic presentation of religious doctrines than one might find in Christianity. He also welcomed the appeal of Buddhism as a religion without God to people of his time for whom the existence and nature of God has little interest. Smart consequently argued for mutual understanding between religions and was convinced that each individual creed can learn from all the others.

See **Buddhism, Christianity, Religion**

Further reading: Smart (1971, 1998)

Socrates (469–399 BC): probably the most widely known philosopher in the West although he left no written texts, apparently preferring instead to communicate with others 'in living speech' as Plato describes it. His life is mostly known to us through the dialogues and letters of Plato, although Xenophon has also written an account of Socrates' life and activities and some of the Greek poet–playwrights have likewise made references to him, sometimes in a sarcastic way. Socrates was an Athenian citizen who lived in Athens when it was at the height of its power under Pericles. He engaged in many public debates and discussions, mainly with the Sophists who taught oratory, and he became famous for his probing questioning approach which often showed up the weaknesses and inconsistencies in opponents' arguments. He claimed to have been divinely mandated to seek wisdom, specifically with regards to the meaning of the Delphic Oracle's declaration to his friend Chaerophon, that he (Socrates) was the wisest person in Athens. In order to establish how that could be so, Socrates took it upon himself to question others about matters which puzzled him. Hence his use of the dialectical question–response procedure which would lead to insight. Plato's *Apology* describes the trial of Socrates where he was charged with not worshipping the gods of the state and of introducing unfamiliar religious practices and of corrupting the young. Socrates defended himself against what he claimed

were trumped up charges by declaring his divine vocation to all present and adding that since he constantly
contributed positively to Athenian society rather than
being punished he should be rewarded. The result was
that Socrates was found guilty and sentenced to death,
which provides the material for Plato's dialogues *Crito*
and, most importantly, *Phaedo* (the dialogue *Euthyphro*
provides a pre-trial drama on the steps of the court as
Socrates is about to enter where he discusses the nature
of piety and of divinity with Euthyphro, his protagonist
there). Socrates' heritage was to demonstrate firstly that
the awareness and acknowledgement of one's own ignorance is a necessary pre-condition for wisdom. His dialectical method emphasised the importance of reasoning and
the value of definitions. He also brought into central focus the importance of morality by constantly addressing
the question as to how we should live together as human
beings. As the inspirational mentor to Plato, one of the
group of young men whom he so impressed by the way in
which he personified all that was best in philosophy and in
life, Socrates' heritage lies in the Platonic dialogues which
depict the philosophic process in the form of dramatically
set conversational exchanges on a whole range of philosophical topics that are still relevant today. The Platonic
Socrates, who is almost always central to these dialogues
as facilitative noetic therapist, retains permanent value
as the iconic figure of Western philosophy. It is notable
too how the religious and theological dimension of the
Socratic role is always present, often implicitly, as a significant aspect that shapes the tone of the discussions that
take place, thereby constituting Plato's writings as explo-
rations of the philosophical implications of the religious
attitude.

See **The Dialogues of Plato**, *Phaedo*, **Plato**
Further reading: Hamilton and Cairns (1963)

Soul: believed to be the spirit or immaterial part of the human being, the source of the intellect and will and that which survives death. It is sometimes equated with the self. For many religions, including Christianity, it signifies the spiritual part of the person that is capable of being saved or redeemed from sin or evil through divine or supernatural means. It is thought to be independent of the body, a spiritual substance or principle, immortal and divinely created. Plato's writings emphasise the importance of the soul or *psyche* as that which essentially defines human existence as spiritual and intelligent. He also writes about a World or Cosmic Soul and Plotinus describes a hierarchy of The One and the Good, Intelligence and Soul where a close union exists between the souls of individuals in a post-mortem state with the Soul of the All from which they originally separated. Aristotle's concept of *psyche* as the substantial principle of life in living things such as plants, animals and humans, distinguished the rationality of the human souls as the unique principle of human intelligence, knowledge and enquiry. The concept of soul was also of great importance to medieval Christian thinkers and to those in the Islamic and Jewish traditions and is found in many other religious approaches in various forms. It still retains significance today principally for religious reasons though it is also of considerable philosophical interest especially in the philosophy of religion.

See **The Afterlife, Aristotle, St Thomas Aquinas, The Body, Boundary Being, Death, Immortality, Mysticism, Near-Death Experiences, Out of Body Experiences,** *Phaedo,* **The Philosophy of Religion, Plato, Plotinus, Psychical Research, Reincarnation, Spirit, Spiritualism**

Further reading: Crabbe (1999); Quinn (1996)

Spinoza, Benedict de (1632–77): Jewish philosopher, born in Amsterdam, who, at the age of eighteen, studied Latin and read the new scientific works of Copernicus, Galileo, Kepler, Descartes and others. He became critical of orthodox Jewish biblical interpretations and was eventually expelled from the Jewish community. He then worked at grinding and polishing lenses, which gave him financial support to pursue his real interests in reading and publishing in the areas of philosophy, theology and science. His early publications included his *Short Treatise on God, Man and his Wellbeing* and, in 1661, his *Tractatus de Intellectus Emendatione* (translated into English as *Ethics and On the Correction of the Understanding* by Andrew Boyle) together with the *Ethics* appeared. Having moved to the Hague where he published his *Cartesian Principles*, Spinoza subsequently returned to Amsterdam. In the meantime, while in Voorberg, he had written his *Tractatus Theologico-Politicus* (1670) which argued that there was no biblical basis for violence or intolerance, but the book was immediately condemned by theologians. He completed *The Ethics*, in Amsterdam but, because it too was seen as controversial, it was only published posthumously. In the *Tractatus*, Spinoza was convinced that if he could know the truth of how things are then he would discover how to act well and live the 'life of blessedness'. The basis of his search for the truth lies in his concept of substance, defined in his *Ethics* as that which consists in itself and is conceived through itself and does not depend on anything else for its existence. Spinoza's *Ethics* maps out in a logico-mathematical way the system or whole which constitutes all of reality. His vision of this all-embracing logical totality makes it clear why a true scientific knowledge of the world can lead one to the knowledge of God and, conversely, why theological knowledge can lead to the understanding of the true nature of the universe. Thus, true science maps reality, discerned as theological in character, and theology provides the key to understanding the scientific logical nature of reality. Thus science and theology map each other as being concerned with the one reality although science begins from nature whereas theology begins with God. Spinoza's *Ethics* is textually structured in a mathematical mode in the form of definitions, axioms and theorems. In Part 1, he declares that there can only be one substance that is conceived through itself and this is God or Nature. The creator and created constitute one substance so that God or Substance as one, is immanent, not transcendent, and God or Nature seen as a whole is entirely free and self-creating. Spinoza thought that everything is logically inter-connected in this system of reality so that to know the truth about the whole system is to understand the logical connections that pertain to all of its parts. Since logical connections are necessary rather than contingent (that is, capable of being otherwise), this constitutes the universe as containing nothing in it that could be otherwise than it is. This necessary determinate and determined structure of inter-relationships between all the elements in the system is divine in origin, which means that everything is logically deducible from God who is free in being self-determining, yet producing things in a logically necessary way. Though it would seem that freedom is threatened, even abolished, in Spinoza's system, he would argue that it is not, providing one employs the correct vantage point from which to view the system. Put simply, this means that one can conceive of reality as divine or natural, depending on one's point of departure and perspective, just as one can look at the human being as either mental or bodily. In the latter case, the mind is envisaged as a mental substantial correlate of the body just as the body can be envisaged as a physically substantial correlate of the mind. Similarly, reality can be seen as either divine or natural, free or determined. The principle underlying this insight also applies to how we conceive of religious and political tolerance. Different religions, for example, represent different ways of conceiving and worshipping God, each of which can be respected in terms of its own approach, in the awareness that all religion essentially aims at knowing, worshipping and loving God. In terms of knowledge, there are three levels, the lowest of which is the knowledge acquired through the senses, the second level consisting of knowledge of general ideas or 'common notions' as Spinoza calls them, such as motion, solidity and mathematical propositions, which, when clearly and distinctly conceived, provide the basis for the third and highest noetic level which is that of intuitive knowledge of the essence of things themselves. Spinoza describes this as 'the intellectual love of God' which sees everything in relation to God, recognised as the source of all things. Intuitive knowledge also perceives the necessary connections between all things. Complete knowledge of this kind is only available to God, and human beings, by comparison, have only partial and limited understanding. However, Spinoza continues to insist that the more we understand particular objects, the more we understand God. Actively seeking knowledge, he declares, is a mark of freedom, defined as the rational understanding of why everything is as it is. Conversely, being deprived of knowledge brings misery since happiness and peace of mind arise from acquiring genuine knowledge. Knowing oneself truly means loving God and the more one understands oneself, the more one loves God. Thus intuitive understanding results in the greatest peace of mind. Spinoza consequently developed Descartes' rationalism in a compelling theological way in which God maps reality and is defined as intrinsic to it. Spinoza's philosophical views, which are clearly theological in tone, define his philosophy as one to which God, science and the essence of religion are central and essential.

See **God, Pantheism, Rationalism, Reason, Theology**
Further reading: Boyle (1986); Helm (1999); Spinoza (1951)

Spirit: from the Latin *spiritus* 'spirit, breath' and from *spirare* 'to breath, to blow', the term spirit, as in 'the human spirit', for example, can be difficult to define. Some equate it with the human soul whereas others such as Descartes seem to have conceived it as the breath of life understood as a fine vapour or air that animates the human organism. It has also been defined as the force or life principle that animates the bodies of living things. In human beings, it is sometimes conceived of as mediating between or being in addition to, body and soul. It has also been perceived as a gift of God or divinity, as the very breath of God, and, for Christians, the spirit as soul implies the immaterial agent/principle/substance that causes consciousness, including intelligence and willing and the biological life functions such as growth and feeling and so on. Spirit thus can mean the disembodied soul (including as a ghost) which may have different manifestations, for instance (1) a soul without a body inhabiting an unseen world or realm such as Hades, heaven, hell, or (2) a soul without bodiliness but appearing to the living in the likeness of an embodied person or (3) a soul without the physical bodiliness which marked its existence in life before death but is now integrated into a 'spiritualised body' (*corpus spirituale*, as Aquinas calls it) in the state of the spiritualised existence of the beatified and resurrected human beings in body and in soul.

See **Death, Heaven, Hell, Immortality, Soul**

Spiritualism: the belief that disembodied spirits of the dead existing in another world or realm can communicate with the living in this world, especially through mediums and the relevant practices and beliefs that are associated with this.

See **The Afterlife, Death, The Occult, Preternatural, Shamanism, Supernatural**

Spirituality: the state, attitude or quality of being dedicated to God, religion or spiritual concerns or values as contrasted with either physical or materialistic concerns and more specifically the religious way of life of certain individuals and communities of whatever religious creed or beliefs.

See **God, Mysticism, The Sacred**

Stein, Edith (1891–1942): born in Breslau, the youngest child in a large Jewish family, she first studied psychology at the University of Breslau in 1911 but, disappointed with its empirical emphasis, decided to study philosophy under Edmund Husserl in Göttingen and, after a break from her university studies during World War I during which she took up nursing duties, she followed Husserl to Freiburg where she finally took her doctorate in 1916 with a dissertation on 'the problem of empathy'. She became an assistant to Husserl during which time she began to work on his manuscripts, organising and preparing them with the aim of putting them together into one coherent whole. On reading the autobiography of St Theresa of Avila, she became a Roman Catholic in 1922, then taught for some years and translated St Thomas Aquinas's *De Veritate* (Disputed Questions on Truth). She tried to reconcile Aquinas's philosophical approach with that of Husserl. She requested an audience with Pope Pius XI to ask him to write a papal enclyclical against Nazi anti-Semitism but her letter was never answered. In October 1933, she entered the Order of Discalced Carmelite Sisters, inspired to do so by her admiration for St Teresa of Avila and St John of the Cross, and took the religious name Teresia

Benedicta a Croce (Teresa Blessed by the Cross). Within the confines of this religious community, she produced her written works, including *Finite and Eternal Being*. In 1938, in the face of the growing Nazi threat, she left for the Carmelite monastery of Echt in the Netherlands to save the Cologne community of sisters from any difficulties for harbouring a Jewish-born Catholic nun. In 1942, following a letter from the Dutch bishops criticising Nazi policies, she was arrested with her sister Rosa who was also in the monastery and died in the gas chambers in Auschwitz on August 9 1942. She was canonised in Rome by Pope John Paul II on October 11 1998. Although her views on the philosophy of religion occur in a number of her writings, her book *Knowledge and Faith* (2000) is of particular interest. In Part I, she compares the views of Husserl and Aquinas on philosophy, faith and supernatural reason and she sums up her observations as follows:

> Both see the task of philosophy as gaining an understanding of the world that is as universal as possible and as firmly grounded as possible. Husserl seeks the 'absolute' starting point in the immanence of consciousness; For Thomas it is faith. (Stein 2000, p. 61)

She adds that whereas phenomenology is concerned with the concept of a possible world and its point of departure for Husserl lies in the transcendentally purified consciousness, St Thomas's concern is 'for the most perfect possible picture of this world', which for him begins from the consideration of God and God's relationship with creation. In Part v of this text, she examines the work of Pseudo-Dionysius as regards his theological views, religious experience, faith and love.

See **Christianity, God, Faith, Judaism**
Further reading: Stein (2000)

Sublimation: the process of directing what are sometimes thought to be primitive or basic human energies, either on an individual or collective basis (to include basic needs for authority and sexual needs), towards what is believed or thought to be more socially or politically acceptable. In the context of the philosophy of religion, Feuerbach put forward the view that the perception that God exists and possesses certain divine attributes is a human construction based on the need to extrapolate from what are considered to be positive aspects of human life (such as love, goodness, justice) to an imaginary ineffable, often personified level of divinity believed to contain in a supremely perfect and absolute manner these qualities to a transcendent degree. Marx and Freud developed this theory with regards to religion being 'the opium of the people' (Marx) or the need for a father figure to love and hate (Freud). The claim that religious belief in God is reducible to sublimation still carries some weight with critics of religious rationality.

See **Don Cupitt, Freud, Feuerbach, God, Karl Marx, Religion, Schleiemacher**
Further reading: Helm (1999)

Substance: from the Latin *substare* 'to stand under', is that which, according to some philosophers, notably those in the Aristotelian–Thomistic tradition, stands independently as an objective entity, which means that a dog is substantially an individual substance of a generic and specific kind of animal species as an existing, living, sensory entity which has certain qualities such as its colour, size, personality and so forth, but which remains substantially an individual dog. Some philosophers such as Descartes have argued that there are mental and physical substances and that human beings consist of both as minds connected to bodies, or rather as minds in bodies, while John Locke stated that though he believed that substances exist, he had no idea of what a substance consisted underneath the qualities or properties exhibited 'externally' ('substance is I know not what'). David Hume was sceptical about the very existence of substance since, according to him, it is not something which provides any impression on which an idea, and therefore knowledge, can be based (much later A. J. Ayer, writing in the twentieth century, for linguistic as well as Humean reasons supported Hume's view). Whether or not one accepts the reality of substance determines one's attitude towards the philosophy of religion, either positively or negatively and agnostically.

See **Aristotle, A. J. Ayer, Anne Conway, Empiricism, Hume, Spinoza**

Further reading: Boyle (1986); Conway (1996); Descartes (1968); Warnock (1996)

Sufism: the name comes from the Arabic word for wool and originates in the coarse woollen clothing worn by some early Sufis to protest against the decadence which they perceived to be prevalent in the seventh and eighth centuries in the caliphate. (The latter term refers to the office, jurisdiction or reign of a caliph, the title given to the successors of Muhammad as rulers of the Islamic world and later to be assumed by the Sultans of Turkey.) The movement emphasises the love of God and has been traced to Christian influences by some scholars although most scholars in the twenty-first century believe it represents a genuine indigenous development within Islam. One of the most important Sufi scholars was al-Ghazali. In medieval

Islam there were a number of Sufi orders that imposed a disciplined way of life on their members but did not demand celibacy. After some time these orders developed into a major force for Islamic missionary activity and the revitalisation of Islamic society. From the early twelfth century Neoplatonic ideas began to influence the Sufi movement, which resulted at times in forms of theological pantheism. By the nineteenth century the Sufi orders dominated society in the Islamic world but were challenged in the twentieth century by the rise of secular nationalism in Muslim countries, many of which like Turkey banned the Sufi orders. At the beginning of the twenty-first century they seem to be flourishing once more and are found in wide sections of Islamic society, though they try to adapt to the modern world. Many new religious movements accept aspects of Sufism through spiritual leaders such as Kalil Gibran, and Westernised versions of Sufi ideas are also to be found.

See **Al-Ghazali, Islam, Mysticism**
Further reading: Netton (2000)

Supernatural: from the Latin *super* 'above' and *natura* 'nature' the term refers to that which cannot be explained by the laws of nature and/or that which is characteristic of or caused by God or divinity, however conceived of. The supernatural, which is by definition beyond this world, is manifested in beings, primarily God who infinitely transcends all that exists, but also other beings who belong to this realm such as angelic spirits or intelligences, for example, and beatified human souls after death, which when reunited with their bodies will continue to exist in a supernatural way forever.

See **The Afterlife, God, Heaven, Religion, Saints, Spirit, Transcendence**

Symbol: from the Greek *symbolon* 'a sign by which one knows or infers something' or 'an outward sign representing a hidden meaning or an abstract idea'. As signs and representations, symbols stand for an object or idea and understanding the nature and significance of the relevant symbolism will depend on such factors as, for example, whether or not one is a member of the group or society for whom the symbolic significance is clear. There is a great deal of symbolism in the religious sector, as one might expect.

See **Metaphor, Paul Ricoeur**

Synagogue: a place of worship or assembly for the Jewish community in which its members pray, study and worship.

See **Judaism**

T

Taoism (sometimes known as Daoism): from the Chinese word *Tao* meaning the path or way in which things exist and change in the world and how the path of our lives should conform to this. It represents an ancient Chinese philosophical and religious approach attributed to Lao Zi and Zhuangzi which advocates a simple honest life and non-interference with the course of natural events. It also includes sorcery and pantheism since Taoism originated in ancient shamanistic traditions though it was also later influenced by Buddhism. Taoists believe that there is an underlying metaphysical and ethical ineffable structure to the cosmos which when recognised by people can enable them to order their lives in accordance with it. The difficulty is that though we may think that we know the nature of reality it is essentially unknowable and unnamable and is unaffected by any of our attempts to grasp it so that even though reality is experienced by us sensorially, it is in itself invisible, intangible and inaudible. The Tao exhorts absence of action, the lack of effort and desire and the absence of partiality, all which will result in harmony, simplicity and obedience. Morality implies a natural and spontaneous identification of nature and the successful ruler is the one who is non-interfering and allows people to act for themselves. Zhuangzi distinguishes between the natural as the source of happiness and virtue, and the social which leads to suffering and evil. The tendency of law and government is to impose uniformity and ignore natural differences and the Taoist ideal is governing through self-government, thus ensuring that each individual achieves the degree of happiness appropriate to him or herself through following the natural path for that individual. Emotions, while part of the natural flow of life, should not distract us from trying to understand why things change and what sort of emotions we might anticipate having and what can lead us to independence from external things. The one who is perfectly happy completely transcends the ordinary world and the distinction between self and non-self. He or she becomes one with the tao or path which is nameless and so becomes nameless too and can govern the world without taking any action whatsoever since being one with the *tao* is to be one with the way the cosmos is and becomes. Zhuangzi also states that the difference between the finite and absolute point of view is that the former can be linguistically expressed whereas the absolute is beyond words. Language cannot express the unity of reality but only the various objects that exist and hence the self non-self distinction. Furthermore, we should not worry about death since it is natural to die as part of the natural process of change and, in any case, the Tao sage will never die being one with the path. Knowledge is paradoxically gained through rejecting knowledge and the more we focus our attention on the *tao*, the less important will the distinctions become. The perspective of children and those who are ignorant may paradoxically represent the wisest point of view. There are some interesting similarities between Taoism and the Socratic concept of learned ignorance and *via negativa* in philosophical and theological literature.

See **Buddhism,** *Via Negativa*

Further reading: Smart (1998)

Teleology: from the Greek, *telos*, 'end', 'purpose' and *logos*, 'the study of' refers to the study of phenomena that exhibit order, design, purposeful behaviour and activities, tendencies, aims and direction, and how these are achieved. Teleological arguments for the existence of God examine the pattern, design and possibility of purpose in the universe, the movements towards a goal or end that various entities show (including non-conscious, non-cognitive and inanimate beings) and the universe as a whole, in order to demonstrate the organisation and intelligent order designed by divine agency, thereby establishing the existence of God.

See **Arguments for the Existence of God**

Theodicy: from the Greek *theos*, 'God' and *dike*, 'justice', theodicy examines attempts to justify God's ways to human beings as regards, for example, divine goodness and justice in the context of allowing natural and moral evil and human suffering to exist and to address such issues as the belief that we live in the best of all possible worlds (Leibniz).

See **Job, Evil, Leibniz**

Further reading: Conway (1996)

Theology: from the Greek *theos*, 'God' and *logos* 'the study of' and refers to the ordered systematic study and interpretation of God's existence, nature and attributes, the revelations, doctrines and beliefs about God or divinity, however conceived of, and the relationship between divinity and the universe and specifically about the divine–human relationship with all that this implies in terms of worship, religious practices and the kind of moral standards and behaviour expected from human beings.

See **God, Philosophy of Religion, Religion**

Theism: from the Greek *theos* meaning 'god', is usually understood as believing that God is both immanent in the universe while also being transcendent.

See **God, Religion**

Thomism (including **Neothomism**): philosophical views influenced by St Thomas Aquinas who synthesised Christian thought with the philosophical approach of Aristotle (and to a lesser extent with that of Plato and Neoplatonism). In the seventeenth and eighteenth centuries the scholastic philosophy which had its origin in the Middle Ages gradually disappeared, perhaps because of its failure to engage with new developments in the experimental sciences and new approaches to understanding the nature of knowledge. It came to be assumed that since the later scholastics were seen to fail in continuing to be philosophically effective their medieval predecessors were equally unworthy of serious attention. However, the inability of modern philosophers (for instance those of the sixteenth and seventeenth centuries) to develop a realistic metaphysics eventually suggested to some in the Roman Catholic tradition that it might be worth while to re-examine thinkers of that creative medieval period of philosophy, especially Aquinas. The pioneer of this

Thomistic revival was Vincenzo Buzzetti (1717–1824) at Piacenza who eventually succeeded in winning over support from a number of clerics and academics including the brother of Pope Leo XIII who became particularly influential in supporting the revival of Thomism and its relevance to modern intellectual needs. Soon scholars in France, Belgium and Germany, such as Gilson and Maritain (a Neothomist), Mercier and Grabmann came to be seen as reputable representatives of Aquinas's philosophical–theological views, though in Italy and Ireland the clerical control of Thomistic thought was constricting and ultimately self-defeating. Thomism is therefore predominantly to be found among Roman Catholic thinkers and manifests itself in a special interest in natural theology and the philosophy of religion, although it also claims that some Christian truths can only be accepted on the basis of faith in God's special revelation. In general, the Thomistic tradition believes that faith and reason are not in conflict but are harmonious partners in the search for knowledge, in particular with regards to how we can come to know God, and that divine grace presupposes nature and perfects it. Pope Leo XIII in the late nineteenth century declared in favour of Thomistic philosophy and theology being studied in Catholic seminaries and universities, which some would argue did a disservice to the philosophical views of St Thomas Aquinas since they came to be perceived by clerics and religious and by Catholic Thomists as dogmatically true almost to the level of infallibility. This distorted the nature of Aquinas's perception of philosophy (and indeed of theology) and allowed critics of Aquinas such as Bertrand Russell to argue (some would say, justifiably) that St Thomas was not a true philosopher since he knew the theologically believed answers at which he wanted to arrive in his enquiries. Neothomists would claim that it is only in the post-Vatican Two era that St Thomas's philosophical investigations have come to be evaluated more critically and indeed with more intellectual respect since it would now seem that the probing questions which he asked and the carefully considered solutions that he provided merit a great deal more academic respect than would have been thought previously possible. Neothomists would also argue that the central tradition of Greek thought was continued and developed legitimately from a theistic point of view by medieval scholastic Aristotelians such as Aquinas and that this tradition has not been made redundant by modern philosophy. However, such a claim has to convince its audience that Thomistic philosophical views are compatible with modern science and capable of dealing constructively with contemporary philosophical developments including philosophical positivism and contemporary theories of language, expressed in a way which can be understood from a contemporary point of view. The development of Thomism is still in progress; the links established with phenomenology, for example, has to be seen as interesting from a developmental point of view on the part of both philosophical approaches. Perhaps, from the perspective of the philosophy of religion, Thomism may have a good deal to offer in terms of critical analysis and sympathy, though its exponents may need to acquire a more confident attitude about its ability to deal effectively with the concerns of religious belief, towards which it was traditionally sympathetic and justifiably supportive.

See **St Thomas Aquinas, Bernard Lonergan**

Further reading: Caputo (1982); Kenny (1993); Quinn (1996)

Tibetan Book of the Dead, The: known as *Bardo Thodol* is used in Tibet as a breviary and is read or recited on the occasion of death. It was originally conceived, not only for the dying and the dead, but also for the living. Its message is that the art of dying, which is the complement and summation of life, is just as important as the art of living (or of coming into birth). In the later part of the text, which sets out the art of reincarnating, it is said that the future of being is dependent, perhaps entirely, upon a rightly-controlled death. The dying should face death calmly, heroically and with a clear mind and especially with the intellect correctly trained and directed. The aim is to acquire a mental transcendence of bodily suffering and infirmity combined with an inner intellectual equilibrium. Plato's writings might be usefully compared with this text also.

See **The Afterlife, Buddhism,** *The Egyptian Book of the Dead,* **Death, The Dialogues of Plato,** *Phaedo, Psyche,* **Soul**

Further reading: Evans-Wentz (1957)

Tillich, Paul (1886–1965): one of the most celebrated theologians of the twentieth century, he was born in the province of Brandenburg in Prussia, Germany and studied at the universities of Berlin, Halle and Breslau. He read the philosophy of Fichte, Kant and Schleiermacher, and later met Heidegger who also influenced his thinking. He was ordained a pastor of the Evangelical Lutheran Church in Brandenburg in 1912 and became Professor of Theology at Marburg, Dresden and Leipzig and Professor of Philosophy at Frankfurt. An outspoken critic of Nazism, he was forced to leave Germany for the USA in 1933 after Hitler's rise to power and was invited to Union Theological Seminary where he became Professor of Philosophical Theology. In 1954 he was appointed professor at Harvard University and in 1962 became the Nuveen Professor of Theology at the University of Chicago. Tillich's concept of theology is Christian. He argued that God is the ground of being and that we must go beyond the concept of traditional theism which views God as a particular, conscious, personal agent capable of action and relationships. Instead, we should regard faith as a state of ultimate concern. A healthy faith is directed to an infinite object compared with the kind of faith that aims at finite objects and thereby gives rise to racism and nationalism. His book *What is Religion?* (1969) analyses in detail the relationship between religion, philosophy, faith, theology and culture and particularly what constitutes the role, if any, which the philosophy of religion has in relation to the subject matter of religion. Religion, he defines, as the 'directedness of the spirit towards the unconditioned meaning' whereas culture is 'directedness of the spirit towards conditioned forms' and inevitably, there is a mutual encounter between them. The philosophy of religion belongs, he thinks, to the cultural or normative sciences which 'sets forth in a creative and productive synthesis what is valid as religion'. In doing so, it employs 'for its normative construction' what is provided by the history of religions and the psychology and sociology of religion. However, it is not identical with these but sets out, according to Tillich, what religion ought to be. His lengthy and probing analysis ends by employing the support of Hegel to point out that 'religion is the beginning and the end of all things, and also the centre, giving life and soul and spirit to all things'.

See **The Bible, Christianity, God, Kant, Philosophy of Religion, Religion, Schleiermacher, Theology**

Further reading: Tillich (1969)

Transcendence: to transcend means in Latin 'to climb over, across or beyond some boundary'. In the philosophy of religion, the reference is to that which is beyond what is given in human experience, forever beyond the grasp of natural human comprehension, consciousness and scientific explanation. That which is divinely transcendent surpasses everything in its degree of ineffability, excellence and superiority and falls outside any given set of categories. The relationship between God's transcendence and immanence is conceptually explored in theology and in the philosophy of religion in terms of speculating how it might be possible to have some understanding of how God or divinity can be beyond this world and the cosmos as a whole, while yet somehow being 'within' it as a creator and omnipresent God.

See **Absolute, Divine, Eternal, Faith, God, The Holy, Immanence, Ineffable, Gabriel Marcel, Mystery, Mysticism, Omnipotent, Omnipresent, Omniscient, Rudolf Otto, Plato, Plotinus, Religion, Theology**

Transmigration (or metempsychosis): refers to the belief that the soul can migrate after death from one body to another. This belief seems to have originated in India around 600 BC and the doctrine was also taught by the Pythagoreans in Greece. It seems too to constitute a belief of Orphism, the Greek mystery religion, and it features fairly extensively in Plato's dialogues and in Neoplatonism. It is also found in the religious traditions of Hinduism and Jainism. It is closely associate with, though not the same as, reincarnation which in Hindu and Buddhist thought is linked with *karma* (the effect of past actions).

See **Buddhism, Hinduism, Jainism, Plato, Reincarnation, Soul**

Further reading: Mascaro (1965)

Transubstantiation: the theory of the Eucharist officially taught by the Church of Rome that during the words of consecration at the Mass or the Eucharistic celebration, the actual substance or essence of the bread and wine is changed into the body and blood of Christ even though the outward appearance (the 'accidents') of the bread and wine remain the same. This is regarded as a miraculous event brought about by the supernatural power of God. Scripturally, it is based on how the words of Jesus Christ at the Last Supper are interpreted, for example in Matthew's Gospel where we are told that after saying a blessing and breaking the bread and giving it to the disciples, Jesus said: 'Take it and eat ... this is my body'. Then taking a cup of wine and giving it to them, he said: 'Drink you all from this ... for this is my blood, the blood of the covenant, which is to be poured out for many for the forgiveness of sins'. (Matt. 26:26–9.) Philosophically it raises questions about how such an event could possibly be philosophically interpreted on the basis of how substance, essence and properties or 'accidents' are understood. It also raises questions for those philosophers who do not accept as valid the concepts of substance or essence, for example David Hume and A. J. Ayer, and there is also the problematic view of substance presented by John Locke who declares that substance is 'I know not what' while yet accepting that it exists.

See **Substance**

Further reading: The Jerusalem Bible

Trinity, The: the Christian belief in a Trinitarian God who is one in divine essence though a Trinity of three distinct divine persons, Father, Son and Holy Spirit. The Father, as First Person of the Blessed Trinity, expresses His divinity in the Word, or Second Person, who is equally God with the Father and who becomes human in Jesus Christ by the power of God, and in the Western Church, the relationship engendered between Father and Son begets the Third Person of the Trinity, the Holy Spirit, also equal in divinity to Father and Son, the First and Second Persons.

However, as regards the latter, the Orthodox Churches differ by claiming that the Spirit emerges from the Son, though equal in divine essence to both Father and Son. The source of the doctrine lies in the New Testament belief that God reveals himself in three forms: as the Father and source of all things, as the Divine Word who became incarnate to reveal the Father and to redeem fallen humankind, and as the Spirit who gives life and unity to the Church and gives witness to the Father and the Son. The Greek fathers spoke of three *hypostases* (or entities) in one *ousia* (being or substance) which became in Latin three *personae* (persons) in one *substantia* (substance) – person meaning here 'an individual substance of a rational nature' (Boethius). The Christian doctrine of the Trinitarian God gave rise to accusations of three Gods though on a positive note it allowed Aquinas to argue, *contra* Aristotle, that one should try to be like God in friendship since God is not a solitary isolated Being (as Aristotle suggests in his account of friendship in *The Nichomachean Ethics*) but rather represents at the absolute ineffable level, friendship and love at its best in the dynamic divine inter-relationship that defines the Trinitarian activity of divinity.

See **Christianity, God**

Further reading: The Jerusalem Bible

Unamuno, Miguel (1864–1936): born in Bilbao in Spain, Professor of Greek and of Comparative Philology at the University of Salamanca. He later became Rector at the university but was relieved of his post for political reasons though subsequently he was re-appointed to it. An independent member of the Republican bloc, he was once more dismissed as Rector by the Nationalists and put under house arrest where alone and distraught at what had happened to Spain, he died in 1936. His classic work, translated from Spanish into English in 1921 under the title *The Tragic Sense of Life*, deals with the individual's response to the fact of his own existence. The 'man of flesh and bone, is at once the subject and supreme object of all philosophy' according to Unamuno, who argues that it is from one's inner biography that philosophical speculation springs. Philosophy is a product of the humanity of each philosopher who philosophises and addresses him or herself to others not only with reason, but with the will, with feelings, with 'the flesh and with the bones, with the whole soul and the whole body'. It is the complete human being who philosophises. 'I feel, therefore I am' or 'I will, therefore I am' expresses the human point of departure for human experience and reflection. God, whether the God of reason or the God of feeling and volition is a human projection, he states, and he goes on to claim that one of the main concerns of human beings is personal immortality. The need to survive and to persist in surviving is fundamental to human life which is defined as a longing for immortality understood as the personal individual continuity of oneself. Human beings are ends, not means, and civilisation addresses itself to each individual 'I'. The craving for immortality is a struggle for continuing personal consciousness and the tragic sense of life emerges from one's awareness that life seems to be a continuing struggle without ultimate victory or hope of victory. Reason doesn't help us here but rather the felt longing for personal continuity, which Unamuno identifies as a value of the heart. All knowledge is at the service of living and primarily in the service of the instinct of personal preservation and he vehemently rejects the notion of knowledge for its own sake. It is the cult of immortality which constitutes religion's point of departure and its means of preservation. Not wanting the self to die but to live forever is the basic human instinct, according to Unamuno. Hope is the response needed – not faith but hope without reason, and it is hope that engenders faith and both together give rise to love. This is what constitutes the longing and hunger for divinity out of which our sense of beauty, of finality and of goodness, arises. The religious sense must become concrete in the hopeful vision of another life. Unamuno invokes the figure of Don Quixote as personifying the ideal way of trying to cope with the tragic context of life in which we all find ourselves since here is a character who maintains his personal quest in impossible circumstances and whose hope seems undimmed. Unamuno's views belong to the existentialist approach to life and remain fascinating, even when quite bleak in tone. What is even more intriguing is that such views are expressed by an eminent Catholic rector of an eminent Catholic Spanish university, whose position seems to be that the solution to the tragic dilemma of life primarily resides in one's humanly hopeful aspiration to live immortally, despite all the apparent evidence to the contrary.

See **Camus, Existentialism, Gabriel Marcel, Nietzsche, Sartre, Simone Weil**

Further reading: Unamuno (1921)

Unmoved Mover, The: sometimes known as Aristotle's God, the unmoved mover or prime mover is responsible for initiating movement or change since Aristotle does not accept that there can be an infinite series of movers or agents of change. Therefore, he claims, there must be some ultimate source of movement or change which is not moved or changed itself but rather attracts other entities to move towards it. This is the first mover or unmoved mover which, for Aristotle, scientifically accounts for how change ultimately occurs. St Thomas Aquinas adopted this in his first way for establishing the existence of God and his second way is somewhat similar in that Aquinas argues that causality can only be explained by an ultimate uncaused cause which, he concludes, people assume God to be. In Aquinas's philosophical–theological view, Aristotle's scientific conclusion that there has to be an ultimate unmoved mover is thus theologically transformed into God as the primary unmoved mover and uncaused cause.

See **St Thomas Aquinas, Arguments for the Existence of God, Aristotle, Negative Theology,** *Via Negativa*
Further reading: Ackrill (1981)

Upanishads: the Hindu scriptures. The term literally means 'to sit near' and can refer to a secret or mystical doctrine or teaching or to the collection of texts that since the eighth century BC has been known as 'the last of the Vedas'. The Vedas began as an oral tradition and only became a written tradition much later. They represent ancient revelations found in a series of hymns, ritual texts and speculations composed over a millennium beginning around 1400 BC. The earliest extant documents are possibly from around the fifteenth century AD and were recorded by Muslim authors. The content and doctrine of the Upanishads range from treatises that promote devotional theism to atheism and thus represent a wide spectrum of philosophical approaches. The thirteen classical *Upanishads* were composed between the eighth and fourth centuries BC though many later works, some of which date from the fifteenth century, also use the name.
See **Hinduism**
Further reading: Mascaro (1965)

Via Negativa: the 'way of negation' or knowing God by knowing that we do not know God. This form of knowledge through ignorance is discussed in, among other texts, Plato's dialogue *Parmenides*, in Maimonides' *Guide of the Perplexed* and in Aquinas's *Summa Contra Gentiles* where he declares that such knowledge leads to the realisation that God is the unique, transcendent, simple supreme being.

See **St Thomas Aquinas, Maimonides, The Dialogues of Plato, Pseudo-Dionysius, Negative Theology**

Further reading: Quinn (1996)

Via Positiva: sometimes known as *via affirmativa* or the 'positive way' referring positively to God by the positive attribution of qualities from the world of experience, for example goodness, justice, mercy and so forth.

See **analogy, St Thomas Aquinas, Feuerbach, Religious Language, Sublimation**

Further reading: Quinn (1996)

Weil, Simone (1909–43): born in Paris of Jewish parents, in her early teens she mastered Greek and several modern languages and subsequently studied philosophy at the Lycée Henri IV where she was taught by Emile Auguste Chartier. One of the first female students at the Ecole Normale Supérieure, from where she received her *aggregation* in philosophy in 1931, she alternated after graduation between teaching philosophy at various schools in France and doing manual work in factories and in the fields in order to understand the real needs of the workers. She took a particular interest in factory workers and in the unemployed and became a revolutionary trade union activist who was sympathetic to Marxism. She served briefly in 1936 as a volunteer on the Republican side in the Spanish Civil War from which she returned disillusioned with ideologies and came to the conclusion that Communism led to the formation of a state dictatorship. Her philosophical approach is marked by a belief in the importance of the individual quest for knowledge and self-enlightenment and is shaped by a synthesis of Marxist and Classical Greek thought, especially that of Plato, all of which is set in the context of an individually pacifist and spiritual religious–mystical approach. Always acutely aware because of her own chosen experiences that industrial factory work was marked by a humiliating form of servitude and low status she came to develop a philosophically positive approach that focused on the importance of human dignity and humility as understood through her concept of 'decreation' which signifies a systematic release of the self from the 'personal'. This is modelled on a view of God as the creator who rejects the need to interfere in the direct control of the universe. This conception of God's incarnation in Jesus Christ as a fundamentally divine self-emptying constitutes the model for those who follow Christ, according to Weil, and demands a response towards human suffering that renounces claims to power combined with a self-participation in the sufferings of the afflicted. Thus, her experiences as philosophy teacher, thinker, activist and writer led her progressively to apply spiritual and religious insights that were shaped by a Christian perspective to the problems of alienated labour. Increasingly drawn towards Christianity from the mid 1930s though she refused to be baptised into the Catholic Church, she

converted from Judaism to Christianity in 1938 and became interested in studying Greek poetry and Gregorian
chant. During the first years of World War II, Weil lived
with her parents in France, then decided to leave for the
USA and from there went to England where she worked
for the Ministry of the Interior with de Gaulle's Free
French in 1943. She refused food and medical help out
of sympathy for the plight of people in Occupied France
and this hastened her death, though there has been debate as to whether her death was suicidal or the result of
mental illness. Although her publications were few, a considerable collection of her writings in the form of essays,
articles and diaries were published posthumously. While
her early pieces concern contemporary problems, her later
work reflects her religious search with a specific focus on
the importance of detachment as a religious attitude for
which God provides the divine exemplar who, in creating
the universe, detached himself from it and surrendered it
to its own law of gravity or necessity. Weil also claimed
that the solution for the feelings of uprootedness experienced by so many people in the society of her time lies in
a social order that is grounded in a spiritual core marked
by physical labour. She was also concerned about how
individual human freedom might be adequately catered
for in various political and social systems, finally opt-
ing for a form of liberalism over socialism. A complex
and very spiritually oriented person with strong leanings
towards asceticism (perhaps partly explainable by her
own psychological makeup derived from her family life),
Simone Weil uniquely combined in theory and practice
her search for a meaningful religious dimension to existence with a strong practical interest in helping those
who were socially and politically oppressed and down-
trodden. Her writings are typically characterised by an
insistent and compelling sense of personal vocation in the

commitment to her way of life, and this is also evident, as one might expect, in her philosophical analysis of religion. One collection of her writings on the subject, published under the title *Intimations of Christianity among the Ancient Greeks*, aims to show that there are Christian implications in classical Greek thought in, for example, the writings of Homer, in Greek tragedies, in Pythagoreanism, in Greek science and especially in the works of Plato, whom she regarded as a mystic and the first to reflect Greek spirituality. God's quest for humankind, she declares, permeates the Greek experience, and Plato, she argues, constitutes the heir to the Greek mystical tradition. A fundamental theme in Greek civilisation, she contends, relates to how the gap might be bridged between human misery and divine perfection. In this context, she believes that Plato did not discover any philosophical doctrine but was only following a tradition. He was inspired by earlier philosophers, not only by Socrates, but by the Orphic tradition and the Pythagoreans and probably, she adds, by the traditions of Egypt and other oriental countries. Weil concludes that Plato personified the form of occidental mysticism. These views of hers demonstrate how she interprets Plato and early Greek philosophy, and perhaps philosophical thought generally, through the lenses of religious mysticism and through those other religious themes and doctrines which define spirituality for her. She emphasises the message of *Theaetetus* 176a as an exhortation to leave the world and become assimilated to God. The Greeks were aware of eternal as opposed to human justice, she claims, and she makes reference to the Platonic references to be like God, which for Weil carry the Christian implication of imitating God in Christ. Plato's wisdom, she concludes 'is nothing but an elevation of the soul to grace'. Other themes such as political leadership and the ideal society, divine love in creation and what constitutes the essence of love, the Pythagorean intimations of mysticism, and Greek science with its concept of the living being as an image of the environment all demonstrate to Weil that Greek thought anticipates and implies the Christian and, therefore, divine world view. Weil's Christian and mystical hermeneutical approach is fascinating and reminiscent at times of how St Augustine writes, and it is evident that both share the view that Platonism in particular represents the kind of philosophical approach which is closest and most sympathetic to the Christian view of reality.

See **St Augustine, Christianity, Karl Marx, Mysticism, Neoplatonism, Plato**

Further reading: Weil (1957)

Whitehead, A. N. (1861–1947): English logician, mathematician and philosopher born in East Kent where his father was a vicar and his boyhood experiences provided him with a strong sense of the continuity of the life of a society over generations and one to which religion is intimately bound up with its way of life. He co-authored *Principia Mathematica* with Bertrand Russell, the seminal work on the logical foundations of mathematics. His philosophical approach tried to combine (1) his logico-mathematical interest in abstract relational systems with (2) a cosmological interpretation of the world based on general notions from the physical sciences and (3) a moral, religious and aesthetic interest in human relationships within societies. Whitehead's religious perspective regarded the human relationship with God as constituting the permanent ground of the world process. He claimed that experience comes to us initially in the form of vaguely connected *continua* rather than in terms of clear cut data and so we begin from a sense that there is 'something going on' in a spatio-temporal context. He proposed an organic philosophical perspective that posited the interconnections between all that exists in reality, including God. His later metaphysical writings also provided an inspiration for process theology. In these later works he argues for a system whose elements are organically related and in relation to which God functions as the ground of possibilities and provides an ideal for actualisation. In Chapters 11 and 12 of his book *Science and the Modern World* (1925) Whitehead explores the relationship between religion and science and claims that since God is the ultimate limitation on possibility we have come to the end of rationality with God. Unlike Aristotle, who metaphysically located God as the unmoved mover, for Whitehead what is known about God must be sought in particular experiences. The interpretation of such experiences will differ according to the relevant system of thought involved, which is inevitably shaped by cultural, historical, social and scientific factors. This results in different ways of naming God, as, for example, Yawveh, Allah, Supreme Being, but Whitehead cautions against metaphysical definitions of God since these, he believes, can be problematic in terms of how divinity comes to be understood (for example as the source of good and also perhaps of evil, or at least as being in collusion with evil, and so forth). With regards to the relationship between religion and science, the historical and contemporary conflicts between them are, Whitehead claims, the result of the fact that both theology and science are each in a process of continuous development. Each represents a powerful way of knowing and both need to be respected and accepted as compatible and interrelated. If conflict and contradiction between the two are identified, it is due, according to Whitehead, to the evolution of knowledge and argues for mutual tolerance

between religion and science, and implicitly between religions themselves. He perceived religion in the twentieth
century to be in decline (and he was thinking specifically
of Christianity here), because its defensive and combat-
ive stance and because of the perception that it functioned
as a social underpinning for political and individual stability rather than as the vision of something that stands
'beyond, behind and within, the passing flux of immediate things'. This is something

> real, and yet waiting to be realised . . . a remote pos-
> sibility, and yet the greatest of present facts; some-
> thing that gives meaning to all that passes, and yet
> eludes apprehension; something whose possession is
> the final good, and yet beyond all reach; something
> which is the ultimate ideal, and the hopeless quest'.
> (Whitehead, 1925, p. 171)

The immediate human response to this religious vision,
claims Whitehead, is worship. This uplifts experience
and when renewed provides enrichment and a purity of
content. The fact of the religious vision, which historically persists and expands, gives ground for optimism he
thinks. The alternative to this would be living a human
life with occasional enjoyment, happiness and fulfilment
in an overall context of pain and misery. Religious worship signifies the need for assimilation and is ideally motivated by love. The ideal religious vision never overrules
but is always present and aimed at eternal harmony and
order. The power of God is the worship he inspires, according to Whitehead, and the form of religion that is
strong is the one whose rituals and modes of thought
facilitate the apprehension of such a vision. Finally, the
worship of God is an adventure of the spirit which seeks

the unattainable and religion dies when the high hopes of such an adventure are repressed.

See **Process Theology, Bertrand Russell**

Further reading: Whitehead (1925)

Witchcraft: a widespread system of beliefs and practices involving what are believed to be preternatural (that is beyond what is normally found in nature) or supernatural (beyond or above the natural) powers and agencies which are thought to influence human activities and events. Witchcraft can be distinguished from sorcery where the latter is understood to involve the exercise of ritual magic with evil intent often using physical objects, spells, potions and poisons. Sometimes the conscious acts of individuals are involved though it can also happen that on other occasions witchcraft can operate without conscious effort as a result of inherited powers and forces. Since the Enlightenment particularly it has been usual, especially among more highly educated people, to consider witchcraft as an irrational system of beliefs belonging to a more primitive past, but anthropologists have shown how central it is to many societies even today and how it does follow a logical pattern. In the West popular belief in witchcraft has largely died out since the seventeenth and eighteenth centuries, although interest has revived in it since the late nineteenth century and continues today with certain groups. In other parts of the world witchcraft has never died out, though its manifestations have changed due to the difference in social setting from modern witchcraft in the West.

See **Shamanism**

Wittgenstein, Ludwig (1889–1951): one of the twentieth century's most important philosophers, Wittgenstein was born in Vienna into a very wealthy family, the youngest of eight children all of whom were very gifted, particularly in music. He studied engineering in Berlin and then in Manchester, and while there became very interested in mathematics, corresponding with Bertrand Russell who invited him to study at Trinity College Cambridge to which he was admitted in 1912. While there he worked out his ideas on philosophical logic in particular, and discussed his views with G. E. Moore, J. M. Keynes and Bertrand Russell. He joined the Austrian army at the start of World War I during which time he also worked on his philosophical and logical ideas which later constituted the content of *Tractatus Logico-Philosophicus* (1921). This remarkable book dealt with what could be said in philosophy and set out what Wittgenstein conceived logic and philosophy to be. Throughout his life he retained a strong interest in exploring the relationship between language, thought and reality, and in the *Tractatus* he seems to have believed that the model for a precise language that could picture reality was a logical form of language. Wittgenstein also acknowledged in this book the dimension of the unsayable (because unthinkable) which shows itself and which he called the mystical. After World War I, Wittgenstein gave to his sisters all the considerable family wealth to which he was entitled and became in turn a primary school teacher, a gardener and a designer/architect of the house being built for one of his sisters in Vienna, during which time he became acquainted with Moritz Sclick, Professor of Philosophy at the University of Vienna, and other members of the Vienna Circle, as well other philosophers and mathematicians. Returning to Cambridge in the late 1920s, he became lecturer in philosophy there and subsequently replaced Moore as Professor of Philosophy. In the post-*Tractatus* period, he changed his philosophical views arguing that language is similar to a game in that it is used differently depending on the context in which it is employed. Just as games differ from each other (as do tennis and football), so too does language, depending on where and with whom it is used and for what purpose. This functional 'games family likeness' theory of language thus replaced the ideal logical model of language set out in the *Tractatus* and was posthumously published in his *Philosophical Investigations* (1953) as were many of Wittgenstein's other writings that were collected and edited after his death. Always unsettled throughout his adult life, he took leave from Cambridge during World War II to become a medical orderly, then, after the war, resigned his Professorship, went to Ireland for two years and then to the USA before finally returning to Cambridge to die there of prostate cancer which had been diagnosed while he was in Dublin. During his early period, Wittgenstein regarded philosophy as an activity, a method of clarification of what is said, always respecting the principle that 'What we cannot speak about we must pass over in silence' (*Tractatus* 7). While his second theory of language allows for the descriptive expressive capacity that language has, nonetheless he retained his earlier view that the purpose of philosophy is elucidation. This is summed up in his famous statement in *Philosophical Investigations* that 'Philosophy is a battle against the bewitchment of our intelligence by means of language' (sect. 109). Philosophy also shows us a new way of looking at reality sometimes by putting before us what we have always known by analysing and placing different elements together in the right order. Philosophy also means 'working on oneself'. On the question of religion, Wittgenstein made a number of important points, many of which are to be found in *Culture and Value* and elsewhere in his writings.

As someone whose grandparents were Jewish and whose own background was Catholic (he gave up religious practice in his late teenage years), Wittgenstein's considerable interest in religious faith as an adult is always respectful and sympathetic. He regarded religious belief as a passionate commitment to a system of reference, as a way of living and a way of assessing life (*Culture and Value* 64e). It is an attitude to life, he states, which religious instruction supports by describing what is involved in its system of reference while also appealing to conscience. Faith is trusting, claims Wittgenstein, and, like philosophy, religion shows us how to look at reality. The methods of religion indicate and imaginatively depict religious truth by using illustration and narrative, and exhorting people to follow its message. Those who believe seize with certainty on their faith and submit to its authority. The human experience of living can educate people to believe in God, Wittgenstein suggests, although he observed that to stay within the religious sphere always involves some struggle. In *Culture and Value* he describes religion as being like 'the calm bottom of the sea at its deepest point, which remains calm however high the waves on the surface may be'. (53e.) It is clear that Wittgenstein remained fascinated throughout his life with the phenomenon of religion, especially as manifested in Judaism and Christianity, though he remained on the sideline as regards commiting himself to religious faith. His position was that of the interested and sympathetic observer who perceived religious belief as providing a worthwhile perspective on human life and on reality generally.

See **A. J. Ayer, Belief, Christianity, Faith, Judaism, Religion, Bertrand Russell**

Further reading: Wittgenstein (1980)

World Religions See **Rudolf Otto, Ninian Smart**

X Y

Yoga: from a Sanscrit term meaning 'to yoke', *yoga* describes a process of spiritual discipline achieved by harnessing spiritual and mental powers to attain self-control and ultimate enlightenment. In the Hindu system of philosophy, certain physical and mental exercises and bodily postures are involved in the practice of yoga and aim to bring about a mystical state of union with the Supreme Being in a state of complete awareness and tranquillity or, at least a form of liberation conceived as a state of perfect isolation. More generally, *yoga* refers to a system of meditation that is essentially common to the Hindu tradition; Buddhism and Jainism and shares many associated assumptions such as the notion of *karma*, *dharma* and some concept of *metempsychosis* (that is the transmigration of the soul from one body to another in a cyclical life pattern).

See **Buddhism, Hinduism, Jainism,** *Karma*

Z

Zen Buddhism See **Buddhism**

Zoroastrianism (also called Mazdaism): a religion from ancient Persia (Iran) that dominated that region before the coming of Islam. Today it is a minority religion. Named after the prophet Zoroaster (or Zarathustra), this dualistic religion may have been founded by the Persian prophet in the late seventh or early sixth century BC and it became the official religion of Persia from the third century BC until the seventh century AD. It is set out in the sacred writings of the Zend–Avesta and is based on the concept of a continuous struggle between Ormazd (or Ahura Mazda) the god of creation, light and goodness, and Ahriman, the spirit of evil and darkness, and it includes a highly developed ethical code. Contemporary Zoroastrians claim that they are monotheists and do not necessarily regard the physical world as bad.

See **Religion**

Bibliography

Ackrill, J. L. (1981), *Aristotle the Philosopher*, Oxford: Oxford University Press.

Alexandrakis, Aphrodite (ed.) (2002), *Neoplatonism and Western Aesthetics*, Albany: State University of New York.

Anderson, James F. (1953), *An Introduction to the Metaphysics of St Thomas Aquinas*, Washington, DC: Regnery Gateway.

Angeles, Peter A. (1981), *Dictionary of Philosophy*, New York: Barnes and Noble Books.

Annas, Julia (1999), *Platonic Ethics Old and New*, Ithaca, NY and London: Cornell University Press.

Al-Ghazzali (1997), *The Incoherence of the Philosophers*, trans. Michael E. Marmura, Provo, UT: Brigham Young University Press.

Arberry, A. J. (1951), *Avicenna on Theology*, London: John Murray.

Armstrong, Karen (1994), *A History of God,* London: Mandarin.

Averroes (2001), *Faith and Reason in Islam*, trans. Ibrahim Najjar, Oxford: Oneworld Publications.

Ayer, A. J. (1936), *Language, Truth and Logic*, Middlesex: Pelican Books.

Babich, Babette E. (ed.) (2002), *Hermeneutic Philosophy of Science, Van Gogh's Eyes, and God: Essays in Honour of Patrick A. Heelan, S. J.*, Dordrecht, Boston and London: Kluwer Academic Publishers.

Barnes, Jonathon (1982), *Aristotle*, Oxford: Oxford University Press.

—— (ed.) (1984), *The Complete Works of Aristotle*, Vols 1 and 2, Princeton, NJ: Princeton University Press.

Bergson, Henri (1977), *The Two Sources of Morality and Religion*, trans. R. Ashley Audra and Cloudesley Brereton, Notre Dame, IN: University of Notre Dame Press.

—— (1983), *An Introduction to Metaphysics: The Creative Mind*, Totowa, NJ: Rowman and Allenheld.

Berkeley, George (1962), *The Principles of Human Knowledge*, ed. G. J. Warnock, Glasgow: Collins/Fontana.

The Jerusalem Bible (1966), London: Darton, Longman and Todd.

Blackham, H. J. (1962), *Six Existentialist Thinkers*, London and New York: Routledge and Kegan Paul.

Boethius (2002), *The Consolation of Philosophy*, trans. Richard H. Green, Mineola, NY: Dover Publications Ltd.

Boyle, Andrew (trans.) (1986), *Spinoza's Ethics and On the Correction of the Understanding*, London and Melbourne: Everyman's Library, Dent.

Buber, Martin (1958), *I and Thou*, trans. R. Gregor Smith, New York: T and T. Clark.

―――― (1988), *Eclipse of God*, Atlantic Highlands, NJ: Humanities Press International Inc.

Burrell, David B. (1986), *Knowing the Unknowable God: Ibn-Sina, Maimonides, Aquinas*, Notre Dame, IN: University of Notre Dame Press.

―――― (2004), *Faith and Freedom: An Interfaith Perspective*, Malden, MA, and Oxford: Blackwell Publishing.

Camus, Albert (1973), *The Myth of Sisyphus*, trans. Justin O'Brien, Middlesex: Penguin Books.

―――― (1960), *The Plague*, trans. Stuart Gilbert, Middlesex: Penguin Books.

―――― (1983), *The Outsider*, trans. Joseph Laredo, Middlesex: Penguin Books.

Caputo, John (2001), *On Religion*, London and New York: Routledge.

Caputo, John D. (1982), *Heidegger and Aquinas: An Essay on Overcoming Metaphysics*, New York: Fordham University Press.

Cheney, Liana De Girolami and John Hendrix (eds)(2004), *Neoplatonic Aesthetics: Music, Literature and the Arts*, New York: Peter Lang.

Chesterton, G. K. (2001), *Orthodoxy*, London: House of Stratus.

Choron, Jacques (1963), *Death and Western Thought*, New York: Collier Books.

Clark, Stephen R. L. (1986), *The Mysteries of Religion*, Oxford: Basil Blackwell.

―――― (1998), *God, Religion and Reality*, London: SPCK.

Cohen, G. A. (2000), *If You're an Egalitarian, How Come You're So Rich?* Cambridge, MA and London: Harvard University Press.

Confucius (1979), *The Analects*, trans. D. C. Lau, Middlesex: Penguin Books.

Conway, Anne [1690] (1996), *The Principles of the Most Ancient and Modern Philosophy*, trans. and ed. Allison P. Coudert and Taylor Course, Cambridge: Cambridge University Press.

Conze, Edward (sel. and trans.)(1959), *Buddhist Scriptures*, Middlesex: Penguin Books.

Copleston, Frederick (1955), *Aquinas*, Middlesex: Penguin Books.

—— (1974), *Religion and Philosophy*, Dublin: Gill and Macmillan Ltd.

—— (1982) *Religion and the One: Philosophies East and West*, London and New York: Continuum.

Costello, Stephen J. (2003), *Credo: Faith and Philosophy in Contemporary Ireland*, Dublin: The Liffey Press.

Crowe, S. J., Frederick, E. (1985), *A Third Collection of Papers by Bernard J. F. Lonergan, S. J.*, New York: Paulist Press and London: Geoffrey Chapman.

Cupitt, Don (1995), *The Last Philosophy*, London: SCM Press.

—— (1997) *After God: The Future of Religion*, London: Phoenix Press.

Davies, Brian (2004), *The Philosophy of Religion*, 3rd edn, Oxford: Oxford University Press.

Dawkins, Richard (1989), *The Selfish Gene*, Oxford: Oxford University Press.

—— (1999), *Unweaving the Rainbow*, London: Penguin Books.

Dawood, N. J. (trans.) (2003), *The Koran*, London: Penguin Books.

de Beauvoir, Simone (1960), *The Mandarins*, Glasgow: Collins Fontana Books.

Derrida, Jacques (1995), *The Gift of Death*, Chicago, IL and London: The University of Chicago Press.

Descartes, R. (1968), *Discourse on Method and the Meditations*, trans. F. E. Sutcliffe, Middlesex: Penguin Books.

Dillon, John (1977), *The Middle Platonists*, London: Gerald Duckworth and Company.

—— (ed.) (1991), *Plotinus: The Enneads*, trans. Stephen MacKenna, London and New York: Penguin Books.

Dodds, E. R. (ed.) (1936), *Journal and Letters of Stephen MacKenna*, London: Constable and Co.

Dodds, E. R. (trans.) (1963), *Proclus The Elements of Theology*, Oxford: Oxford University Press.

Dru, Alexander (ed. and trans.) (1960), *The Journals and Letters of Kierkegaard 1834–1854*, London and Glasgow: Collins Fontana Books.

Durkheim, Emile [1912] (1965) (1915), *The Elementary Forms of Religious Life*, New York: The Free Press and London: Collier Macmillan Publishers.

Eliade, Mircea (1959), *The Sacred and the Profane*, trans. Willard R. Trask, San Diego, New York, London: Harcourt Brace & Company.

—— (1977), *From Primitives to Zen*, London: Collins Fount Paperbacks.

Eusebius (1965), *The History of the Church*, trans. G. A. Williamson, Middlesex: Penguin.

Evans, C. Stephen (2002), *Pocket Dictionary of Apologetics and Philosophy of Religion*, Downers Grove, IL: InterVarsity Press.

Evans-Wentz, W. Y. (ed.) (1957), *The Tibetan Book of the Dead*, Oxford: Oxford University Press.

Fakhry, Majid (1997), *A Short Introduction to Islamic Philosophy, Theology and Mysticism*, Oxford: Oneworld Press.

—— (2002), *Al-Farabi, Founder of Islamic Neoplatonism*, Oxford: Oneworld Publications.

Frazier, James (1993), *The Golden Bough*, Ware: Wordsworth Editions Ltd.

Freyne, Sean (2004), *Jesus, A Jewish Galilean*, London and New York: T and T Clark International.

Gadamer, Hans-Georg (2000), *The Beginning of Philosophy*, trans. Rod Coltman, New York: Continuum.

Gilby, Thomas (trans.) (1951), *St Thomas Aquinas Philosophical Texts*, London: Oxford University Press.

Habermas, Jurgen (2003), *The Future of Human Nature*, Cambridge: Polity Press.

Hamilton, Edith and Cairns, Huntington (eds) (1963), *The Collected Dialogues of Plato, Including the Letters*, Princeton, NJ: Princeton University Press.

Hanratty, Gerald (1997), *Studies in Gnosticism and in the Philosophy of Religion*, Dublin: Four Courts Press.

Helm, Paul (ed.) (1999), *Faith and Reason*, Oxford and New York: Oxford University Press.

—— (2003), *Faith with Reason*, Oxford: Clarendon Press.

Hick, John (1957), *Faith and Knowledge*, New York: Cornell University.

—— (1989), *An Interpretation of Religion*, London: Macmillan.

Hodgson, Peter C. (ed.) (1984), *Hegel Lectures on the Philosophy of Religion*, Berkeley: University of California Press.

Hume, David [1777] (1975), *Enquiries Concerning Human Understanding and Concerning the Principles of Morals*, ed. L. A. Selby-Bigge, 3rd edn rev. by P. H. Nidditch, Oxford: Clarendon Press.

Hyman, Arthur and Walsh, James J. (eds)(1973), *Philosophy in the Middle Ages*, Indianapolis IN: Hackett Publishing Company.

James, William (1956), *The Will to Believe and other essays in popular philosophy*, New York: Dover Publications.

Jamil-Ur-Rehman, Mohammad (1921), *The Philosophy and Theology of Averroes*, Baroda: Arya Sudbarak Printing Press.

Kant, Immanuel [1793] (1960), *Religion Within the Limits of Reason Alone*, 2nd edn, trans. Theodore M. Greene and Hoyt H. Hudson, New York and London: Harper Torchbooks, Harper and Row Publishers.

Kenny, Anthony (1980), *Aquinas*, Oxford: Oxford University Press.

—— (1986), *The God of the Philosophers*, Oxford: Clarendon Press.

—— (1992), *What is Faith?* Oxford: Oxford University Press.

—— (1993), *Aquinas on Mind*, London and New York: Routledge.

—— (2004), *The Unknown God*, London and New York: Continuum.

Kierkegaard, Søren (1985), *Fear and Trembling*, trans. Alistair Hannay, Middlesex: Penguin.

—— (1989), *The Sickness Unto Death*, London: Penguin Books.

Leaman, Oliver (1988), *Averroes and His Philosophy*, Oxford: Clarendon Press.

—— (1995), *Evil and Suffering in Jewish Philosophy*, Cambridge: Cambridge University Press.

—— (1999), *Key Concepts in Eastern Philosophy*, London and New York: Routledge.

—— (1999a), *A Brief Introduction to Islamic Philosophy*, Cambridge: Polity Press.

—— (2000), *Eastern Philosophy Key Readings*, London and New York: Routledge.

Leibniz, Gottfried Wilhelm (1973), *Leibniz Philosophical Writings*, ed. G. H. R. Parkinson, trans. Mary Morris and G. H. R. Parkinson, London and Melbourne: J. M. Dent and Sons.

Lesky, Albin (1965), *Greek Tragedy*, trans. H. A. Frankfort, London: Ernest Benn and New York: Barnes and Noble.

Levinas, Emmanuel (1985), *Ethics and Infinity: Conversations with Philippe Nemo*, trans. Richard A. Cohen, Pittsburgh, PA: Duquesne University Press.

—— (1998), *Of God Who Comes to Mind*, trans. Bettina Bergo, Stanford, CA: Stanford University Press.

McConica, James (1991), *Erasmus*, Oxford: Oxford University Press.

MacCulloch, Diarmaid (2003), *Reformation*, London: Allen Lane.

MacKenna, Stephen (1936), *Journals and Letters of Stephen MacKenna*, ed. E. R. Dodds, London: Constable and Co.

McInerney, Ralph (1998), *Thomas Aquinas Selected Writings*, London: Penguin Books.

Maimonides, Moses (1963), *Guide of the Perplexed*, trans. Shlomo Pines, Chicago, IL and London: The University of Chicago Press.

Marcel, Gabriel (1948), *The Philosophy of Existence*, trans. Manya Harari, London: The Harvill Press.

───── (1950–51), *The Mystery of Being*, Vols 1 and 2, South Bend, IN: Gateway Editions.

───── (1964), *Creative Fidelity*, New York: The Noonday Press.

───── (1978), *Homo Viator*, Gloucestor, MA: Peter Smith.

Marx, Karl (1977), *Economic and Philosophic Manuscripts of 1844*, London: Progress Publishers and Moscow: Lawrence and Wishart.

Marx, Karl and Engels, Friedrich (1969), *Basic Writings on Politics and Philosphy*, ed. Lewis S. Feuer, Glasgow: Collins The Fontana Library.

Mascaro, Juan (trans.) (1962), *The Bhagavad Gita*, Middlesex: Penguin Books.

───── (1965), *The Upanishads*, Middlesex: Penguin Books.

Maurer, Armand (trans.) (1987), *Thomas Aquinas, Faith, Reason and Theology*, Toronto: Pontifical Institute of Mediaeval Studies.

Murdoch, Iris (1992), *Metaphysics as a Guide to Morals*, London: Chatto and Windis.

───── (1997), *Existentialists and Mystics*, ed. Peter Conradi, London: Chatto and Windis.

Nagel, Thomas (1987), *What Does it All Mean?* New York: Oxford University Press.

Netton, Ian Richard (2000), *Sufi Ritual: The Parallel Universe*, Richmond: Curzon Press.

Newman, John Henry (1959), *Apologia Pro Vita Sua*, London and Glasgow: Collins Fontana Books.

───── (1979), *An Essay in aid of a Grammar of Assent*, Notre Dame, IN and London: University of Notre Dame Press.

Nietzsche, Friedrich [1872] (1956), *The Birth of Tragedy and the Genealogy of Morals*, trans. Francis Golfing, New York: Doubleday Anchor Books.

O'Meara, Dominic J. (1995), *Plotinus: An Introduction to the Enneads*, Oxford: Clarendon Press.

O'Meara, John J. (1997), *Understanding Augustine*, Dublin: Four Courts Press.

O'Neill, Onora (2002), *Autonomy and Trust in Bioethics*, Cambridge: Cambridge University Press.

Otto, Rudolf (1923), *The Idea of the Holy*, trans. John W. Harvey, Oxford: Oxford University Press.

Paine, Tom (1984), *The Age of Reason*, Amherst, NY: Prometheus Books.

Plantinga, Alvin (ed.) (1968), *The Ontological Argument*, London and Melbourne: Macmillan.

Polanyi, Michael (1958), *Personal Knowledge*, London: Routledge and Kegan Paul.

—— (1967), *The Tacit Dimension*, London: Routledge and Kegan Paul.

Quinn, Patrick (1996), *Aquinas, Platonism and the Knowledge of God*, Aldershot: Avebury.

Ricoeur, Paul (1995), *Figuring the Sacred*, trans. David Pellauer and ed. Mark J. Wallace, Minneapolis, MN: Fortress Press.

Rowe, William L. (1998), *The Cosmological Argument*, New York: Fordham University Press.

Russell, Bertrand (1961), *Religion and Science*, London: Oxford University Press.

Ryan, John K. (trans.) (1960), *The Confessions of St Augustine*, New York and London: Doubleday Books.

Sanders, N. K. (1972), *The Epic Of Gilgamesh*, Middlesex: Penguin Books.

Sartre, Jean Paul (1965), *Nausea*, Middlesex: Penguin.

—— (1946), *Existentialism and Humanism*, trans. Philippe Mairet, New York: Methuen Press.

Seckel, Al (ed.) (1986), *Bertrand Russell on God and Religion*, Buffalo, NY: Prometheus Books.

Sirat, Colette (1990), *A History of Jewish Philosophy in the Middle Ages*, Cambridge: Cambridge University Press.

Smart, Ninian (1971), *The Religious Experience of Mankind*, London and Glasgow: The Fontana Library.

—— (1989), *The World's Religions*, Cambridge: Fontana.

—— (1997) *Dimensions of the Sacred*, London: Fontana Press.

Spinoza, Benedict de (1951), *A Theologico-Political Treatise*, New York: Dover Publications.

Stein, Edith (2000), *Knowledge and Faith*, trans. Walter Redmond, Washington, DC: ICS Publications.

Swinburne, Richard (1981), *Faith and Reason*, Oxford: Clarendon Press.

Tillich, Paul (1969), *What is Religion?* New York: Harper Torchbooks.

Unamuno, Miguel de (1921), *The Tragic Sense of Life*, trans. Amalia Elguera, Glasgow: The Fontana Library, Collins.

Von Hügel, Friedrich (1933), *Essays and Addresses on the Philosophy of Religion*, 1st and 2nd ser., London: J. M. Dent and Sons Ltd.

Wallis, R. T. (1972), *Neoplatonism*, London: Gerald Duckworth and Co.

Wallis Budge, E. A. (trans.) (1987), *The Egyptian Book of the Dead*, New York: Dover Publications.

Warnock, Mary (ed.) (1996), *Women Philosophers*, London: Everyman J. M. Dent.

Weil, Simone (1957), *Intimations of Christianity among the Ancient Greeks*, London and New York: Ark Paperbacks.

Whitehead, A. N. (1925), *Science and the Modern World*, New York: Mentor Books, New York Library.

Wittgenstein, Ludwig (1980), *Culture and Value*, trans. Peter Winch, Oxford: Basil Blackwell.

Wood, Allen W. (ed.) (2001), *Basic Writings of Kant*, New York: The Modern Library.